IMAGES
of America

BELLE FOURCHE

On the cover: Please see page 36. (Courtesy of the Tri-State Museum.)

IMAGES
of America

BELLE FOURCHE

Jordan Wilms and Mary Buchholz

ARCADIA
PUBLISHING

ISBN 978-0-7385-6152-3

Published by Arcadia Publishing
Charleston, South Carolina

Printed in the United States of America

Library of Congress Catalog Card Number: 2008921892

For all general information contact Arcadia Publishing at:
Telephone 843-853-2070
Fax 843-853-0044
E-mail sales@arcadiapublishing.com
For customer service and orders:
Toll-Free 1-888-313-2665

Visit us on the Internet at www.arcadiapublishing.com

Contents

Acknowledgments

These people have been most helpful: Mary Ellen Warren, Dick Rosander, DeEtte Goss, Doug and Pat Engebretson, Irene Gardner, Barbara Dailey, and Lorraine Klingler. This book would not have been possible without the previous county history and rodeo books. Most especially, we are grateful for the beautiful vintage pictures that were donated to the Tri-State Museum and allowed this book to happen.

INTRODUCTION

The late 1800s was an interesting time in what is now western South Dakota. Because settlement of the Black Hills area was delayed until after gold was found by Gen. George Custer in 1874, the settlement of this area is well documented and gives a great view into what life was like in the West during the second half of the 19th century.

Each western town in this area has its own unique and interesting history, and Belle Fourche is no different. Its history is dotted with interesting and sometimes famous characters. The town is built on what was once Seth Bullock's ranch. Although Bullock is better known for his days in Deadwood, he can be considered the founding father of Belle Fourche and served an important part in the creation of the town. Belle Fourche also portrays some classic stereotypes of an old Western town, including being the site of a bank robbery by members of the Hole in the Wall Gang. Today the rich history here is cherished by its citizens and preserved in a great local museum.

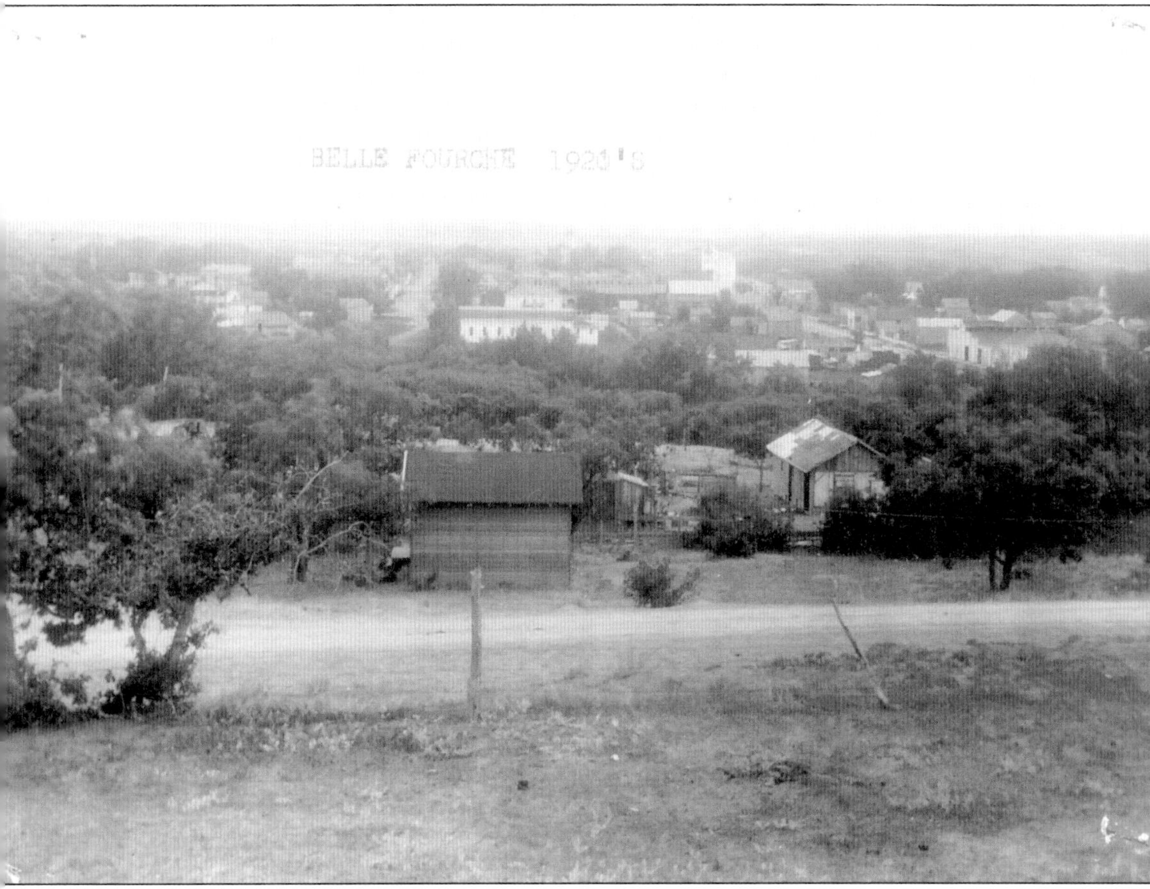

This overview of Belle Fourche shows the town looking from the north sometime during the 1920s. Some of the town's prominent features can be seen, including the Butte County Courthouse, mill, and Saloon Street.

One

Downtown Life

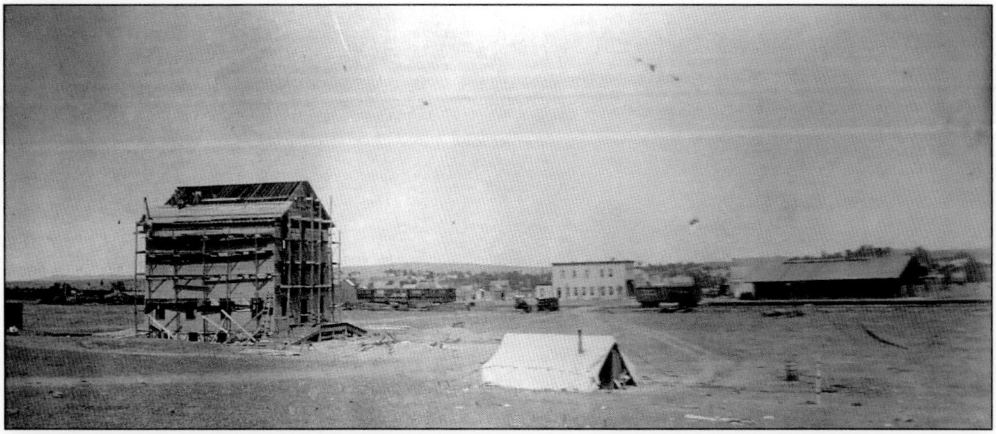

Belle Fourche was in its infancy when this photograph was taken around 1891. On the right side are a railroad car and the depot. Belle Fourche was founded when Seth Bullock offered free right-of-way to the railroad if it built through his ranch. His offer was accepted because nearby Minnesela was asking for a large sum of money for the right-of-way.

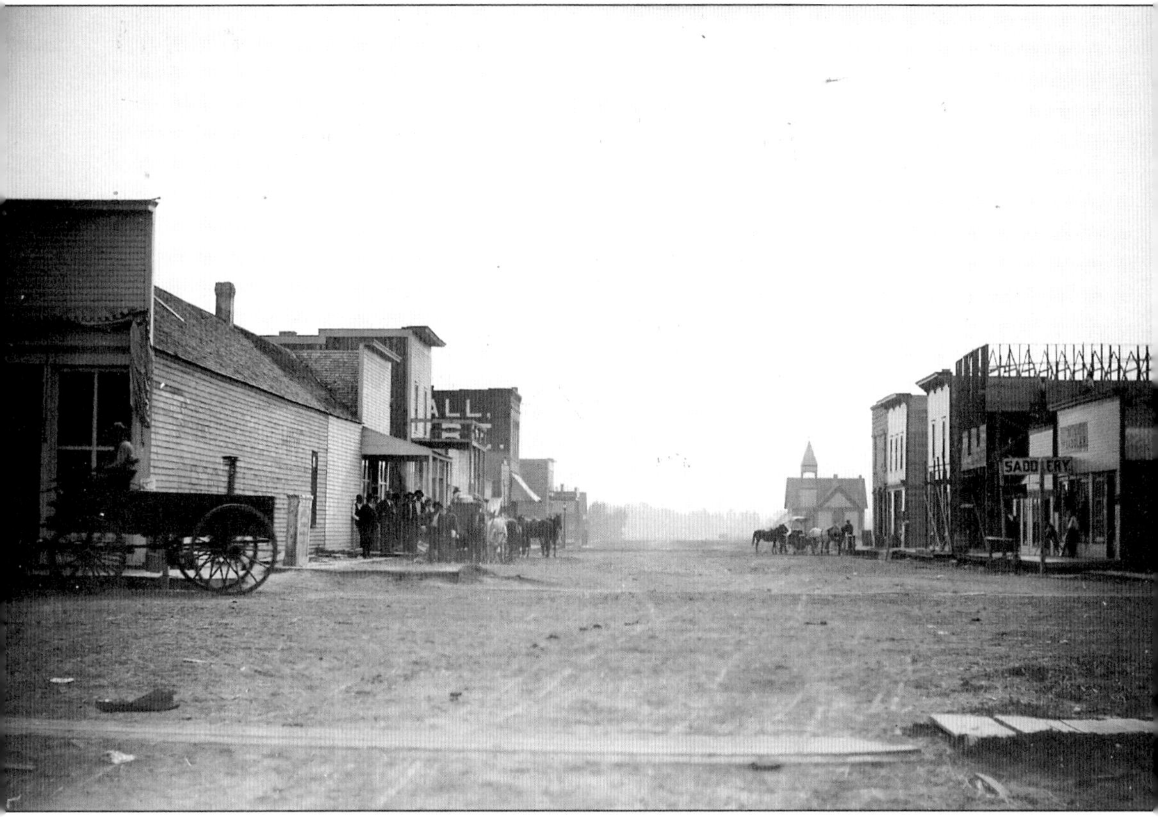

This view of State Street is one of the earliest photographs of downtown on record. Construction of many new buildings can be seen on the right side of the street. This 1894 photograph was taken before the great fire of 1895 that destroyed most of the businesses, especially on the left side of the road. Only the Ferrall Hardware building at the corner of State and Sixth Streets survived the fire on the north side of the street. Notice that many of the buildings here are made of wooden frames. Following the fire in 1895, many of the new buildings in the downtown area were constructed of stone or brick. The white building in the distance on the right is the Methodist church.

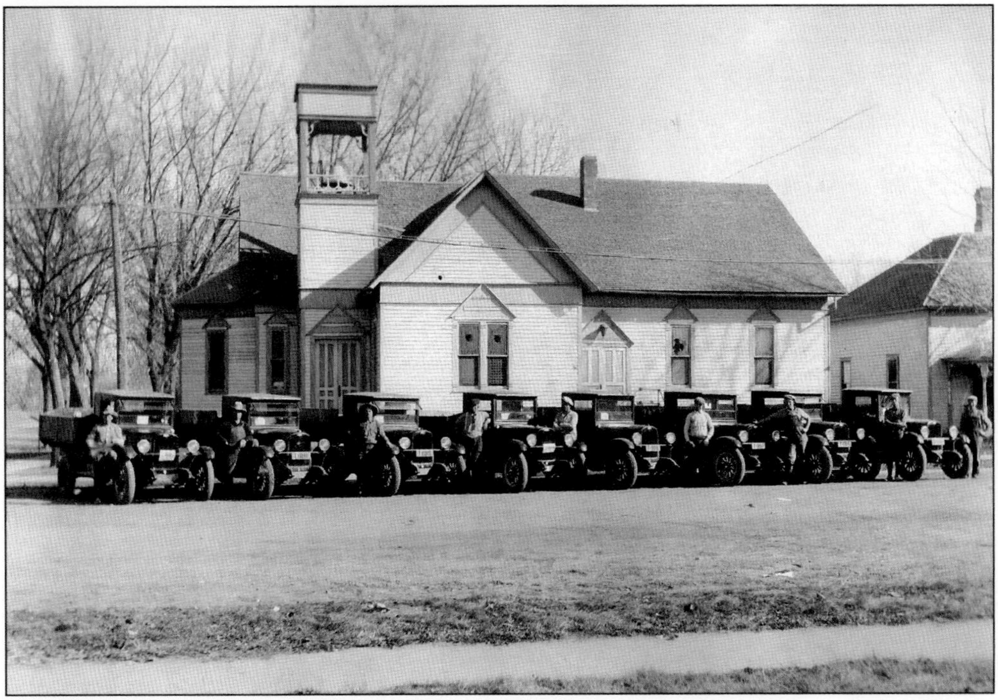

The Methodist church in Belle Fourche was the first church established in Butte County. Dedicated in 1894, it became the center of many activities. The original church was torn down, and a new church was constructed.

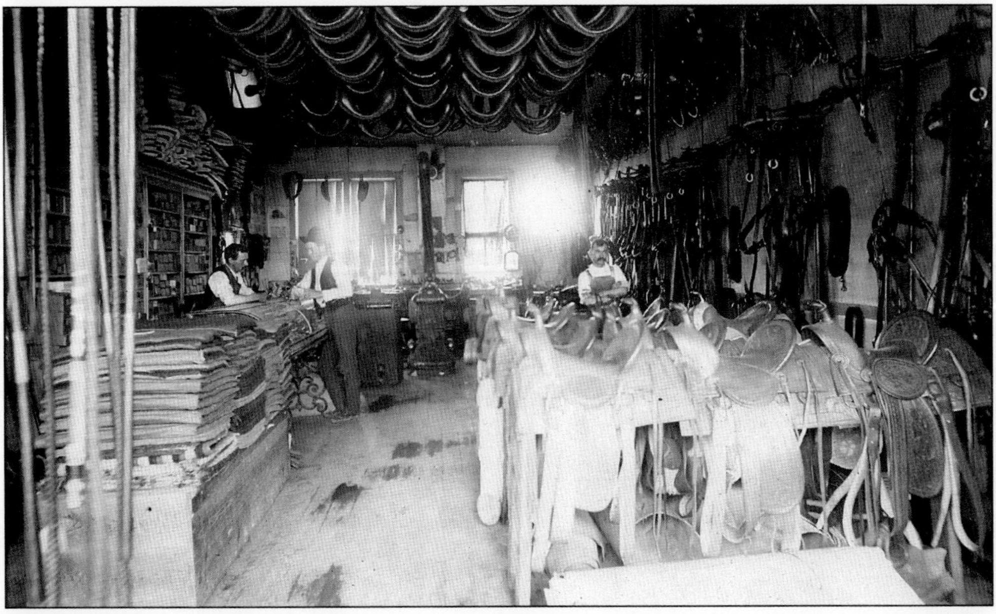

Early Belle Fourche was an important cattle shipping point for a very large area around the town. At one point, it became the largest shipping point for cattle in the world. Early businesses in Belle Fourche catered to the needs of the cowboys coming in off the open range. Opened in 1890, this was the first saddle store in Belle Fourche.

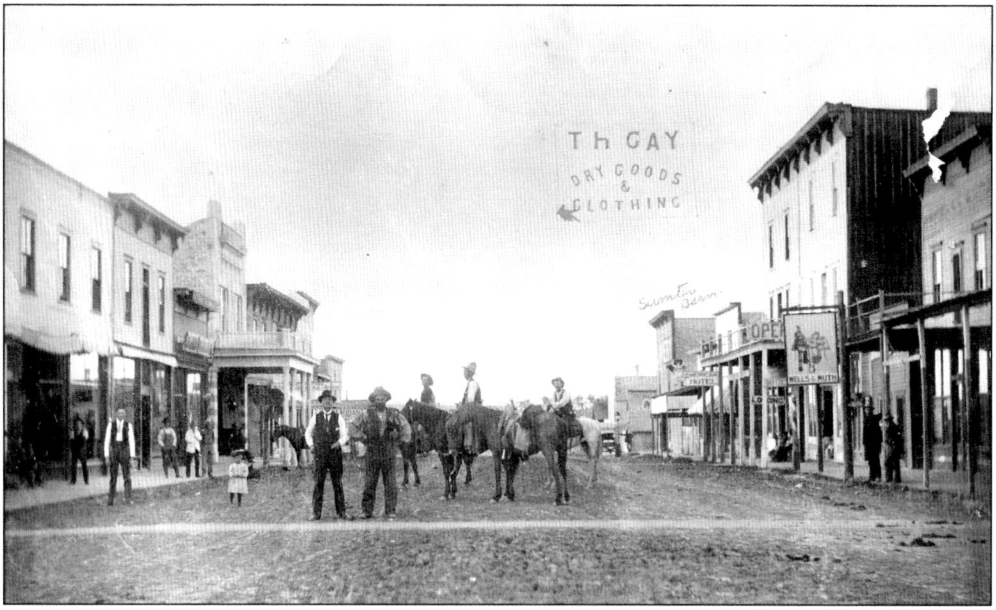

This photograph looking north on Saloon Street, now Fifth Avenue, shows cowboys out on the street sometime before the 1895 fire. This part of the town was where many saloons and brothels were to serve the cowboys as they came into town at the end of a cattle drive. On the east side of the street is the American Hotel. This was one of the earliest hotels in Belle Fourche; however, it had a very short life. It was built in 1893 and burned down in the great fire in September 1895.

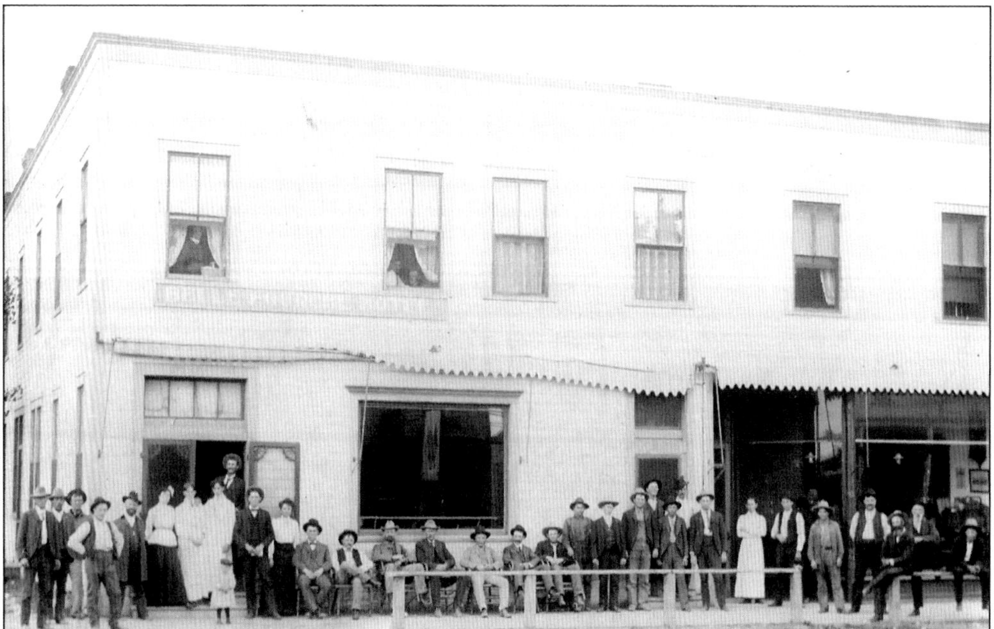

D. P. Roberts, the person first sitting from the left, ran a saloon in Belle Fourche almost from the birth of the town right up until the beginning of Prohibition. He originally worked for the VVV cattle company and came to the Black Hills in 1881. Roberts lived in Belle Fourche until his death in 1942.

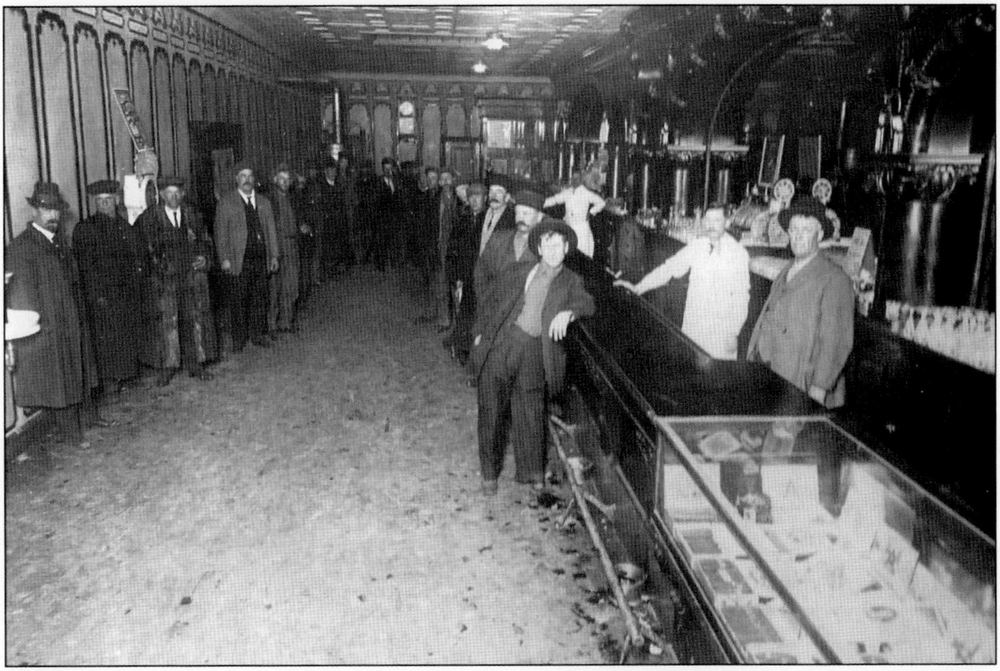

Roberts's saloon was a busy place when this photograph was taken. The beautiful back bar was made of cherry wood and was imported to Belle Fourche in 1901. It has survived longer than the saloon and was still being used in town until it was sold only recently.

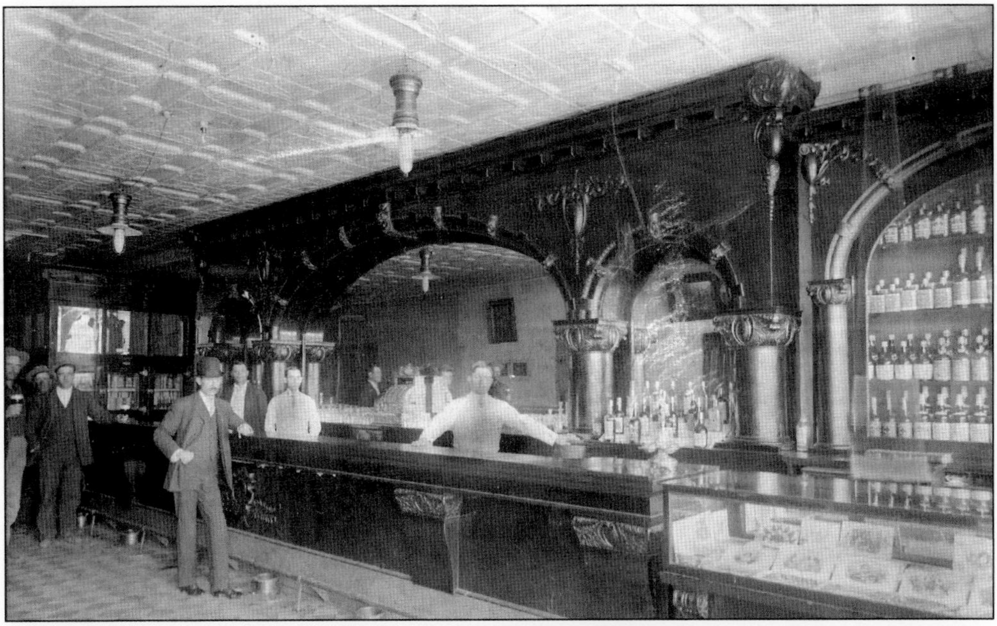

Another of the many saloons on Fifth Avenue was that of Bruce Sebastian. Following the fire in 1895, Sebastian moved a building from Minnesela to Belle Fourche and opened his saloon. He eventually moved to this location and had an intense rivalry with Roberts. Each tried to outdo the other by adding fancy fixtures to their bars.

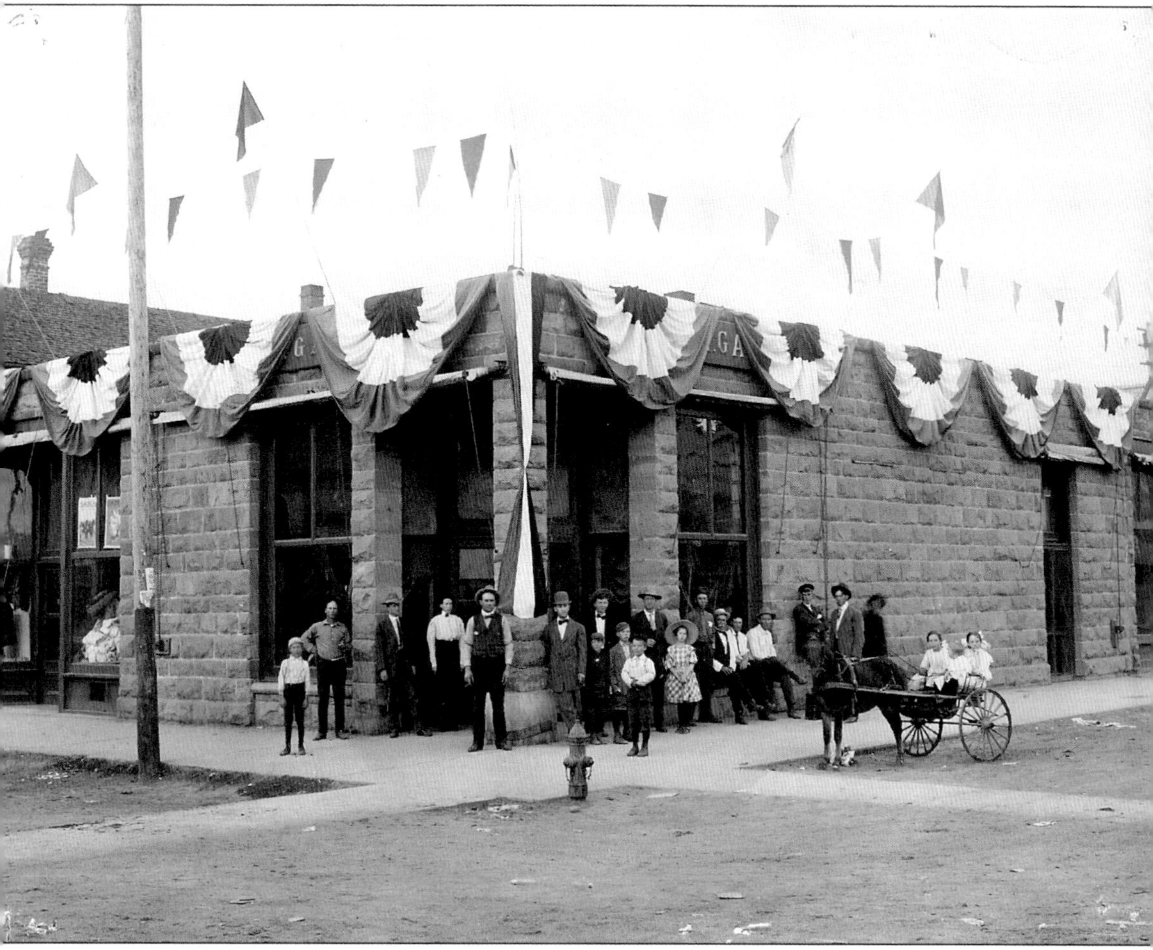

The fire that ravaged the city in September 1895 left the citizens of the young town of Belle Fourche with a choice—rebuild or move on. Following the fire, the citizens of Belle Fourche showed they had staying power and built a total of 14 new businesses, costing almost $30,000. Many of the original wooden buildings were replaced with more permanent stone buildings. One of these businesses was here on the corner of State and Fifth Streets. Finished in 1896, this building originally housed the T. H. Gay Clothing Store. Over the years, several other businesses were housed here. This building still stands on the busy corner. Many of the new buildings on State Street in Belle Fourche were built of sandstone quarried near the town by John Scotney.

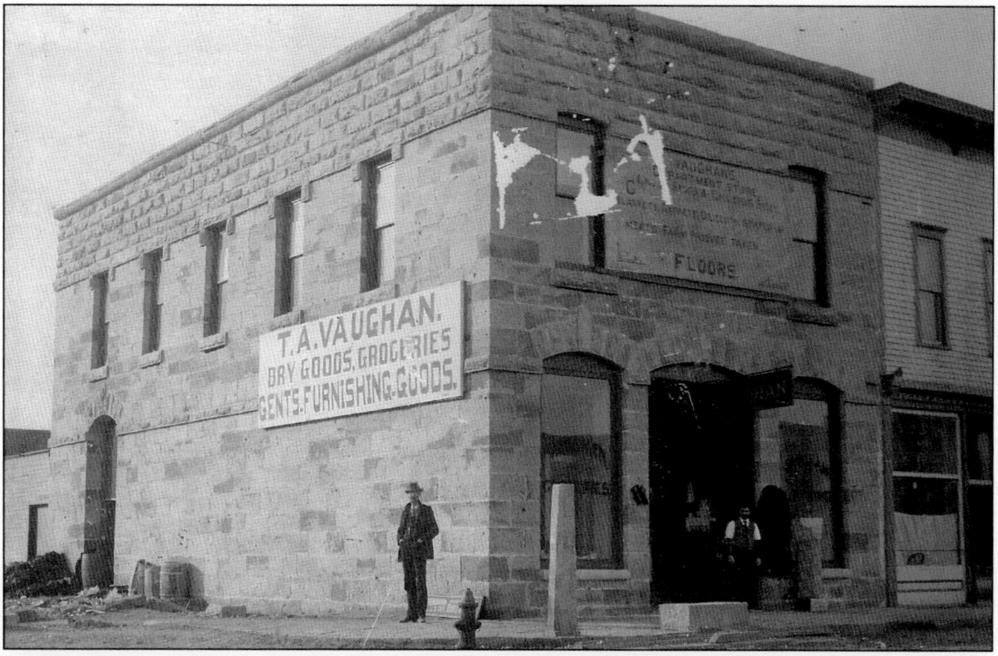

Built by Scotney, the T. A. Vaughan store, which later became a grocery store, was one of the earliest buildings for many years. This building, along with the one directly across the street from it, was one of the few buildings to survive the fire in 1895. This beautiful sandstone building is still standing on State Street and looks much the same as it did over 100 years ago.

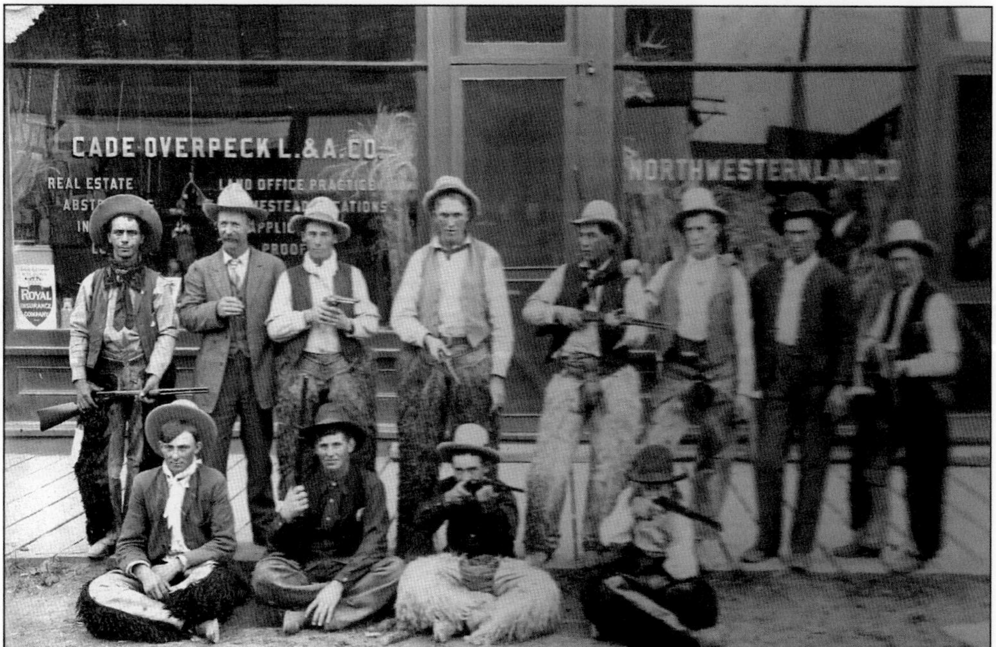

This 1908 photograph shows that although Belle Fourche was a bustling little town and the open range days were over, it was still a cowboy sort of town. The VVV cowboys are posed for a photograph here on Fifth Avenue in front of the Cade-Overpeck Land Title Company.

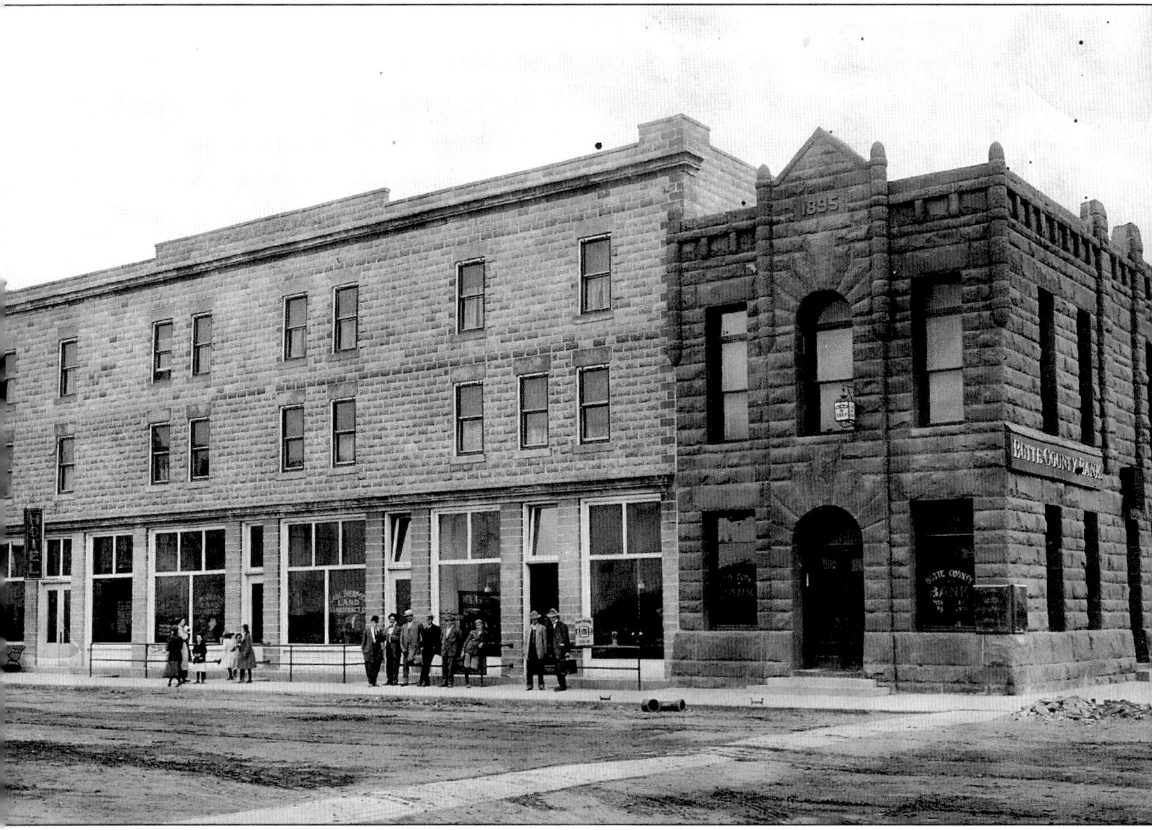

These buildings were mainstays on State Street for most of the 20th century. The Butte County Bank was established in 1891 in Minnesela. It moved to Belle Fourche when Minnesela began its decline after the railroad chose Belle Fourche. This building was constructed in 1895 and was a great example of the sandstone buildings that once dominated State Street. This bank was also the site of the famous botched Belle Fourche bank robbery by the Hole in the Wall Gang. The robbery turned out to be a mostly drunken chain of mistakes, and the gang made off with about $97. The Hampton Hotel was opened in 1910 and was the prominent hotel in Belle Fourche until the construction of the Don Pratt in the late 1920s.

One character who took part in the botched robbery of the Butte County Bank was Tom O'Day. O'Day was a member of the Hole in the Wall Gang. His horse ran off during the robbery, and he was apprehended for his part in it.

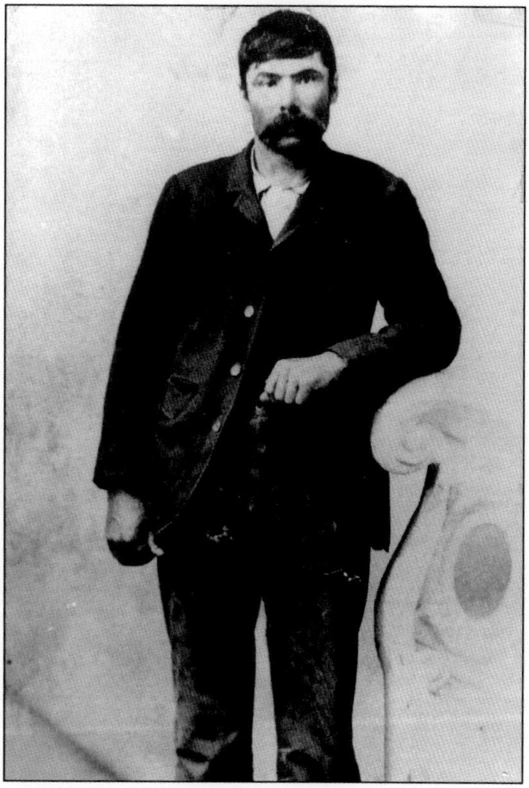

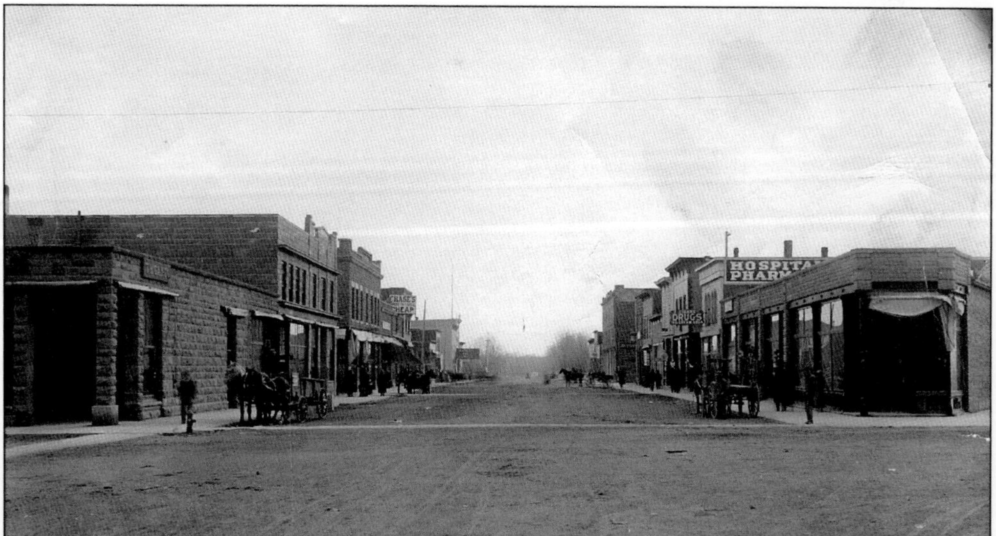

Here is State Street in 1910. Notice that the streets have not yet been paved, and horse-drawn wagons still dominate the street even with the emergence of the automobile. However, it did not take long before the automobile became more prominent.

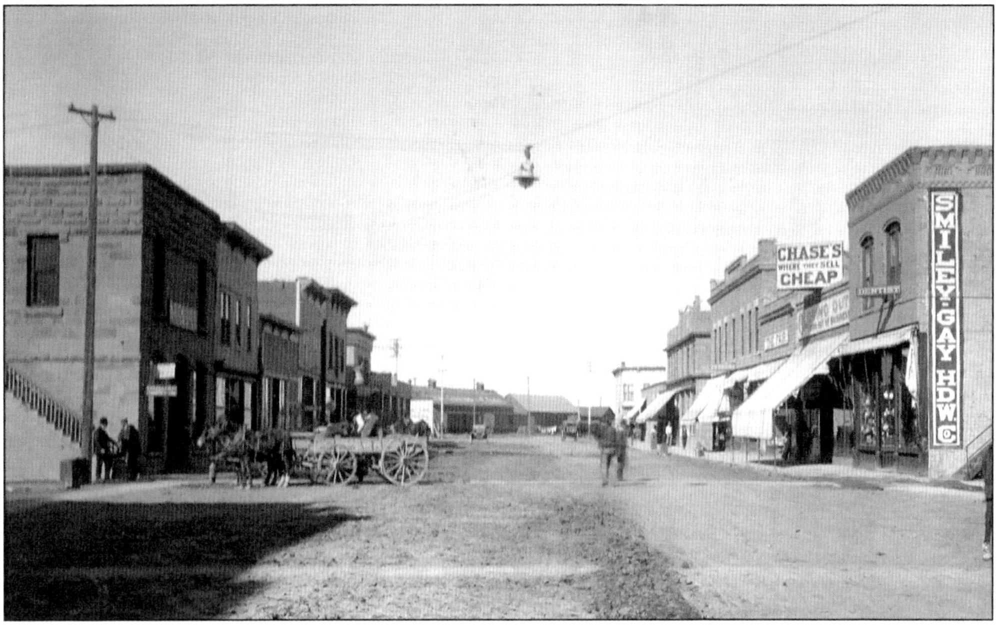

This photograph, taken only a few years after the previous picture, shows that some improvements have been made in the city. There are now electric lights above the streets, and there is a car in the center of the road in the distance, although wagons are still the dominant form of transportation.

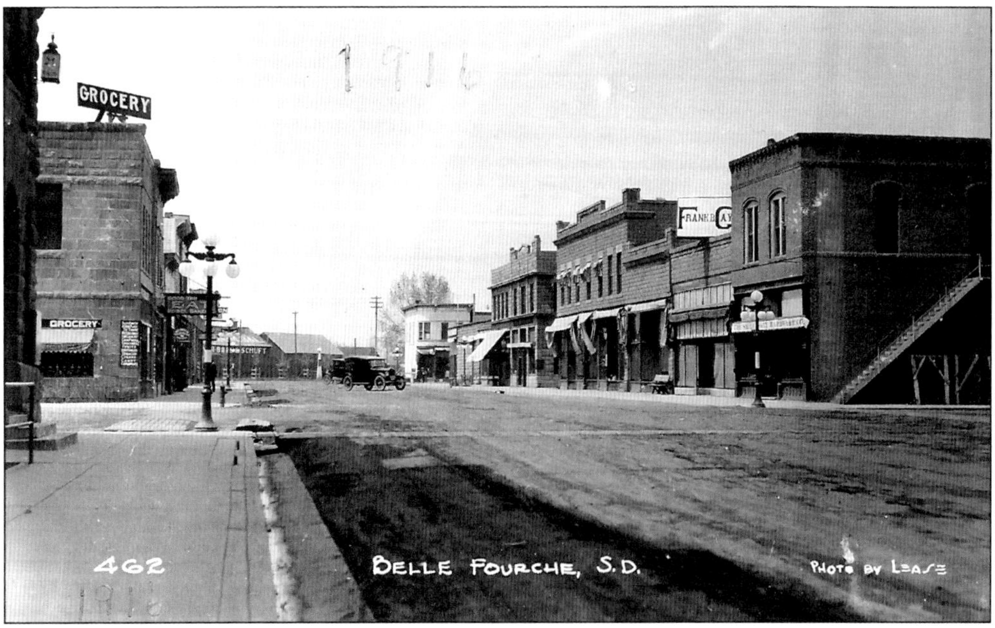

Seen here around 1916, there are electric streetlamps along the entire path of the road, and although still unpaved, it looks much smoother than a few years before. Notice now that there are no wagons on the street, as they have been completely replaced by cars.

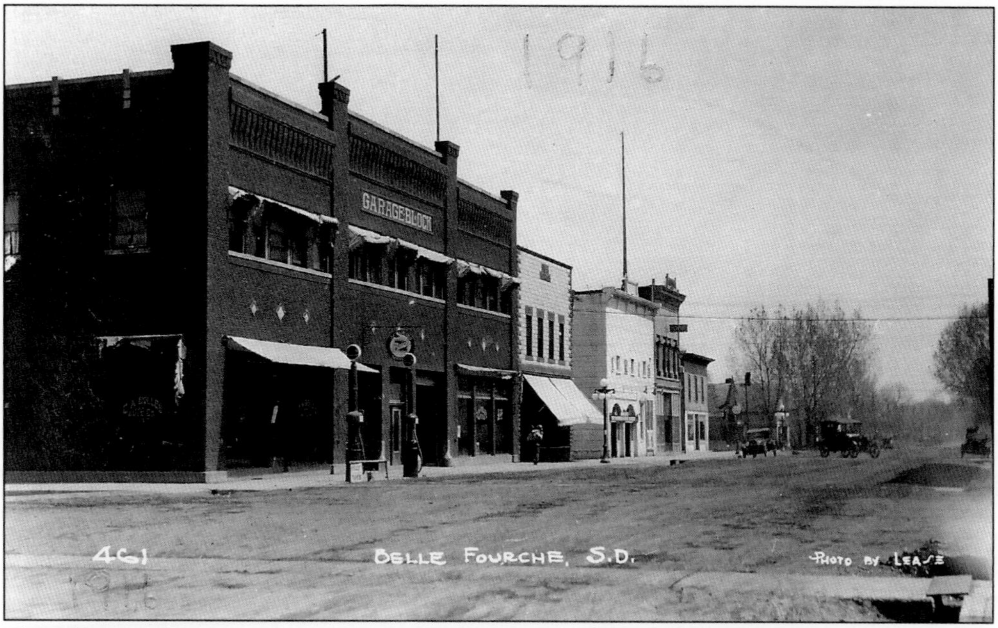

This photograph shows the east end of Belle Fourche taken in the same year as the previous photograph. Here is the Garage Block building, which became a bank in 1937. Notice also the Iris Theater farther down the block.

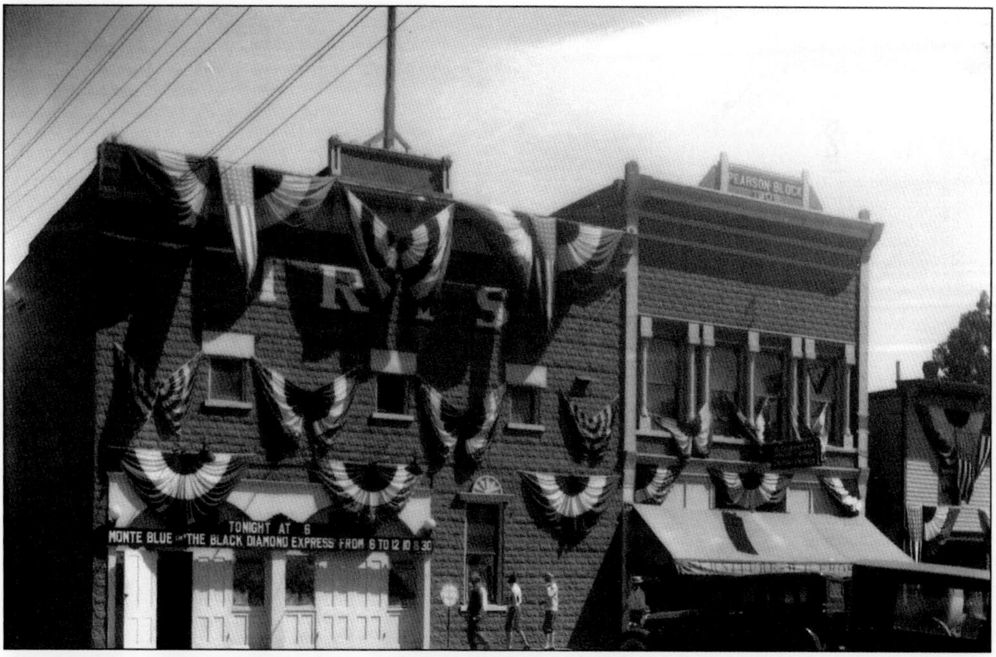

The Iris Theater was built in 1905 as the Pearson Opera House and was a center of social life in early Belle Fourche. It was renamed the Iris Theater in 1915 after the building was remodeled to house projectors for motion pictures and meet state fire codes. This building was torn down in 1930 to make way for the Belle Theater.

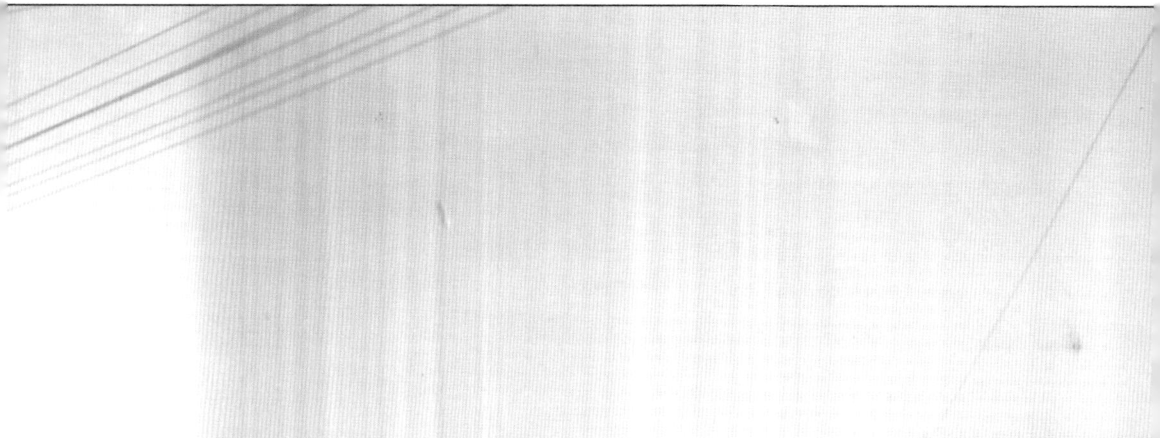

This view looking north on Saloon Street shows Belle Fourche sometime after the 1895 fire. On the right side of the street is a sign that reads, "Dreamland." This was the Dreamland Theater, originally under the management of O. K. Burroughs, which was opened to compete with the Pearson Opera House. For a few years, it succeeded by putting on vaudeville acts as well as showing the new motion pictures, while the Pearson Opera House focused more on showing live plays and musicals. The remodeling of the Pearson Opera House to accommodate motion pictures made it difficult for a small town the size of Belle Fourche to support two theaters, and the Dreamland shut down shortly afterward and became a secondhand store.

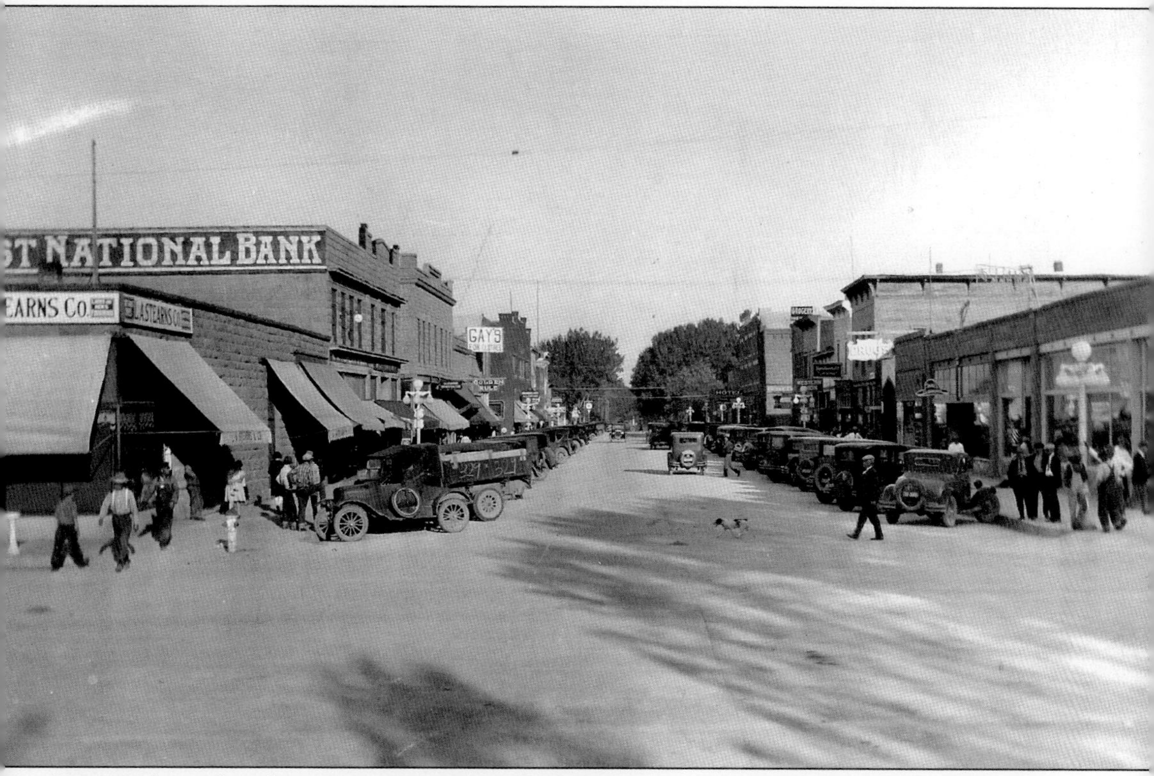

Here in the mid- to late 1920s, State Street has become a busy thoroughfare, and it seems that one would be hard-pressed to find an open parking place on the street. Most of the buildings in this photograph are still around today, especially those on the north side of the road. This photograph was taken shortly after the downtown area had been paved for the first time, around 1925. Belle Fourche was a growing community and served as a hub for ranchers throughout the immediate area and parts of Montana and Wyoming. The slanted parking on the sides of the street is still used today, which makes this photograph exciting in that it would closely resemble a photograph taken of State Street from the same position today.

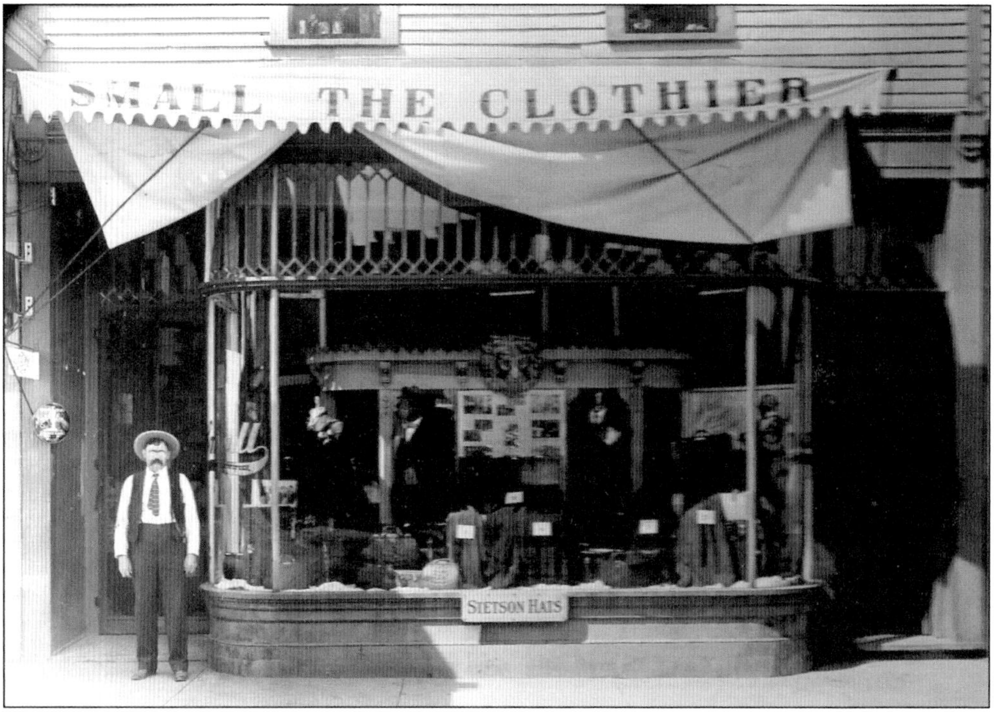

Charles Small was a prominent businessman and pioneer in the early years of Belle Fourche. The storefront seen here was built after a second fire burned Small's store in 1906. In the early years, Small catered to the cowboys who came through Belle Fourche on the big cattle drives.

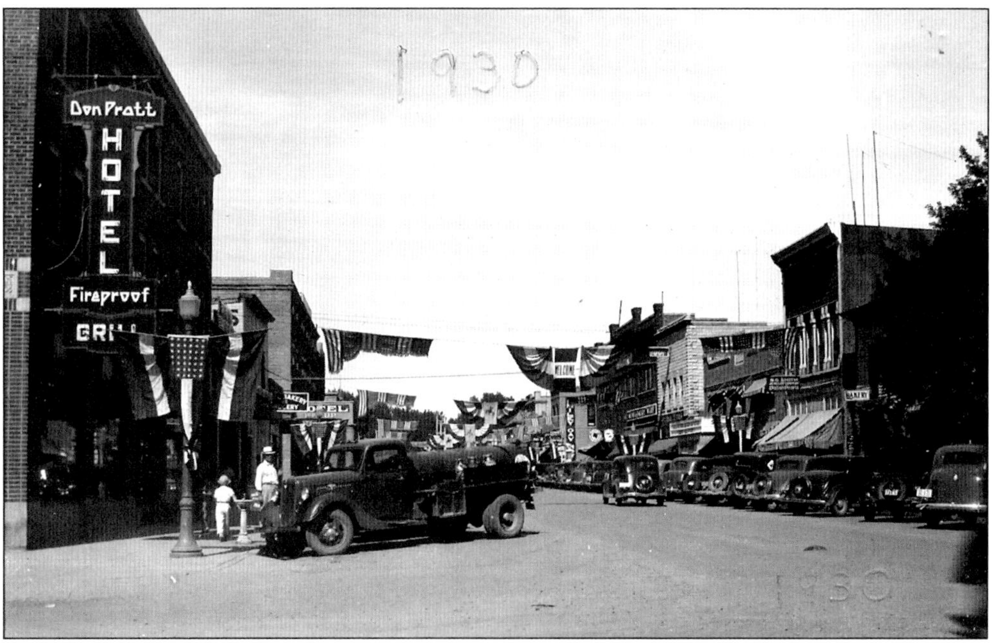

This photograph shows State Street looking west from the corner of Seventh Avenue. Here are some of the new buildings on the block, including the Belle Theater and the Don Pratt Hotel.

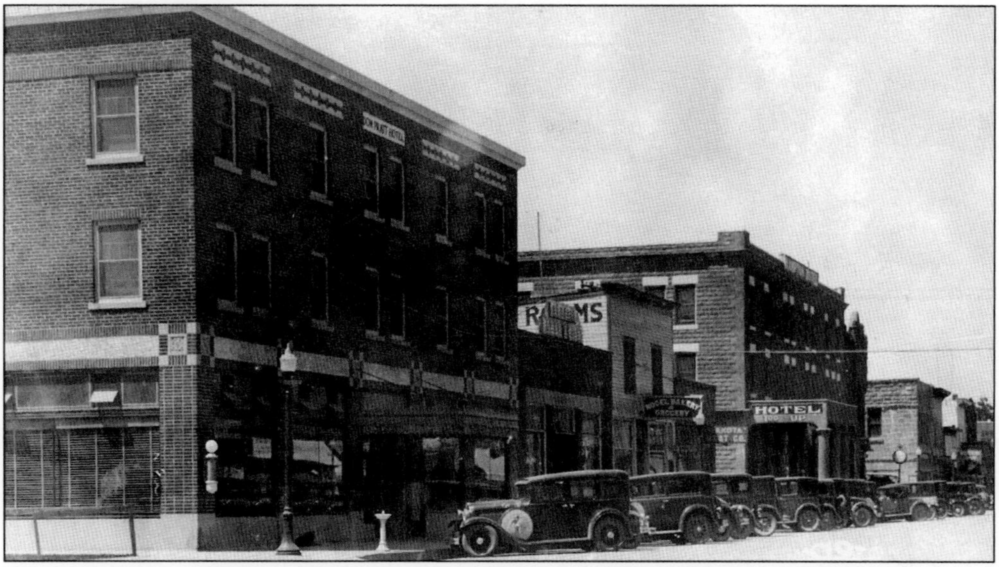

The development of the sugar beet factory in Belle Fourche brought the need for a new and elegant hotel. The Don Pratt Hotel was built the late 1920s and became a successful hotel and convention center. The building still stands today but is no longer used as a hotel.

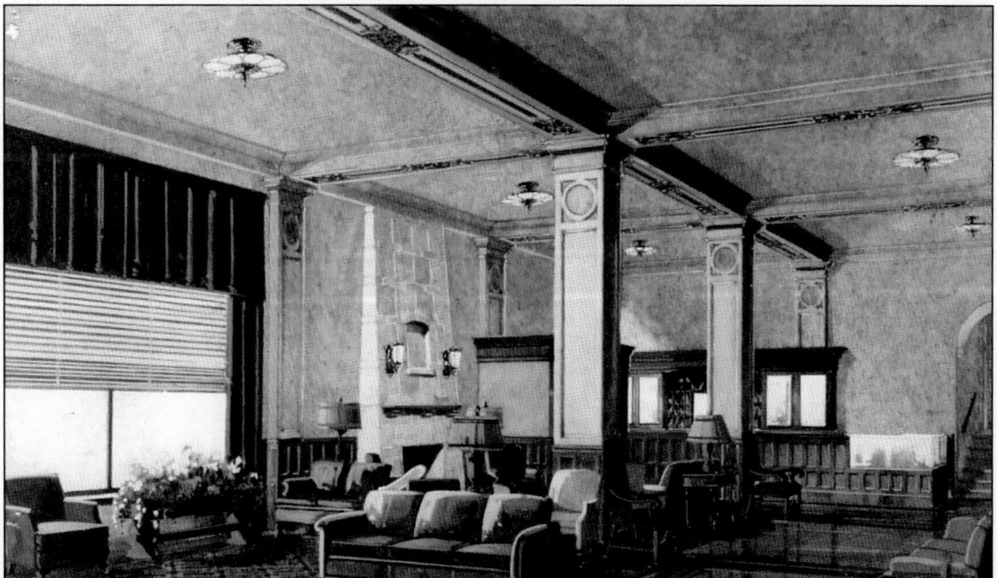

The Don Pratt Hotel was built to be more luxurious than any other hotel in Belle Fourche and to accommodate the VIPs that the sugar mill brought in. This view of the elegant lobby gives a glimpse into the hotel that featured a guest dining room and grill as well as 60 rooms.

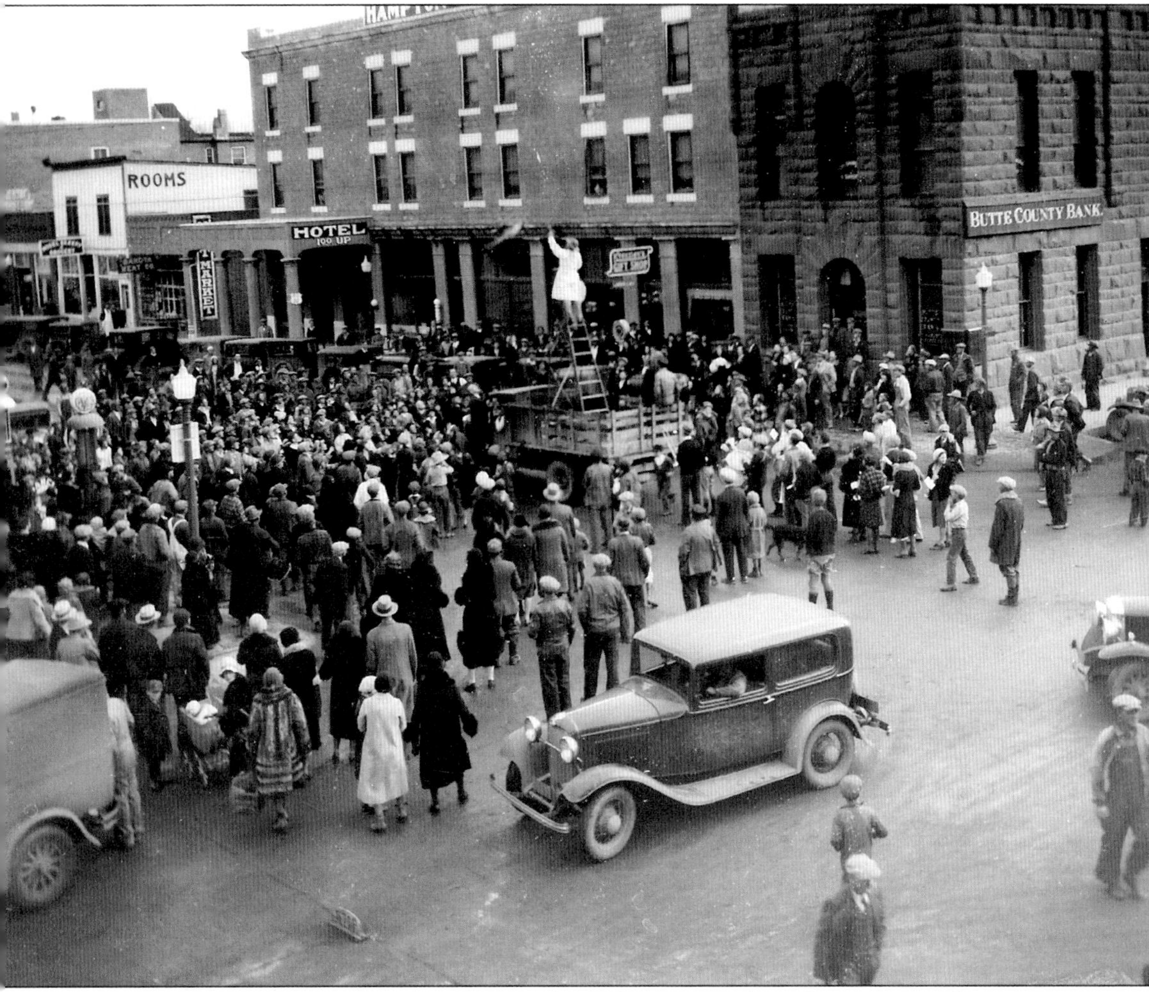

This is an interesting photograph taken from the corner of Sixth Avenue and State Street sometime between 1932 and 1937. Although the event here has not been identified, it must have been a rather large community event, as there is a large crowd and a band is standing behind the truck in the street. This event was odd in part because of how large it was, yet research in period newspapers reveals nothing, and locals who lived in Belle Fourche at the time do not remember such an event. Closer examination of the crowd shows that many of the people seem to be smiling or laughing. It is possible that this was some sort of traveling comedian or magician who happened to stop in Belle Fourche while traveling through the West.

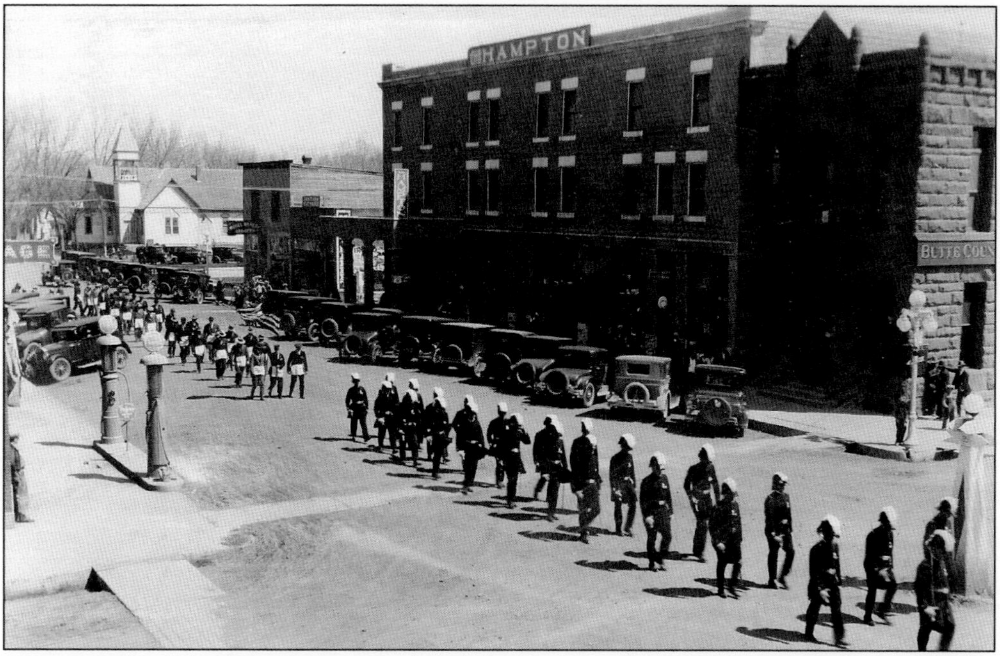

This view shows the Butte County Bank and the Hampton Hotel. These two buildings were the center of many of the photographs taken in the early 20th century in Belle Fourche, especially when there was an event happening in the area. Since that time, these two buildings were torn down and replaced with more modern buildings.

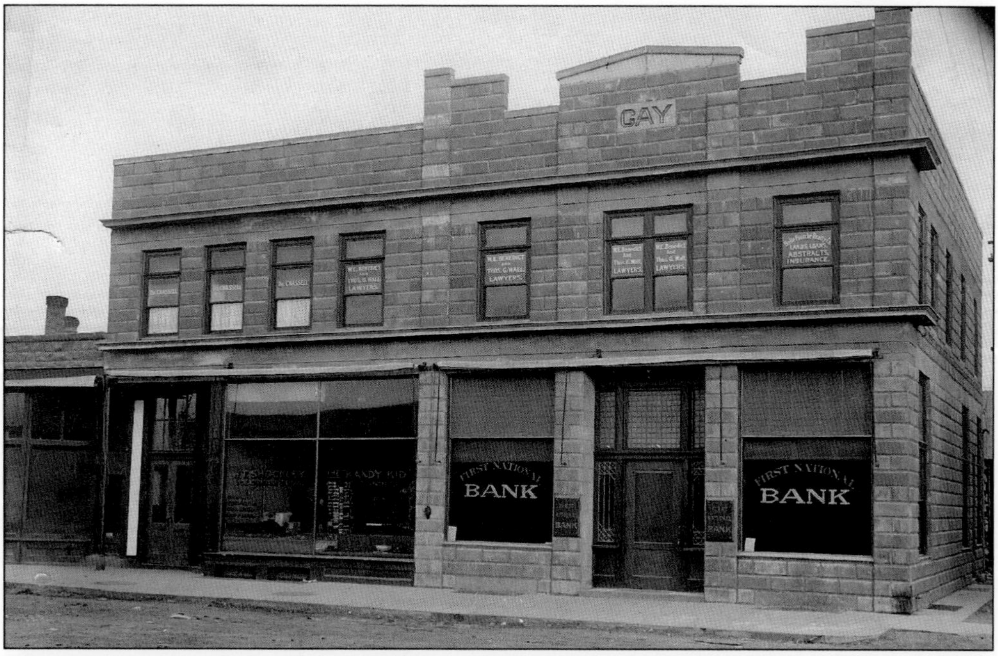

Thomas H. Gay constructed this building around 1908 to be the First National Bank of Belle Fourche, of which he became the president. Gay was an early settler of Belle Fourche, coming to the area with his brother Arthur in 1892. Another brother, Frank, also came to Belle Fourche in 1898 and ran a men's clothing store until 1930.

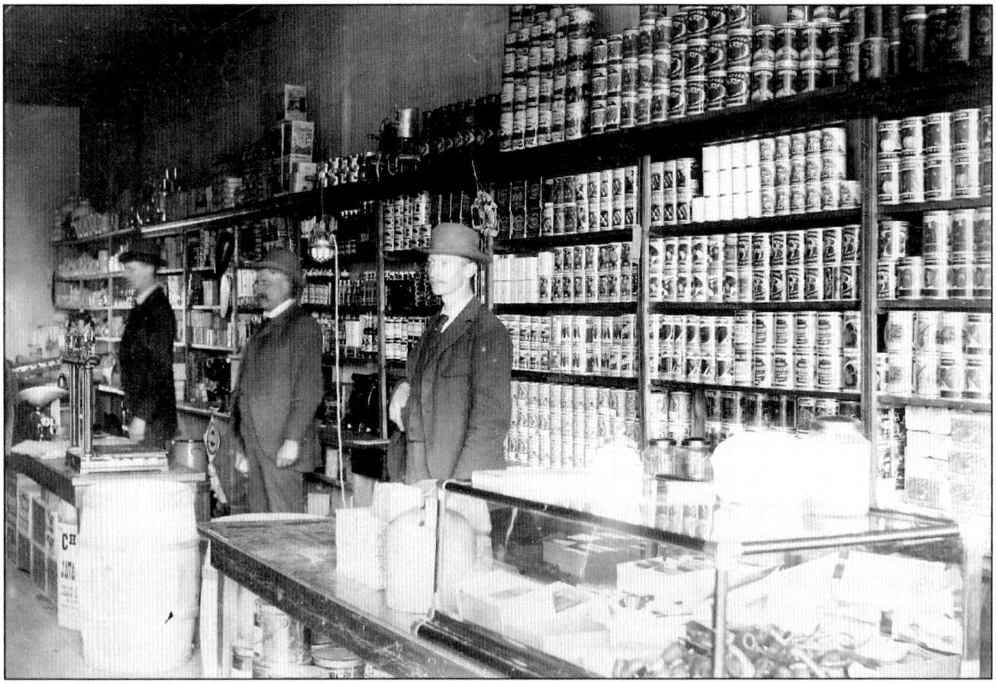

This photograph shows the Gay brothers inside their first store in Belle Fourche around 1894. Arthur and Thomas H. Gay ran a hardware store together until Thomas became the president of the First National Bank.

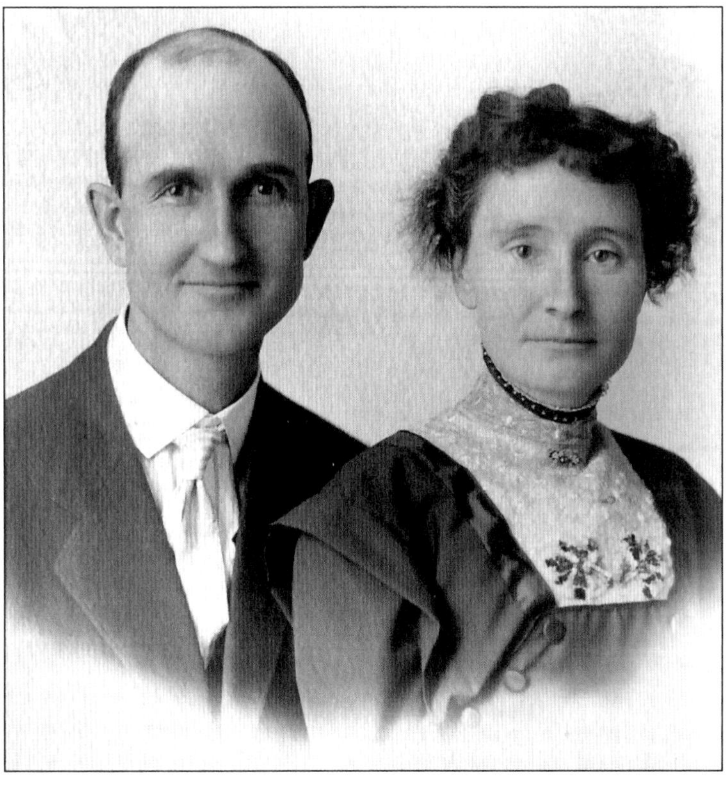

H. E. Frost came to the Black Hills in 1898 and worked at Arnold Grocery in Belle Fourche. After starting his own furniture business in Belle Fourche with his brother-in-law in 1905, Frost went to Omaha to study to become a licensed embalmer.

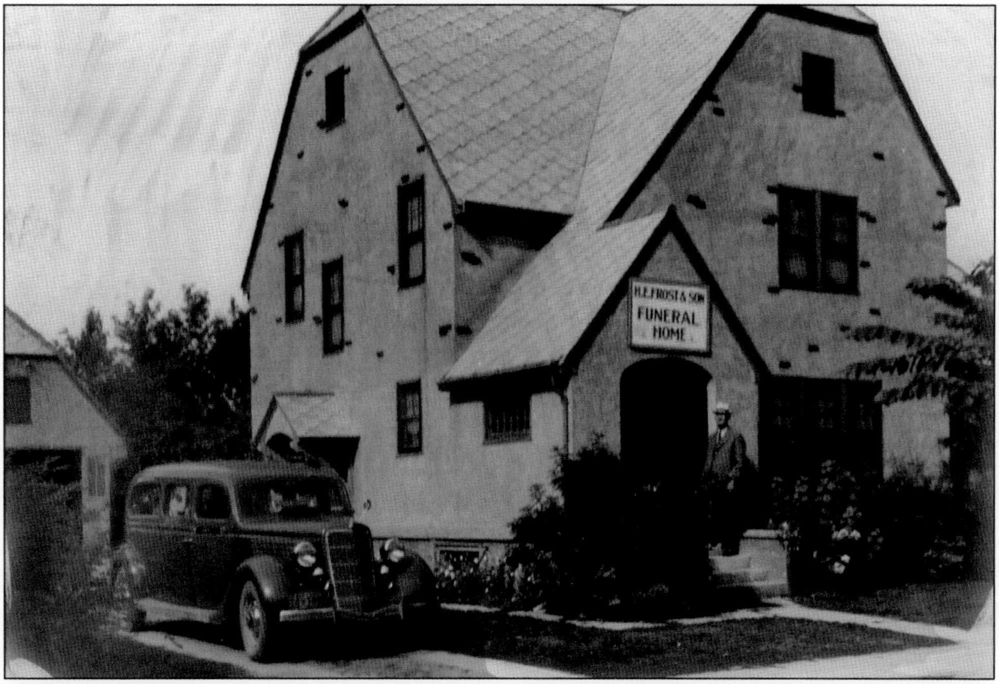

Frost Funeral Home, shown here in 1935, was an important business in Belle Fourche. During the flu epidemic in 1919, Frost Funeral Home did 75 funerals in only 74 days. Frost died in December 1949.

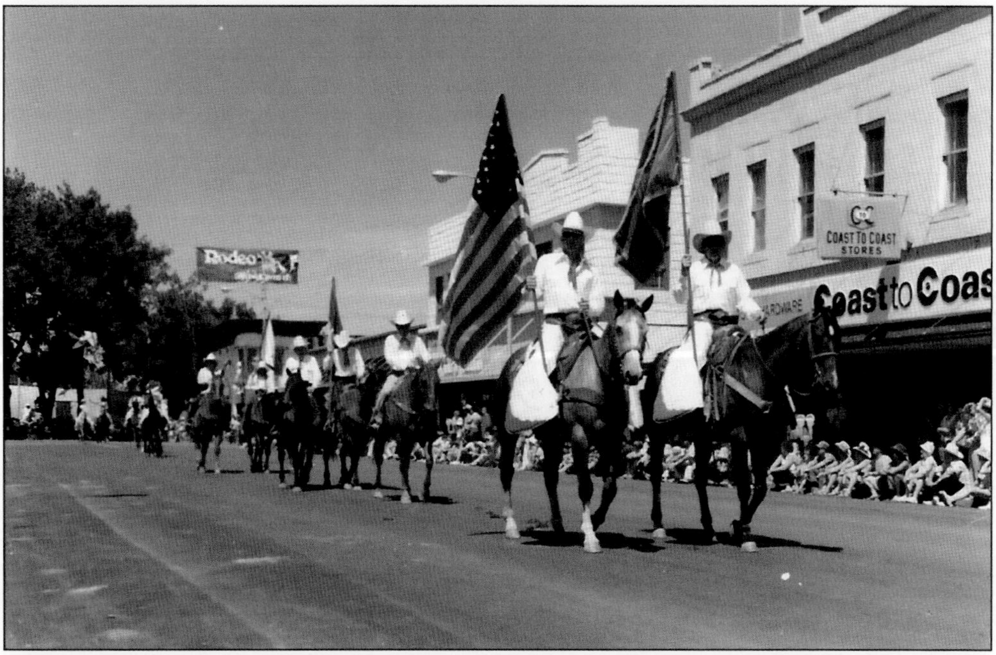

The Fourth of July Round-up Rodeo parade runs right through downtown Belle Fourche. Shown here in 1984, many of the buildings on the west end of State Street are still there. Belle Fourche prides itself in its history, and downtown shows a glance into the past with all the historical buildings that are still standing.

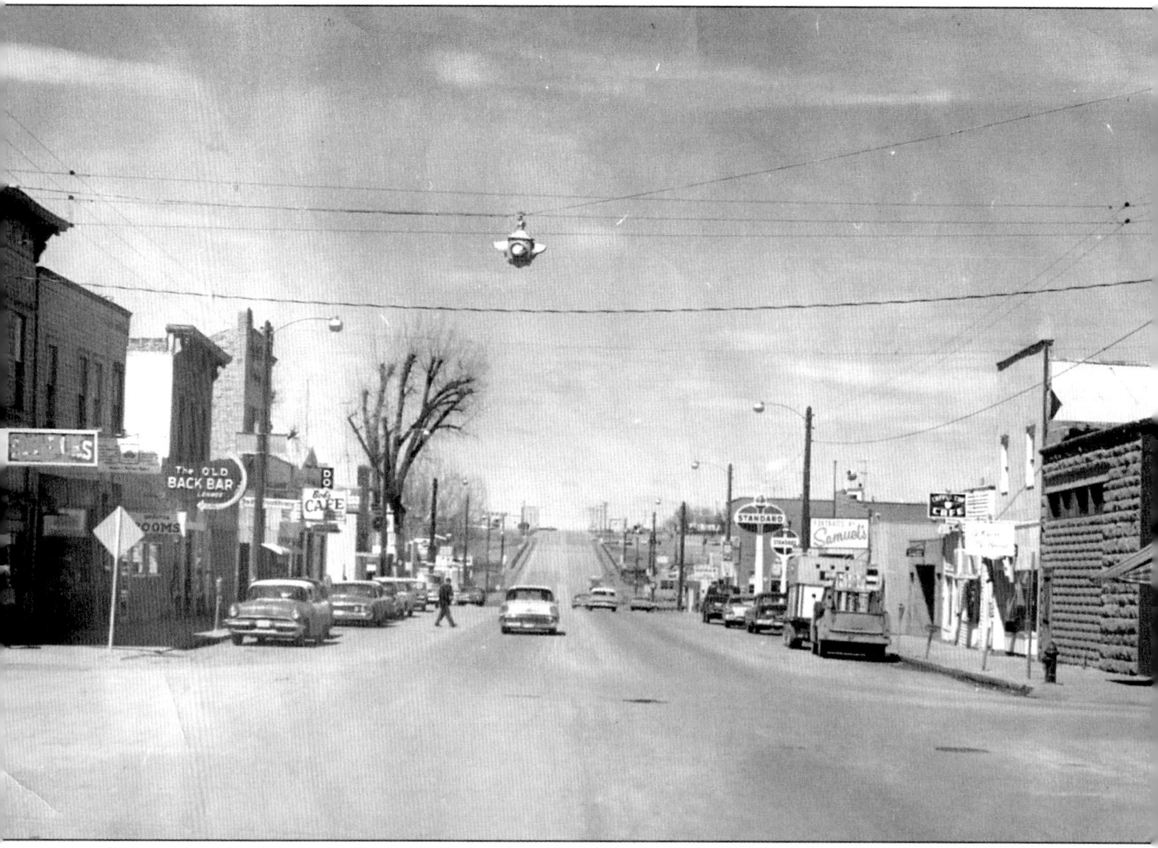

This view, looking north on Saloon Street around 1950, shows what changed over 50 years. Most of the buildings visible in earlier photographs are gone. Some were destroyed in the 1895 fire, and some were simply replaced with newer buildings over the years. Saloon Street became Highway 85 and Fifth Avenue, which is a very busy street. Even today, Highway 85 is a major north-south corridor for truckers and tourists alike. Thousands of vehicles travel this road every day, and with the railroad still running through the heart of the town, cars sometimes back up along this route during midday. There are plans to change this road into a four- and five-lane road that will help to ease traffic flows through town.

Two

Black Hills Roundup

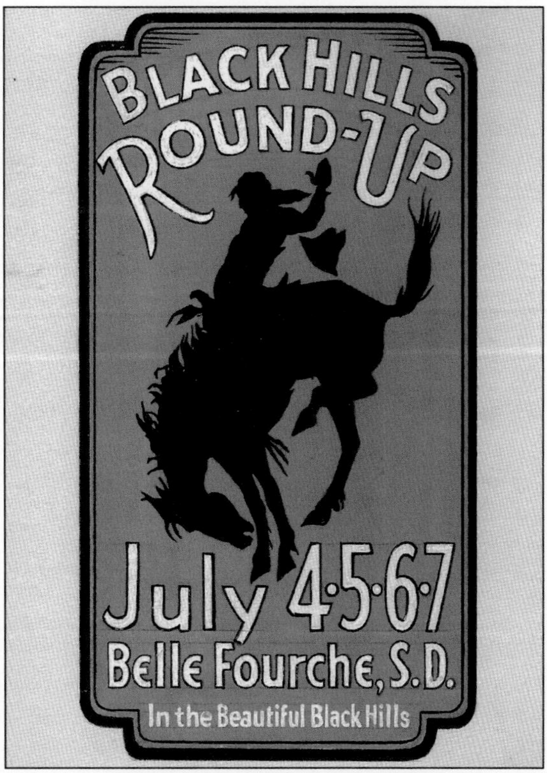

The Fourth of July celebration was first known as the Tri-State Roundup beginning in 1918 and then became the Black Hills Roundup. Both titles were used until 1930, when it became officially known as the Black Hills Roundup. In 2008, the Black Hills Roundup will celebrate its 89th year.

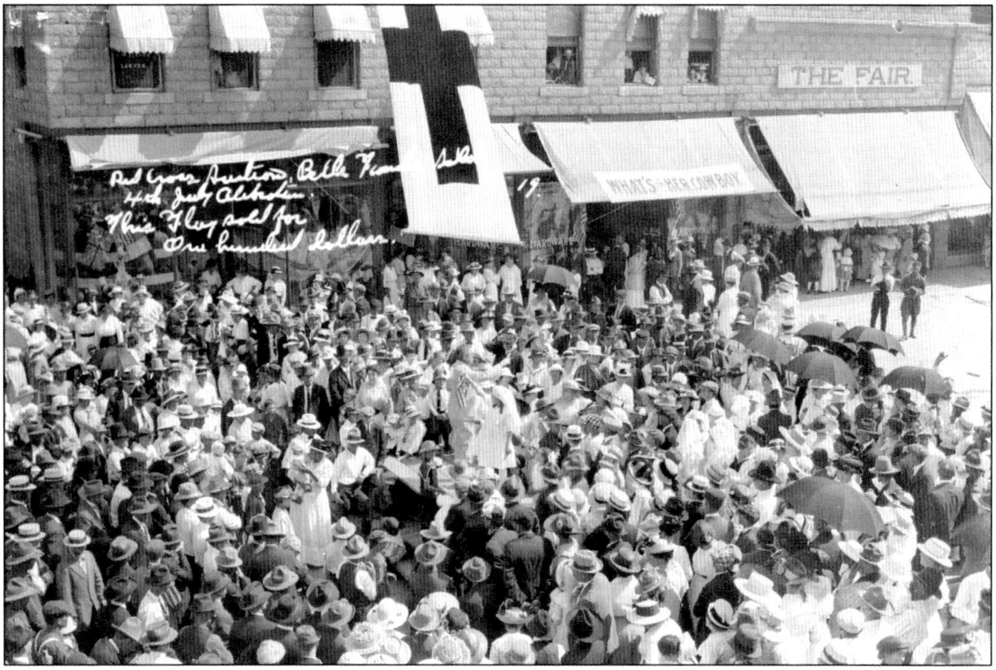

World War I; a Red Cross blood drive; an enthusiastic, patriotic community; and an auction were the ingredients that produced the annual Fourth of July rodeo and celebration. The auction featuring donuts, pet antelope, chickens, and other prizes raised nearly $20,000. Alcester Rose's pet lamb brought $5,425 as cowboys and townsmen bought and resold the lamb over and over. The money raised was wired to Pres. Woodrow Wilson with an offer to send the lamb. Wilson accepted the money but declined the lamb with thanks.

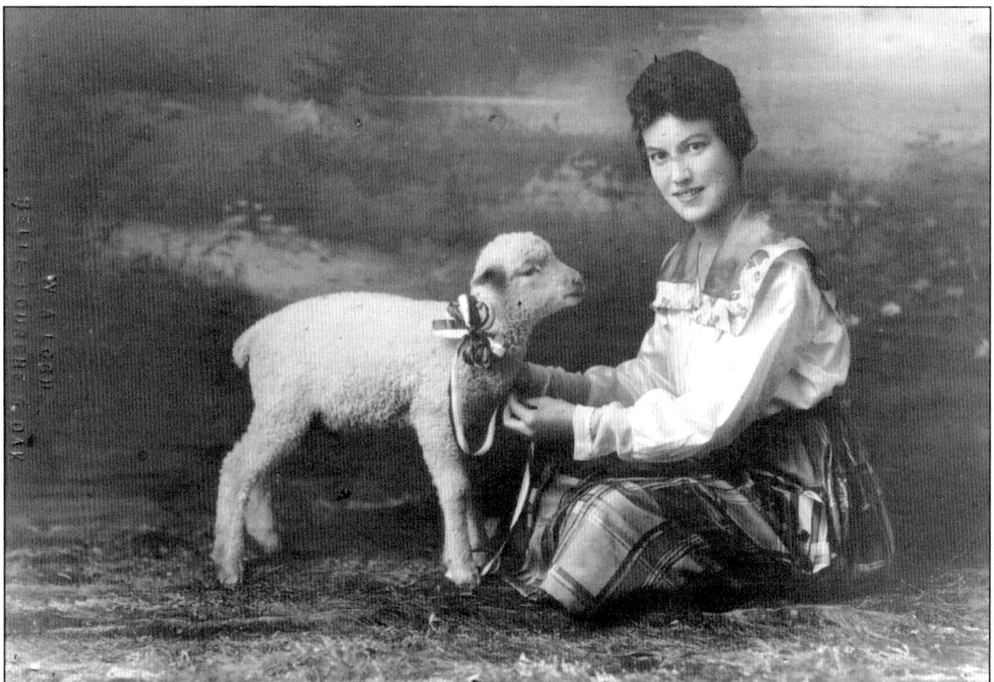

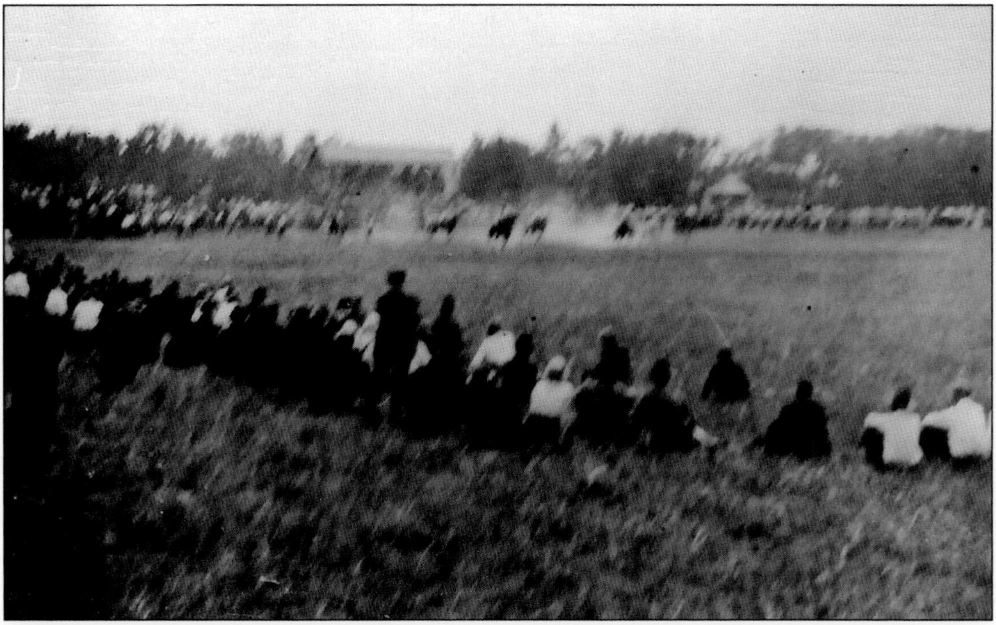

The day continued with a rodeo held at the fairgrounds along the Belle Fourche River. In the days before the Fourth of July, a reported crowd of 20,000 poured into Belle Fourche (which had a population of only 2,000) by train, car, wagon, and horseback to enjoy two days of the rodeo and entertainment. For these early rodeos, there were no chutes. The rider mounted the bronc, which was held by another horse and rider. There was no eight-second ride; the contest ended when either the rider or the bronc gave up. Al Garrett is trying to stay on Sure Fire.

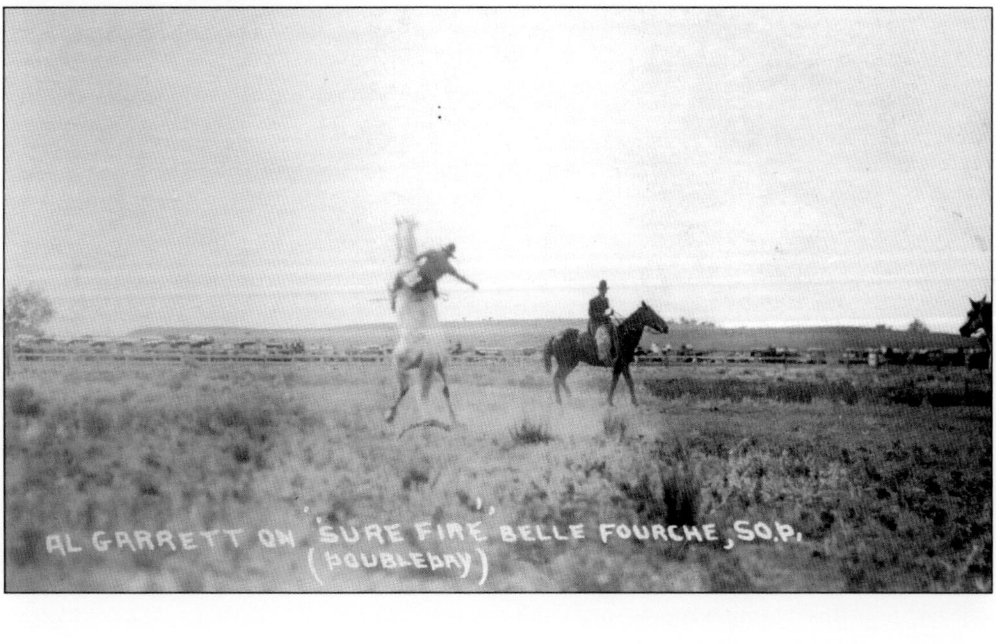

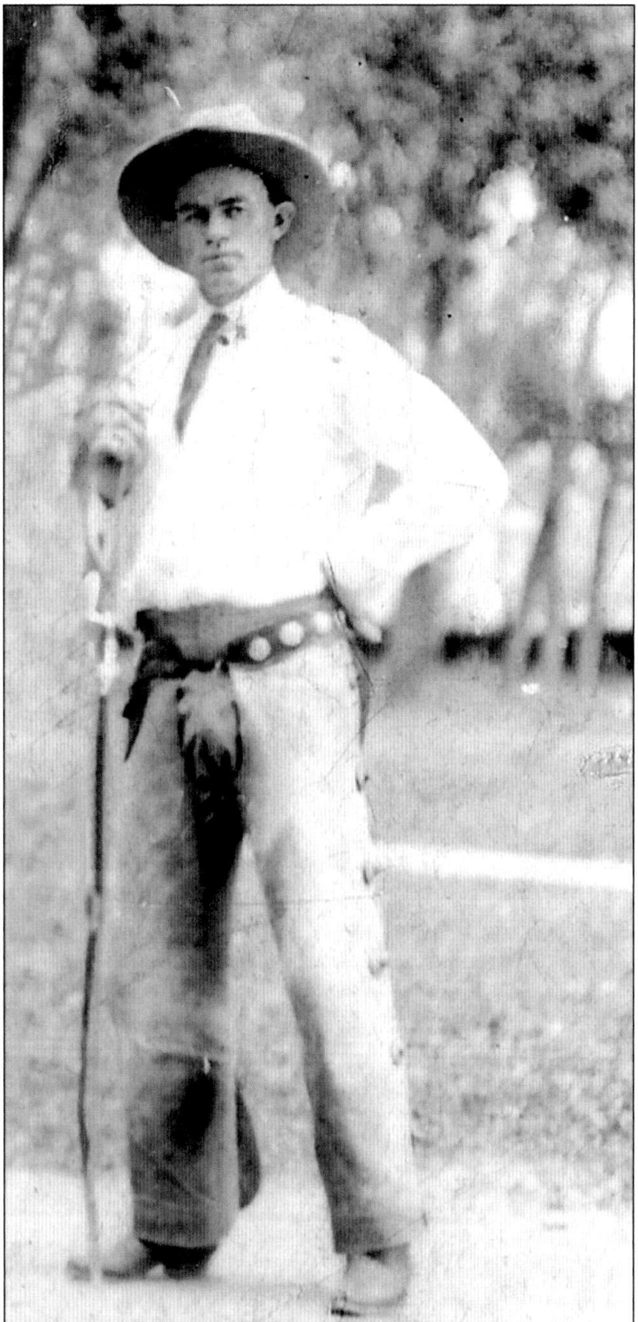

The crowd came to see a contest between world champion bronc rider Sam Brownell and a local outlaw bronc named Tipperary that was owned by Charles Wilson of Camp Crook. Brownell rode but disqualified himself because of a hand change. This rule was enacted by the committee from Belle Fourche; at the Cheyenne Frontier Days the hand change was allowed. Wilson's horses were famous, and Wilson was widely recognized as a rodeo promoter. Brownell was from Cheyenne, Wyoming, and moved to Belle Fourche in 1921. He and Wilson formed a partnership to produce rodeos in the Dakotas and furnish stock.

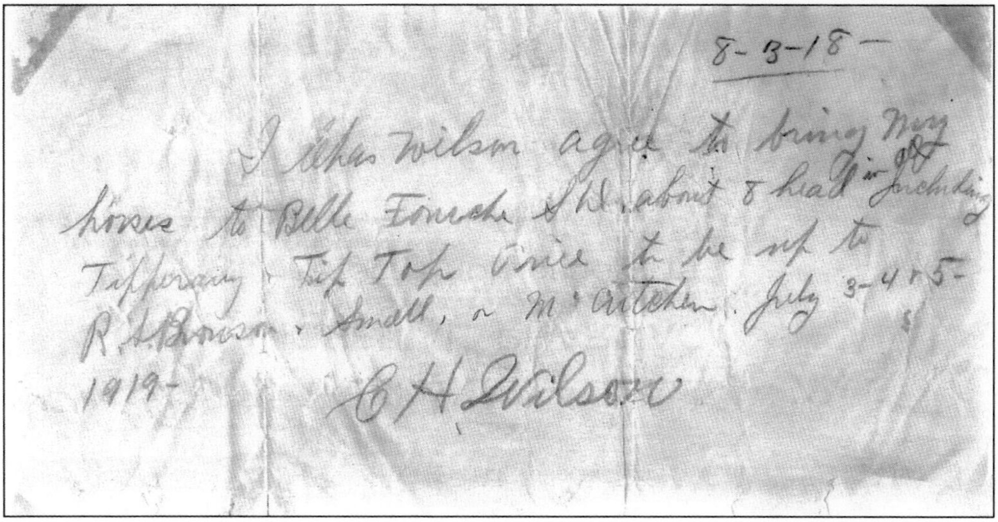
8-3-18-

I Chas Wilson agree to bring my horses to Belle Fourche S.D. about 8 head in all including Tipperary & Tip Top once to be up to R.L. Brownell, Small, or McCutchen July 3-4 & 5- 1919-

C H Wilson

Plans for the 1919 rodeo began when Wilson agreed to bring his broncs Tipperary and Tip Top to the next year's rodeo. The contract between Wilson and the Belle Fourche Commercial Club was written on a scrap of paper in pencil. Brownell agreed to ride. Wilson also brought Baldy, a great snubbing horse. A snubbing horse was a horse used to hold a bronc so the contestant could safely mount. The bronc was sometimes blindfolded until the rider mounted and the horse was released. The 1919 rodeo was another success, and the horses Tipperary and Tip Top ruled.

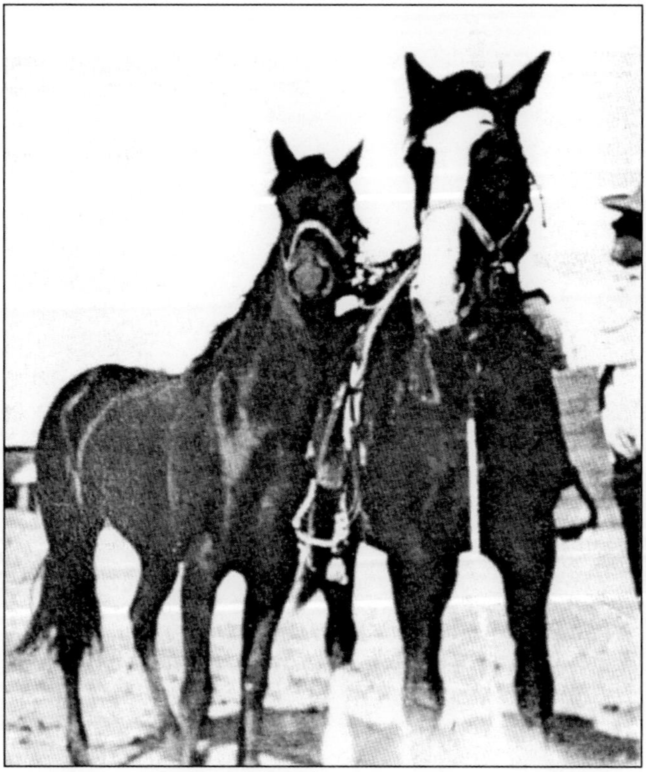

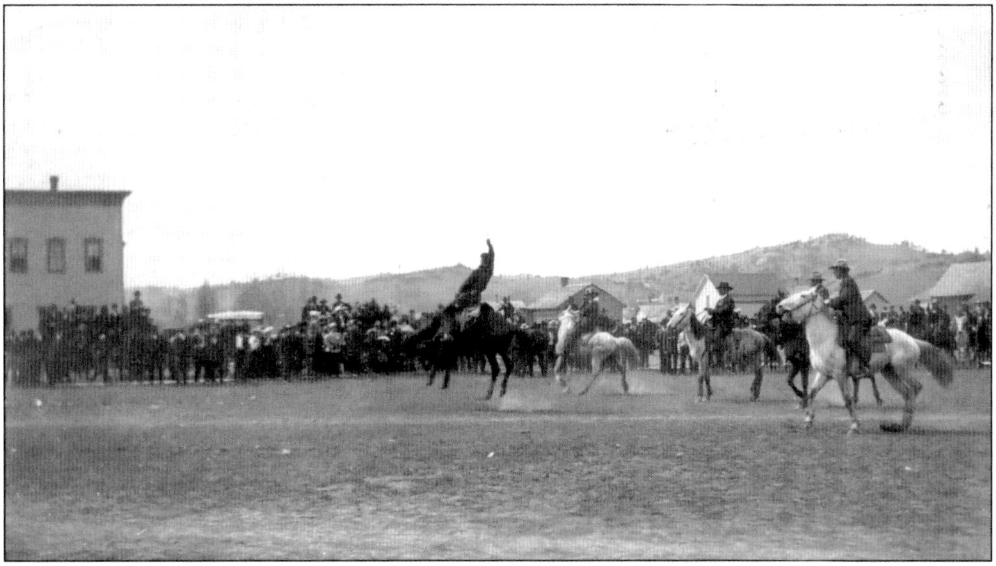

Before the 1918 Tri-State Roundup was organized, early-day rodeos were a way of life. They took place wherever people or buggies formed an arena. The cowboys were just showing off their skills learned and practiced in their employment on the ranches. Betting and bragging rights were parts of cowboy life. Riders, ropers, and doggers challenged each other. A dogger was a rider who wrestled a steer to the ground. Many of these events took place on Belle Fourche streets. The horses and riders formed the arena. Buildings can be seen behind the crowd. One of the first hotels is pictured on the left.

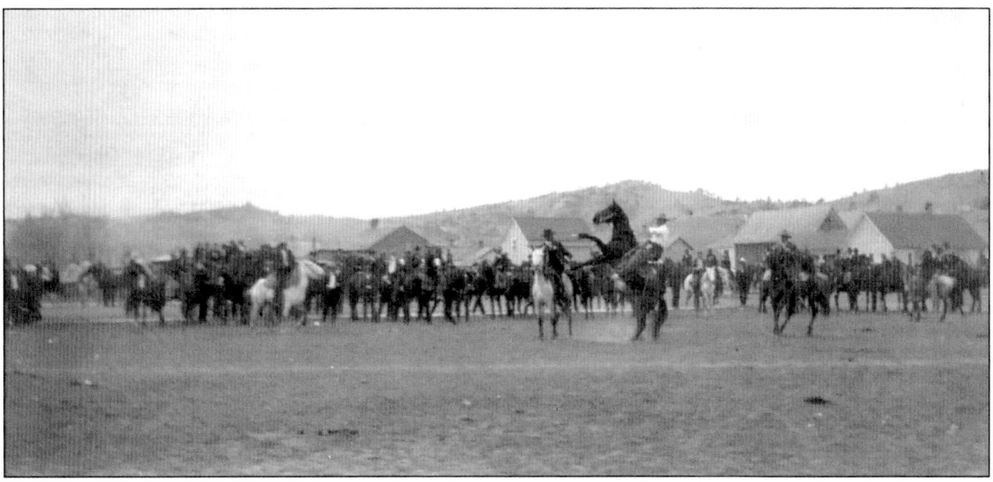

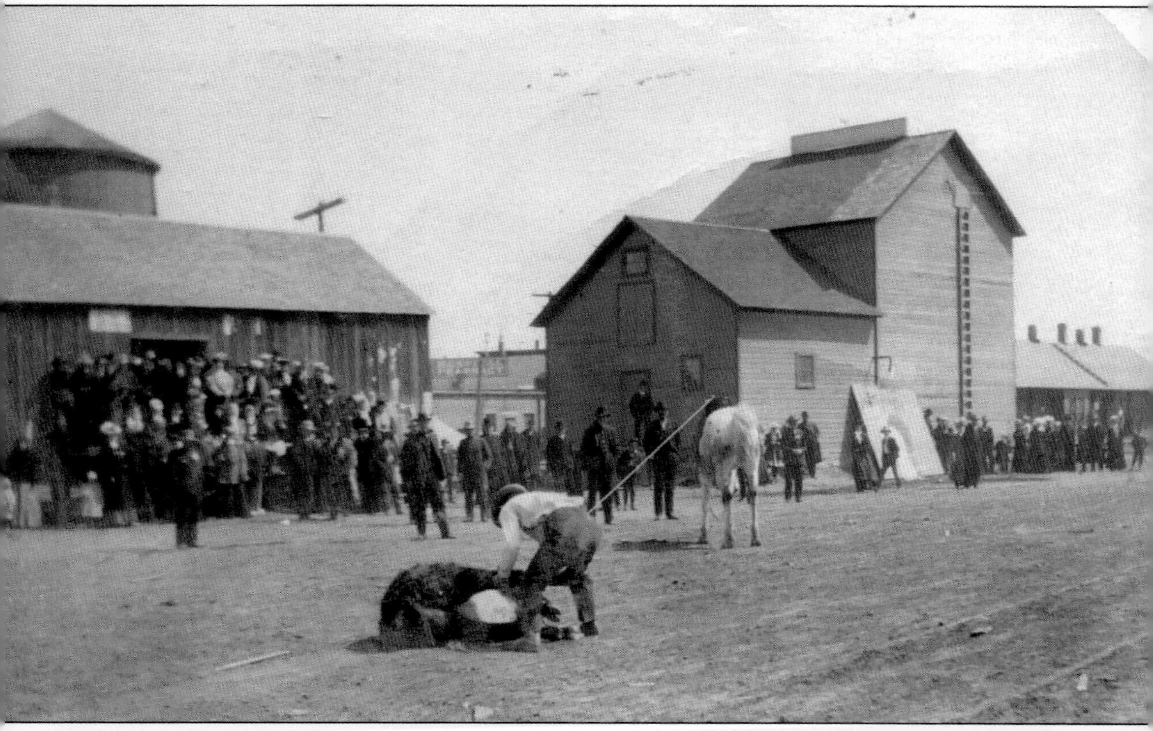

The rules were simple: choose a bronc, ear him down, climb aboard, nod, and start the race. It took two or three cowboys to "ear a horse." One cowboy grabbed the horse by the head and bit the horse's ear to control him. While the horse was distracted, the other two saddled him and the rider climbed aboard. Injuries to horses and riders were common in this process. Today's method is safer. A horse is run into a chute that is just big enough for him to stand, and the cowboy works from above the horse where he has more control and ability to calm it and prevent it from hurting itself and others. Tie-down roping was also done without chutes, fences, or a timer. This picture was taken on Roundup Street with the railroad water tank on the left. The flour mill and the depot are visible behind the spectators.

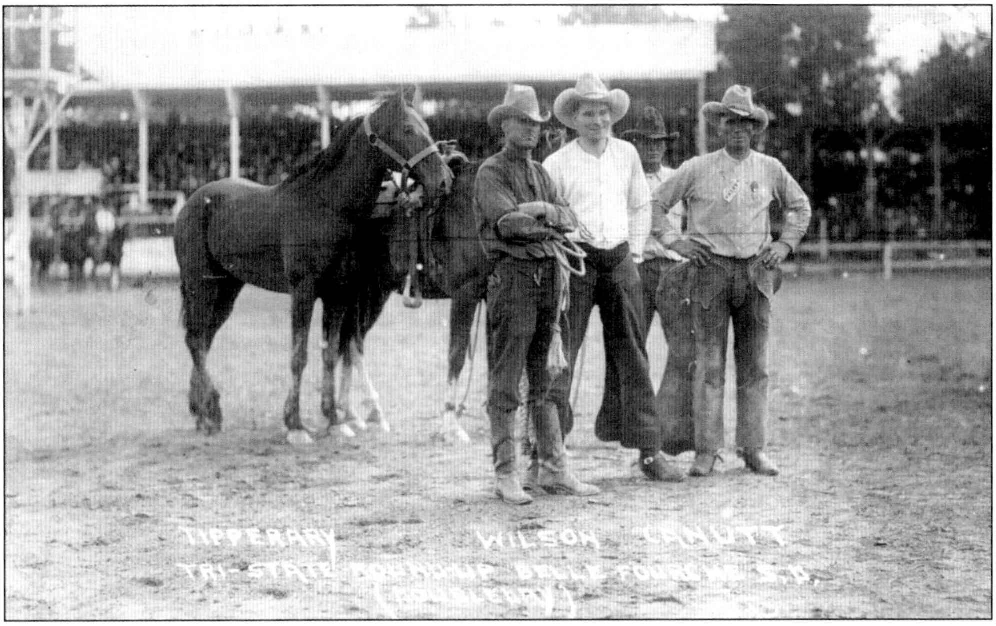

Another world champion bronc rider, Yakima (Enos) Canutt challenged the outlaw bronc Tipperary in 1920. This time the cowboy won. Many said it was because of a very muddy arena that year. The following year, Canutt attempted to ride Tipperary again. Many observers reported that he lost a stirrup, but the judges were on the wrong side of the horse. Canutt went on to star in early Westerns in Hollywood. He returned to Belle Fourche on the centennial celebration in 1985. Standing in front of the newly built grandstand is Tipperary with owner Charles Wilson and rider Canutt. The Tri-State Roundup grandstand was located on the fairgrounds near the Belle Fourche River.

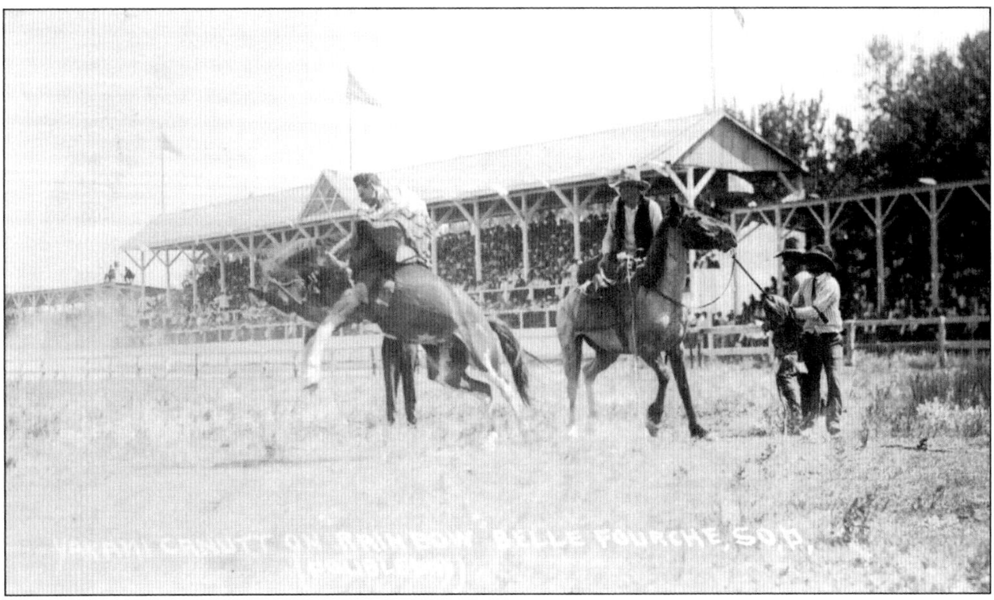

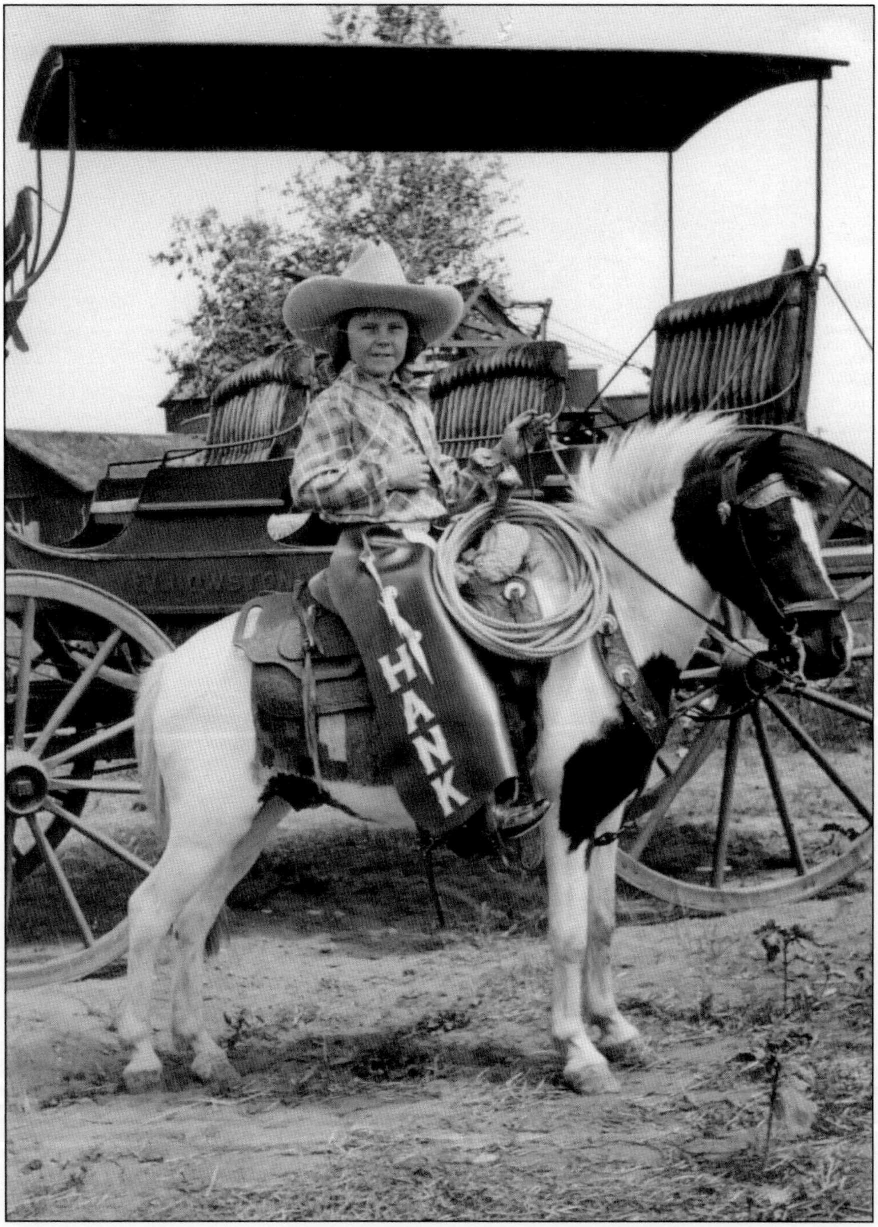

Entertainers were hired for this rodeo and became an important part of the events. The Keenens, including father, Tin Horn Hank, mother, Dessie, and son Carl Little Tin Horn Hank, all did trick roping and riding. The mother and father also rode rough stock. Tin Horn Hank also clowned when the whole family performed at the Tri-State Roundup in 1928. Little Tin Horn Hank was three years old. According to Paul Hennessey's *"Tin Horn Hank" Keenen and the World's Youngest Cowboy*, son Carl developed his talent for roping and riding starting at age two. When he was four, he began training his horse, Bill. Crowds loved the little blond-curled boy. The family continued to act in rodeos, the West show, the circus, and in vaudeville. Vaudeville was being replaced by talking movies, so the Keenens started to perform in the movies. Little Tin Horn Hank was used as a second for Shirley Temple and Jackie Cooper. When he was 15, he had a terrible accident at Red Lodge, Montana, and never was at the top of his craft after that.

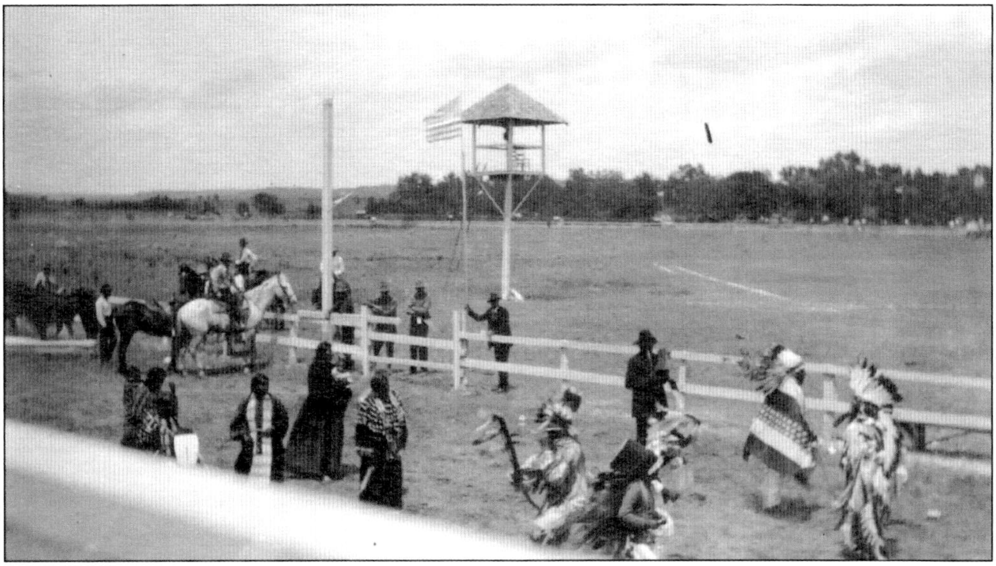

Native Americans from local South Dakota reservations camped along the river, displaying their customs in the tent area. They performed traditional dances in front of the grandstand in their colorful native dress. They also participated in the Fourth of July parade. The officials sat in the crow's nest, judging the contestants. The judges had to enter the crow's nest by climbing a ladder. Leonard Stroud was another rodeo star who performed both on rough stock and as a trick rider. He competed in the Tri-State Roundup for many years. He challenged Tipperary twice and failed dismally each time. He finished his career as a stock and performer contractor. Mayne Stroud, his wife, was also a trick rider and roper.

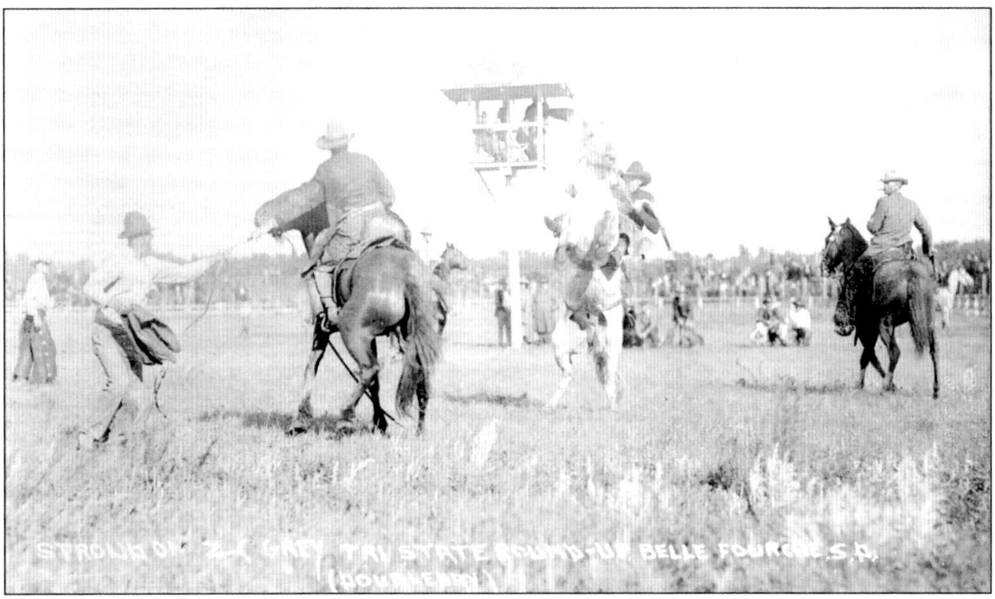

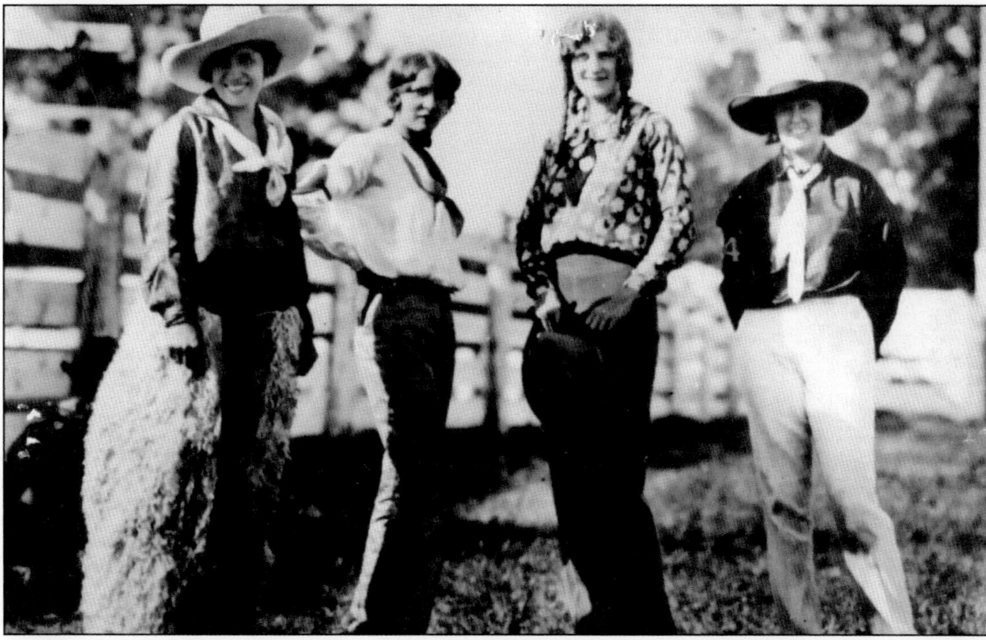

Cowgirls were decorative, but they also competed in cowgirl races, trick riding, and even riding broncs. Their stirrups were tied under the horse's belly. Dessie Keenen refused to hobble her stirrups as that cramped the riders' movements. She rode in the 1921 roundup and won second place. The ladies also rode steers and calves. Tad Lucas wore angora chaps. Lucas, who grew up in Cody, Wyoming, came to be a world champion cowgirl by outriding Sioux Indians at the age of 14; she went on to win 20 national trick riding titles. She was the first woman inducted into the Cowboy Hall of Fame. Grace Runyon from Weta, South Dakota, did clever roping and riding stunts. Prairie Rose Henderson won the bronc riding championship at Cheyenne, Wyoming, and Keenen won second. Years later, Henderson was caught in a Wyoming blizzard and perished. They identified her body by her championship belt buckle.

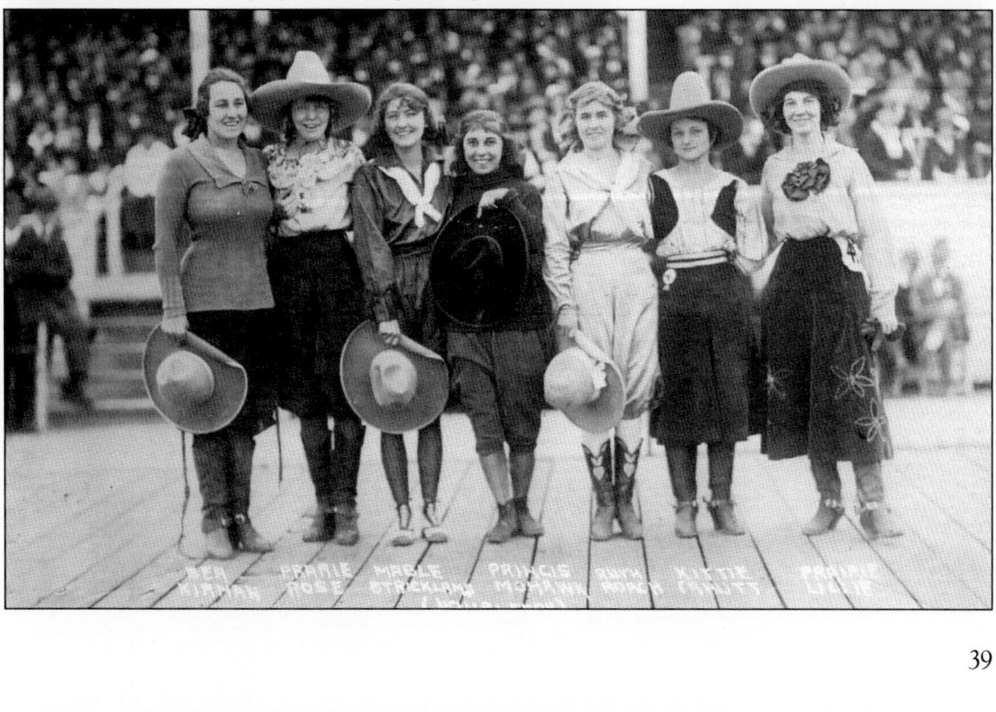

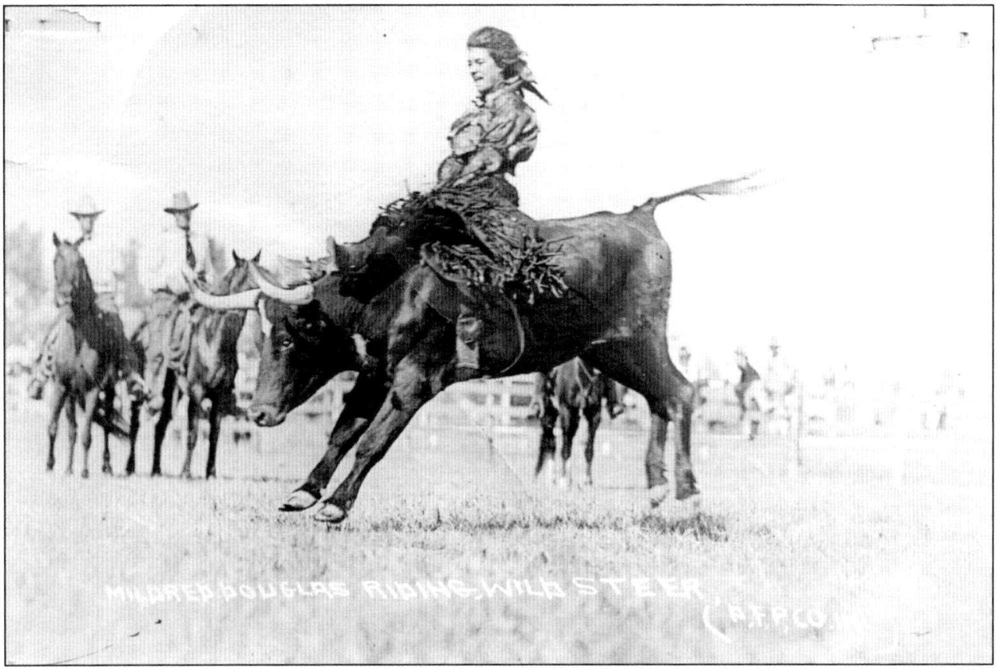

Mildred Douglas appeared in the rodeos from 1916 to 1926. She came from Connecticut. She rode both broncs and steers. Almost all the events in the early 1920s were both men and ladies events. The events consisted of whatever the group that organized the rodeo decided to do. Fox Hastings ran away from a convent school to join a Wild West show. She became the first woman steer wrestler in 1924.

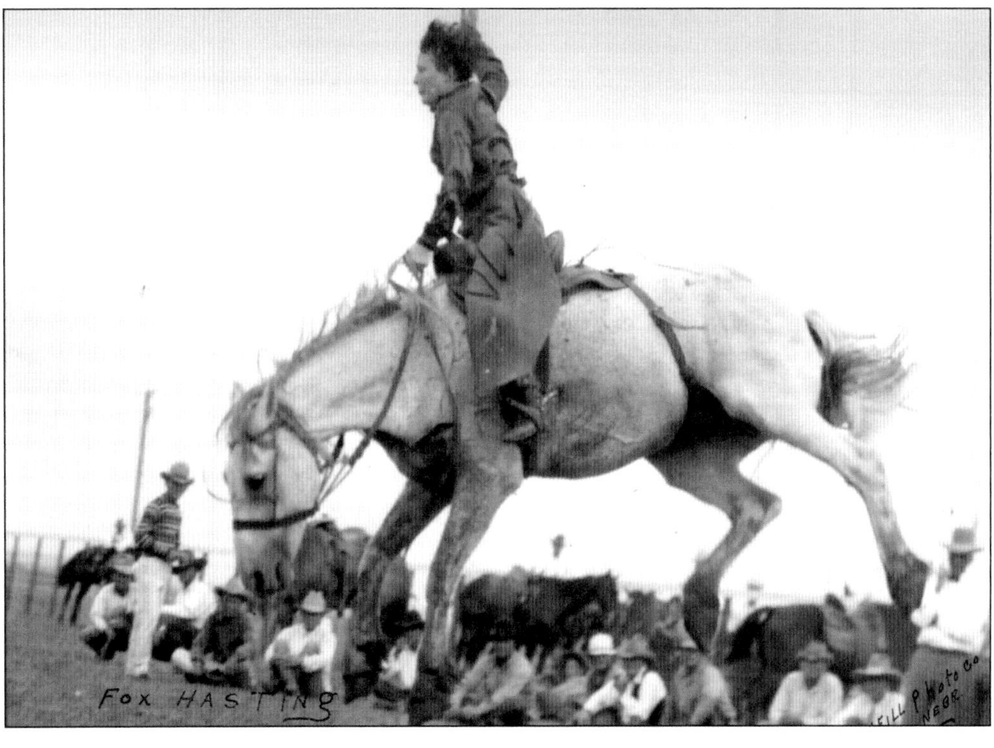

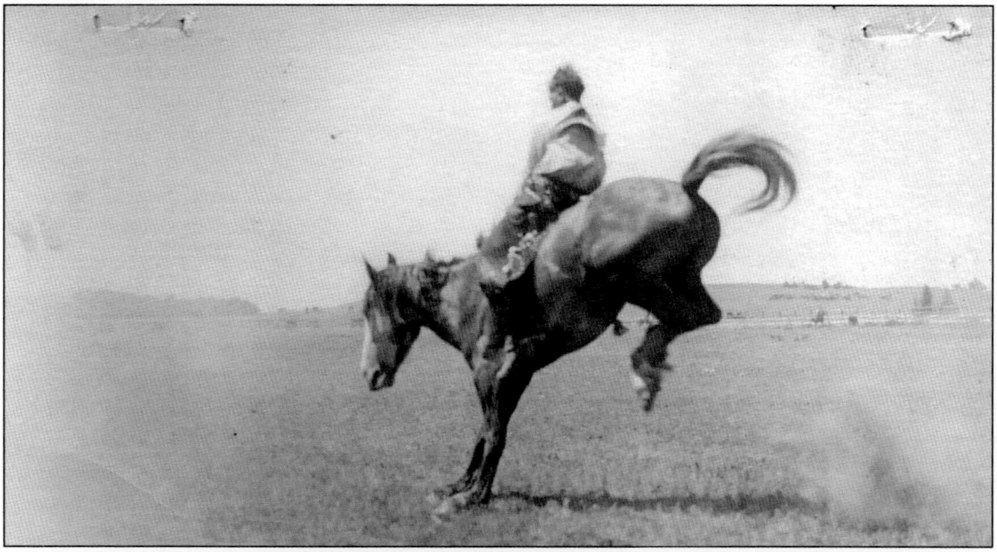

Bareback riding was rough. The guys could use both hands, and they needed both. They only had a rope; there was no suitcase handle as is used today. They rode until the horse quit or the cowboy bucked off. Rules varied and were determined by the organizers. Today's rules are consistent from rodeo to rodeo. Bareback riders must use only one hand or they are disqualified. Fred "Fritz" Kentsler from Mud Butte, South Dakota, was the Tri-State Roundup champion in 1920. He won $450 in this purse. He attempted to ride Tipperary that year but failed. He stuck it out for only 30 yards before hitting the ground.

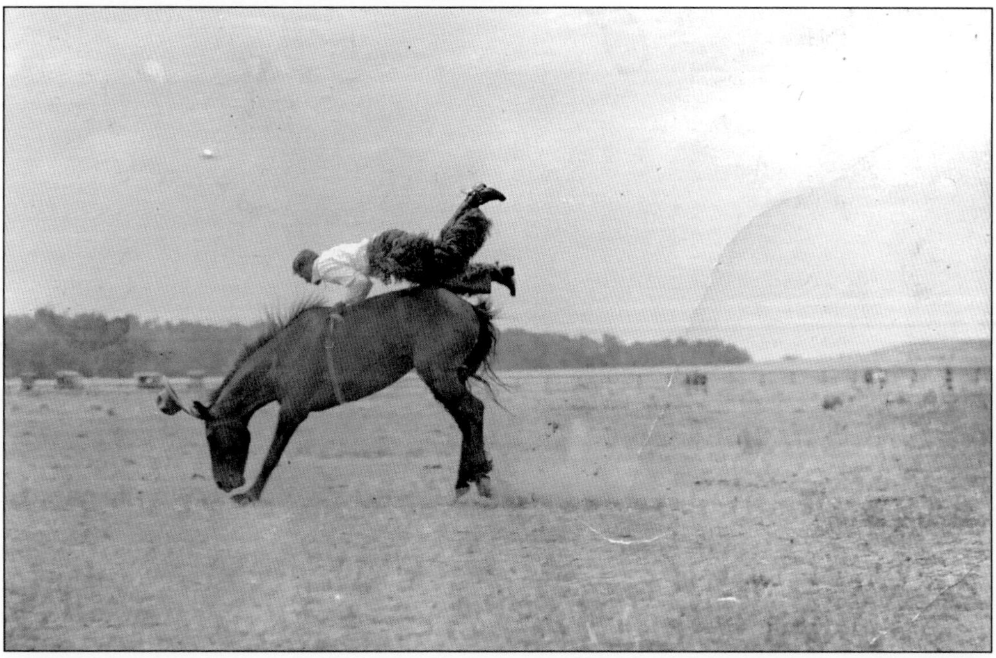

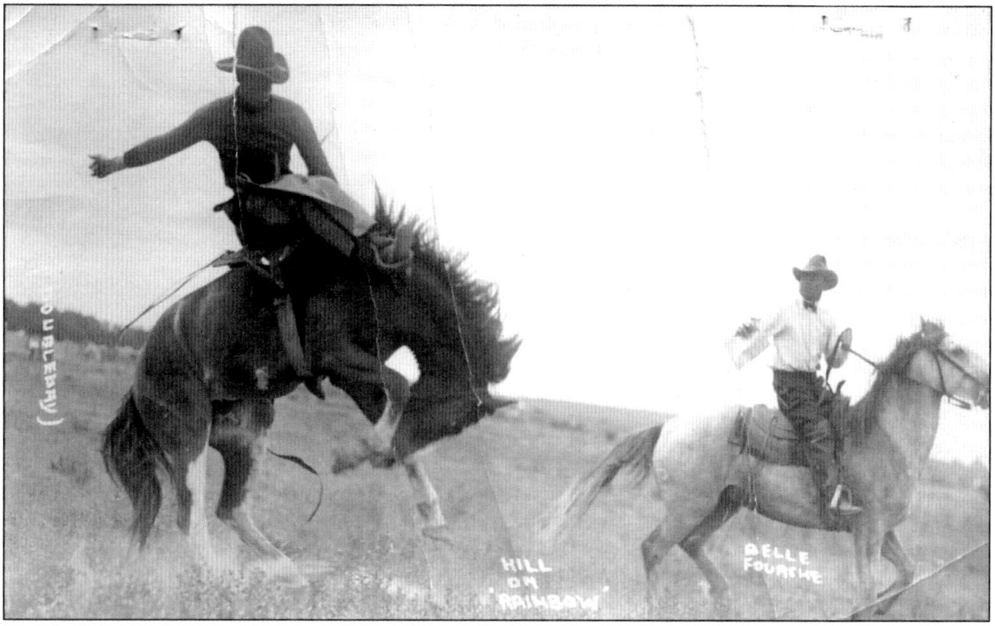

Saddle bronc riders used their own stock saddles. Horses were flanked to make them buck and had a halter and rope. Entry fees were per event, and purses or winnings were $40 for first, $20 for second, and $10 for third in the early days. Entry fees were $6 in Belle Fourche in 1921. This picture of Kit McCorey (below) was used by the Madison Square Garden for publicity and was painted four stories tall. His brother Howard was considered to be the better bronc rider, but the photographer caught a terrific picture of Kit on Topper. Doubleday Photos are famous rodeo photographers.

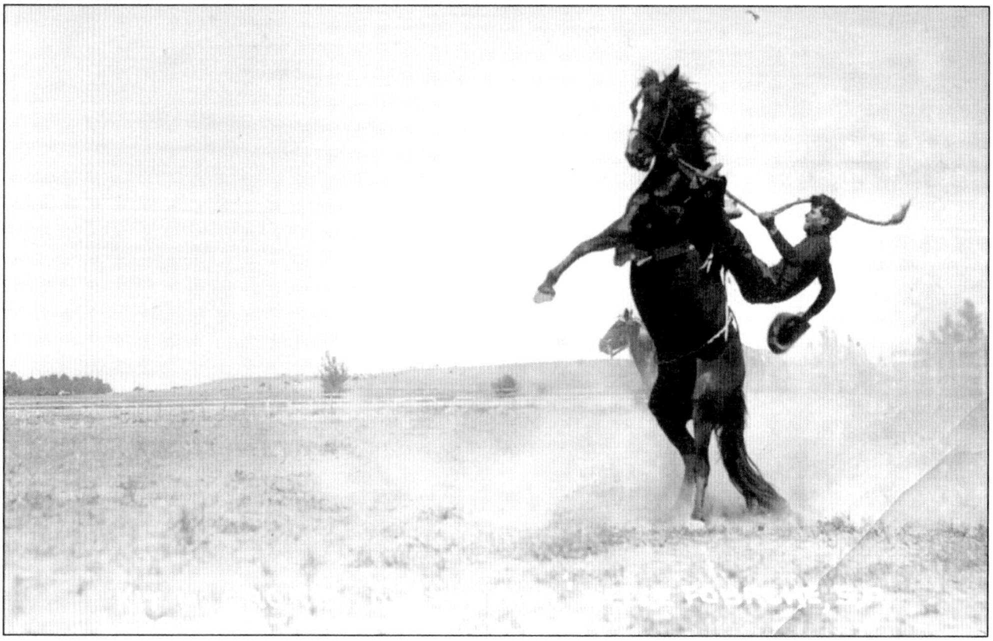

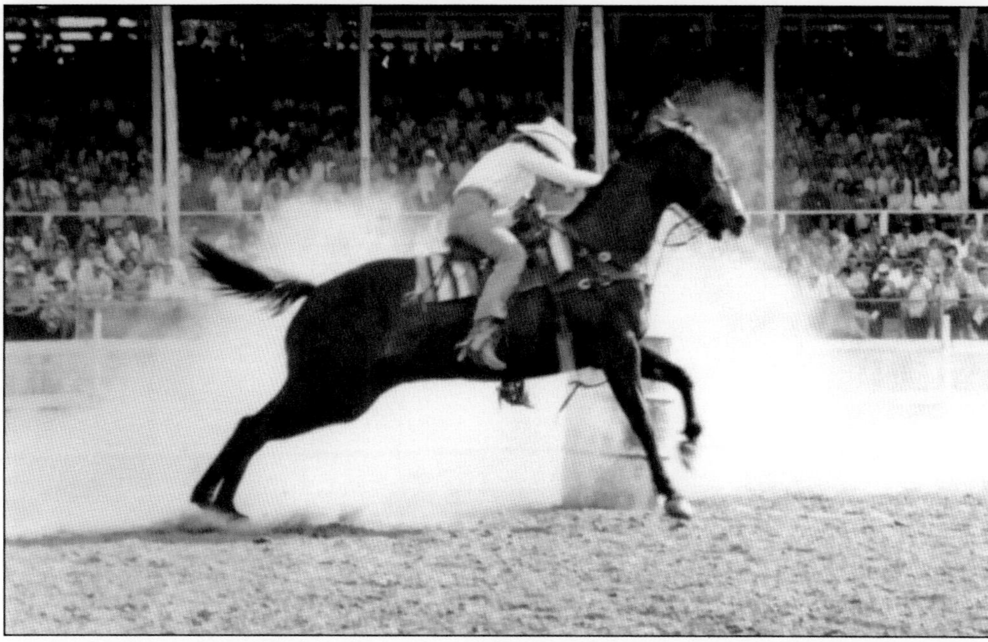

Later attractions were added to the rodeo, including ladies barrel racing and a queen contest. Barrel racing originally developed as an event for women. While their husbands roped or rode bulls and broncs, the women barrel raced. Not much is known about the exact dates and details of barrel racing developments. It is believed that it first saw competitive light in the state of Texas. The Girls Rodeo Association (GRA), instituted in 1949, was the first body of rodeo developed specifically for women. Rosalie Anderson Ridley of St. Onge, the first Miss South Dakota, was honored at the Black Hills Roundup. The first South Dakota queen contest was held at Rapid City Range Days in 1956 and moved to the Black Hills Roundup in 1964. Diane MacKaben, the 1980 South Dakota queen, was crowned 1982 Miss Rodeo World. The first Miss Rodeo America, Marilyn (Scott) Freimark, visited the roundup in 1956.

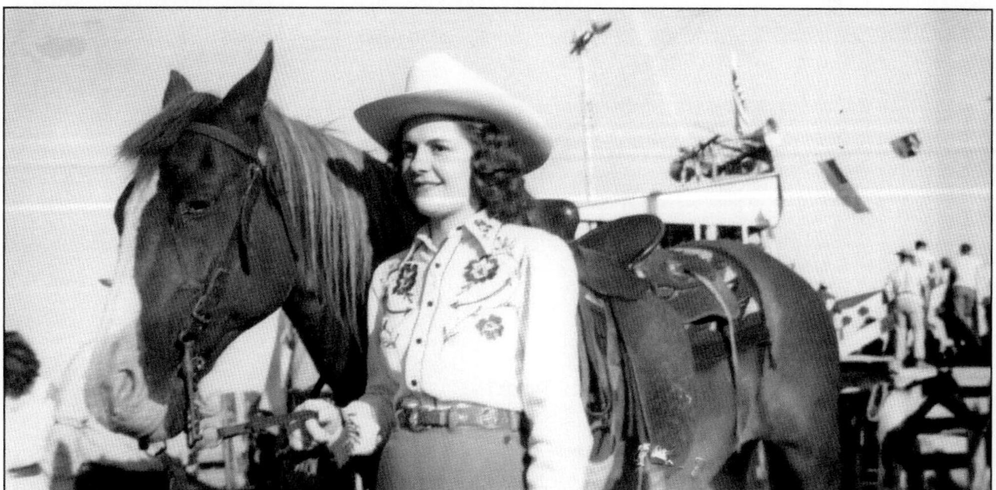

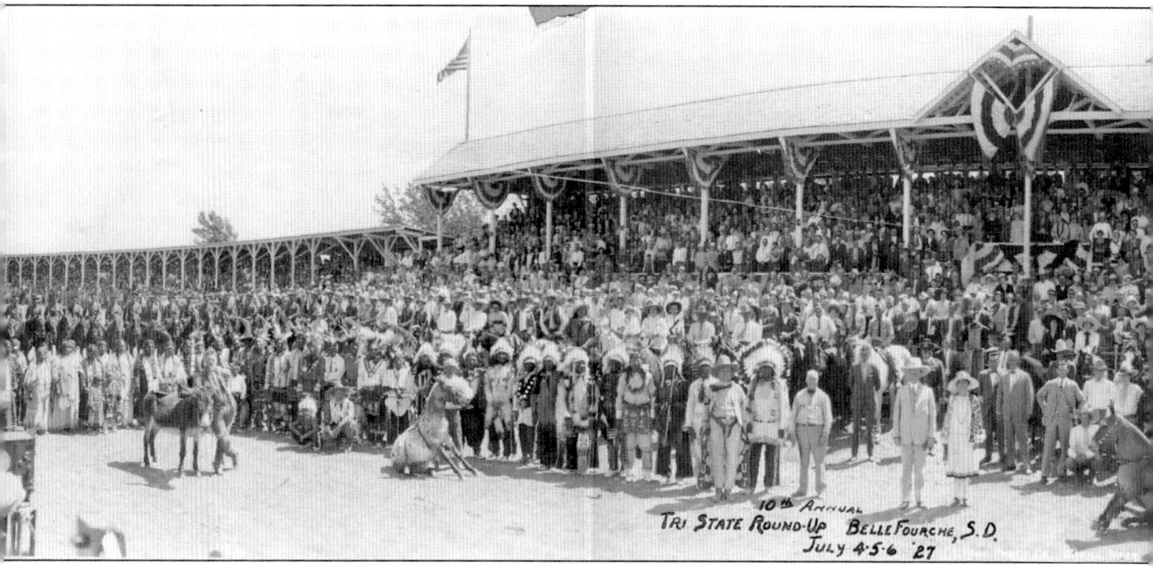

Few rodeos have entertained a president of the United States. The Black Hills Roundup had that honor in 1927 when Pres. Calvin Coolidge and his wife, Grace, were summering in the

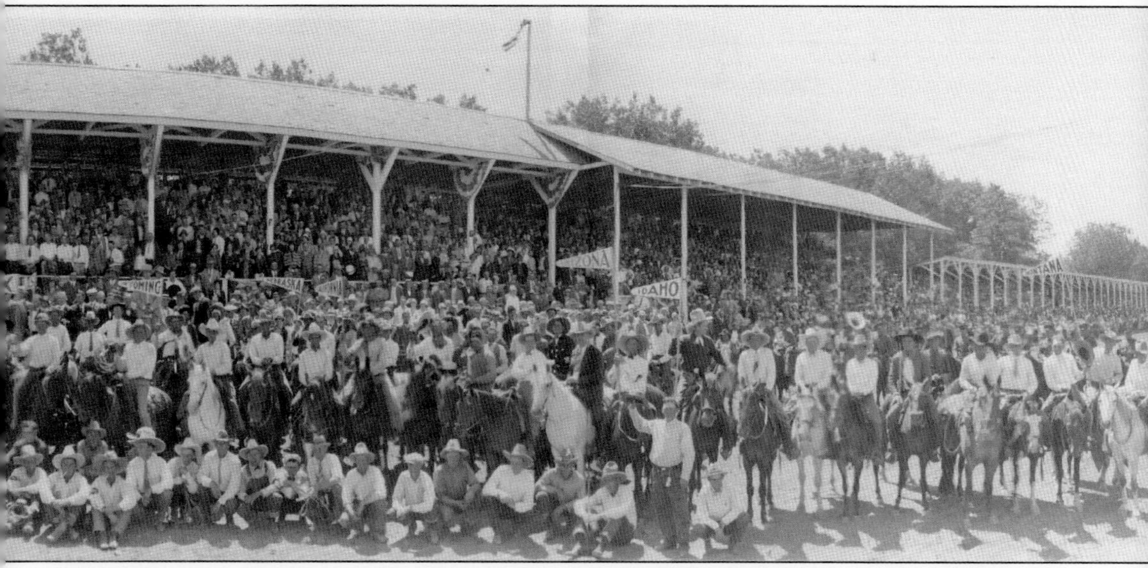

Black Hills. The official party intended to stay only one hour, but before the hour had expired, the president sent word to hold the train, and he stayed all afternoon.

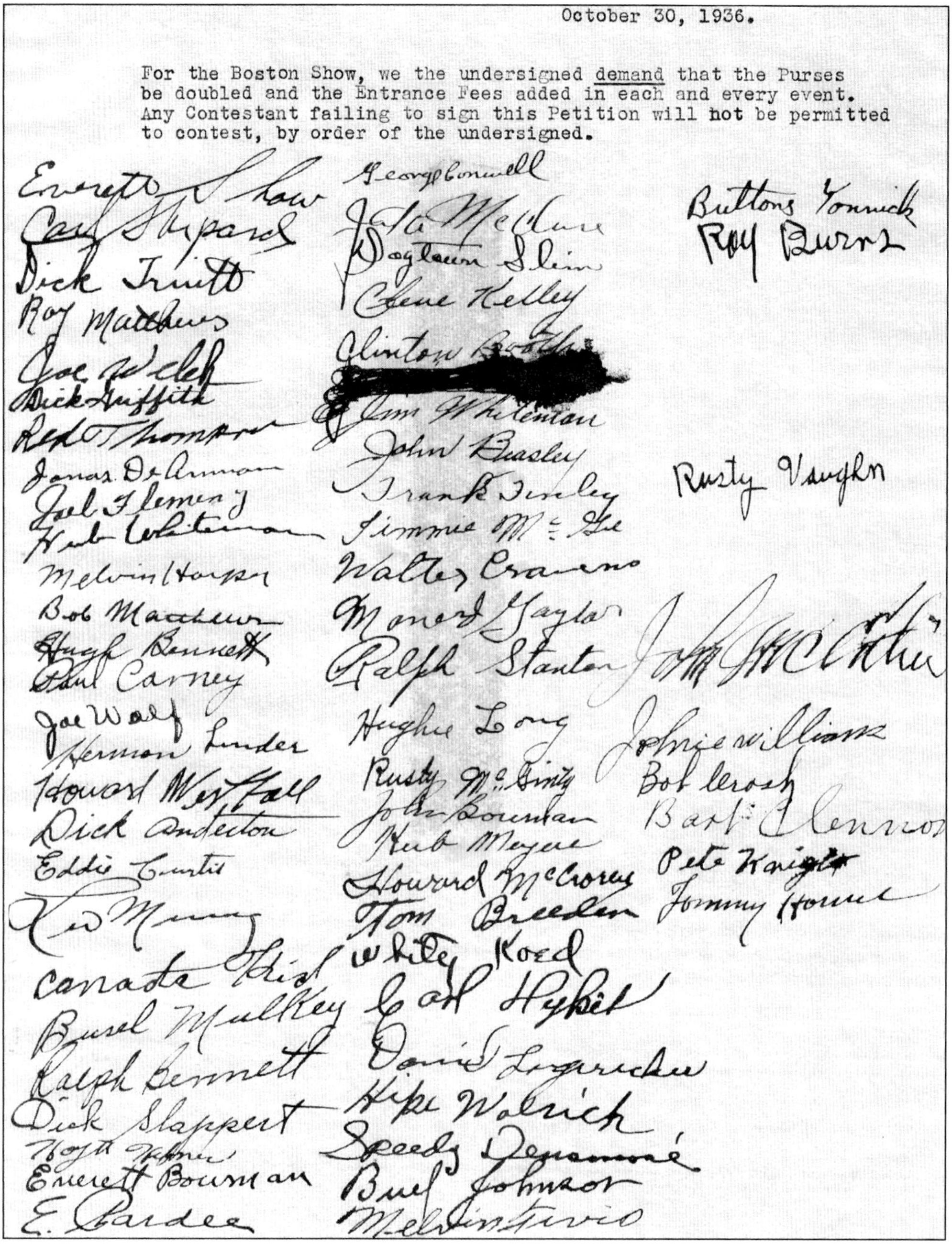

October 30, 1936.

For the Boston Show, we the undersigned demand that the Purses be doubled and the Entrance Fees added in each and every event. Any Contestant failing to sign this Petition will not be permitted to contest, by order of the undersigned.

In 1936, this petition was signed by 61 rodeo participants, which forced rodeo organizers to increase and uniform purses for all events. Another issue was unfair judging. It was signed in Boston. This petition caused the formation of the Cowboys' Turtle Association, now the Professional Rodeo Cowboy Association (PRCA). It was called the turtle because they said it took them so long to wake up to the unfair practices. One of the local area signers was Howard McCrorey of Deadwood. He was a participant as a dogger at the Black Hills Roundup in 1936. There were five McCrorey brothers all involved in rodeo during the early years.

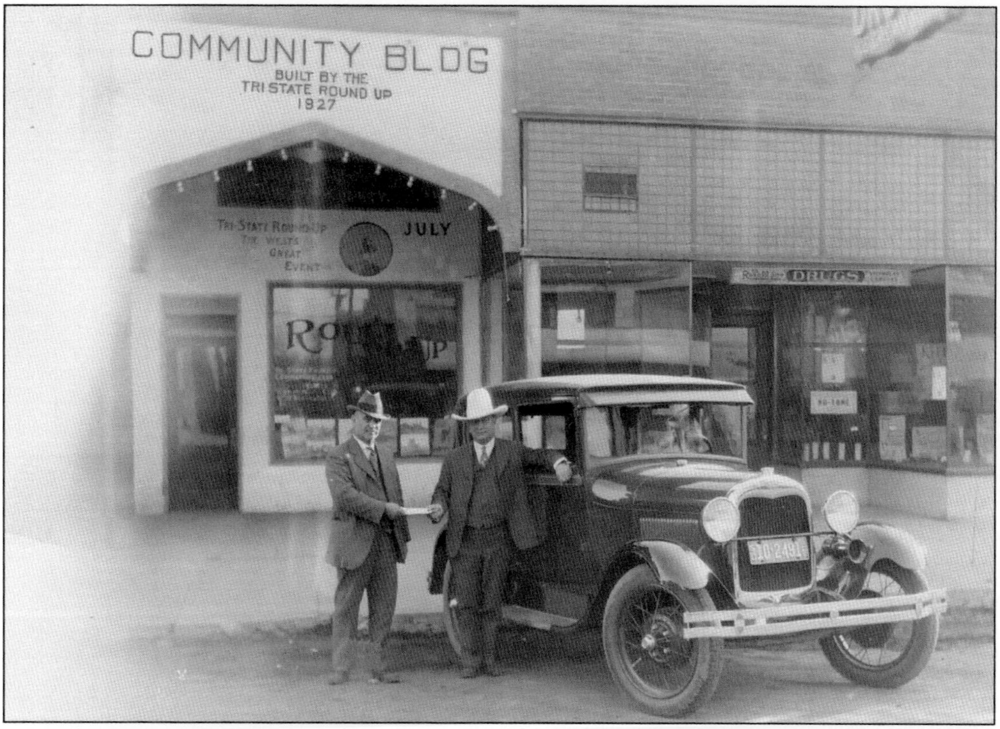

After the 1918 rodeo, a local group formed the Tri-State Fair and Sales Corporation. Over the years, the event and facilities have changed and expanded. Some of the directors are Dave R. Evans, one of the founders; C. F. Harshfield; D. Wayne George; Art Richie, stock provider and co-owner of Tipperary after Charles Wilson died; Gam Ouren; and Abe Blumenthal.

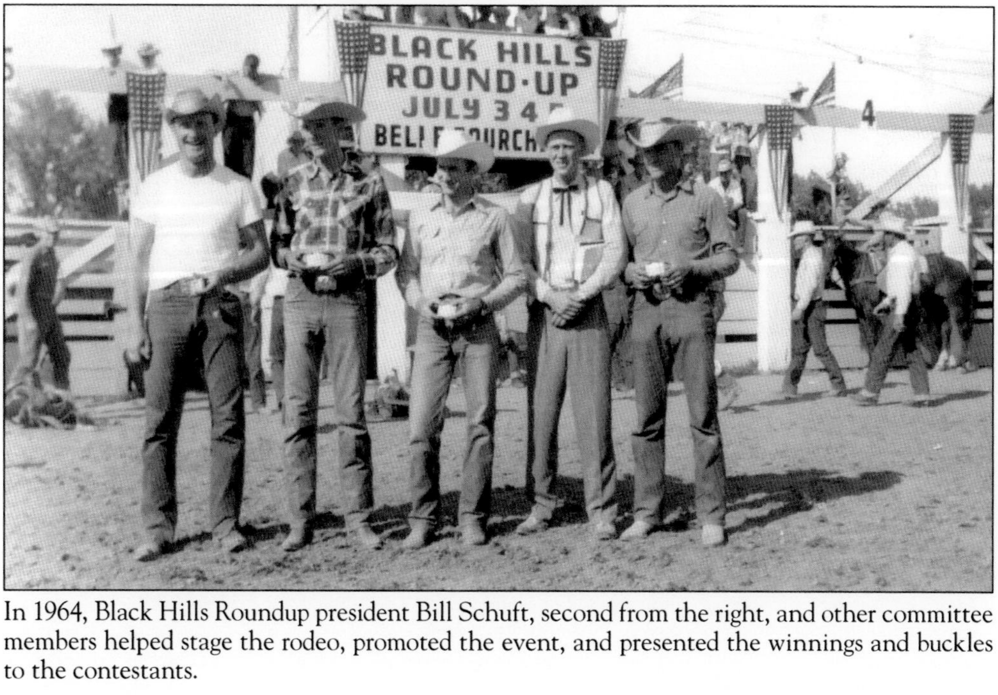

In 1964, Black Hills Roundup president Bill Schuft, second from the right, and other committee members helped stage the rodeo, promoted the event, and presented the winnings and buckles to the contestants.

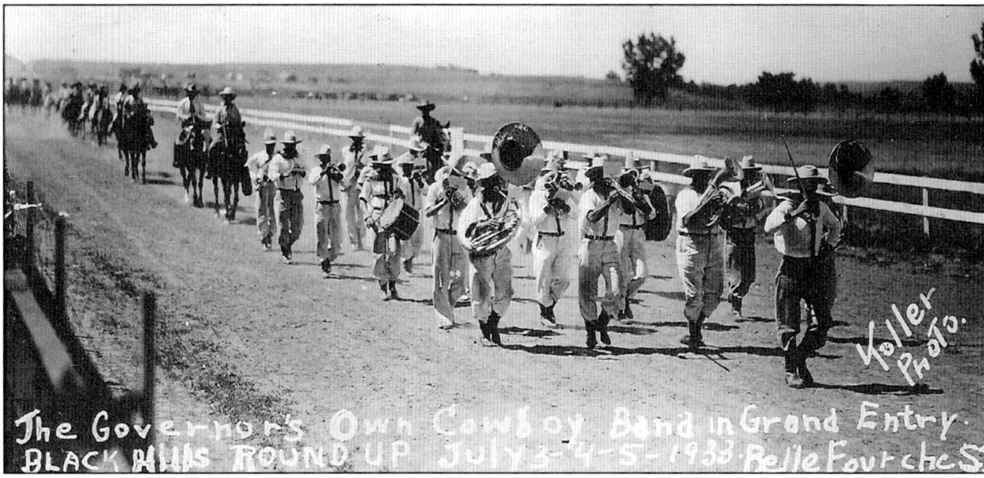

The Cowboy Band has been a cornerstone of the Fourth of July events at Belle Fourche since 1931. The Cowboy Band has become a legend in its own time, playing at the roundup and other annual events. The first Cowboy Band uniforms consisted of Western hats, white shirts, and white pants with black belt loops. In the early 1940s, band members wore red shirts and white leather chaps. The downtown parade has been a mainstay of the celebration since 1918.

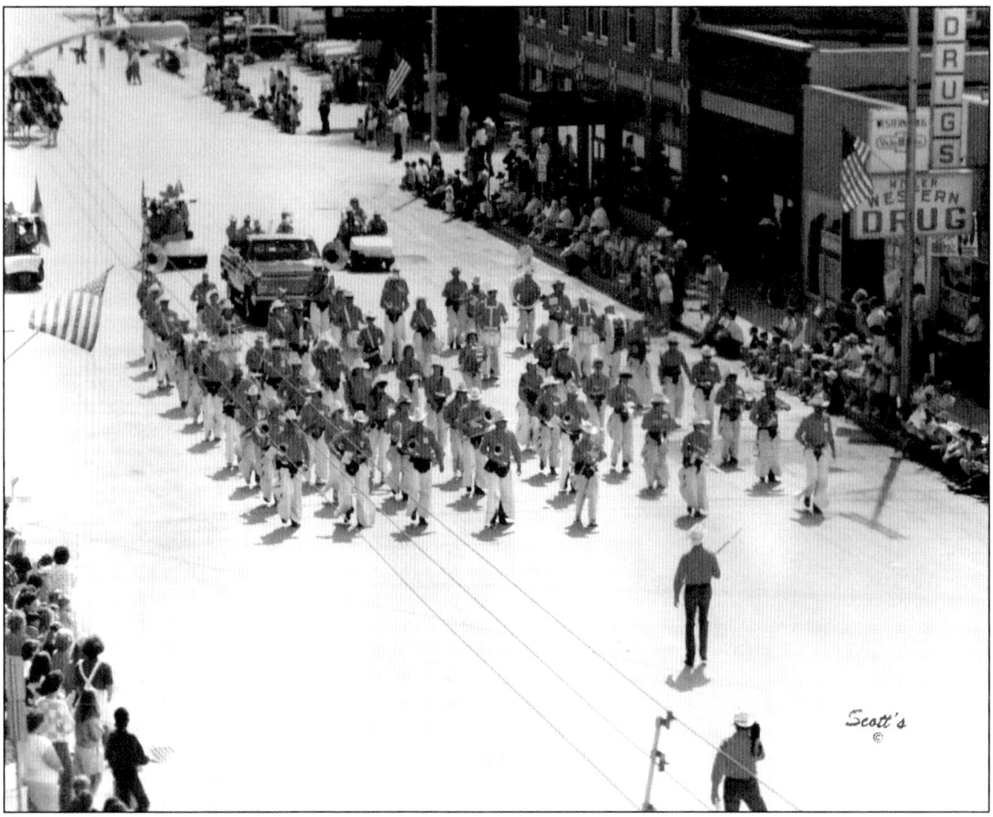

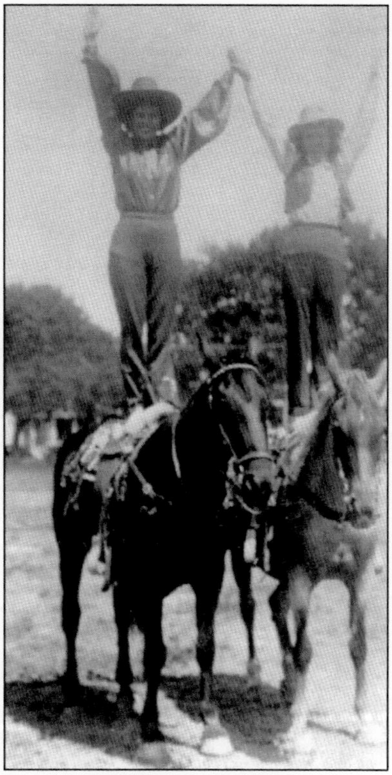

Fidelia (Gilger) Tope and Rosemary (Seymour) Tope were trick riders who performed in area rodeos. They always dreamed of trick riding as little girls. From 1939 through 1948, the sisters were a favorite act as trick riders on their matched strawberry roan horses and they performed rope tricks. During those years, the girls made $50 a day; gasoline was 20¢ a gallon, and hotel rooms cost $1.50 to $3. Both ladies married area ranchers and remained in the area.

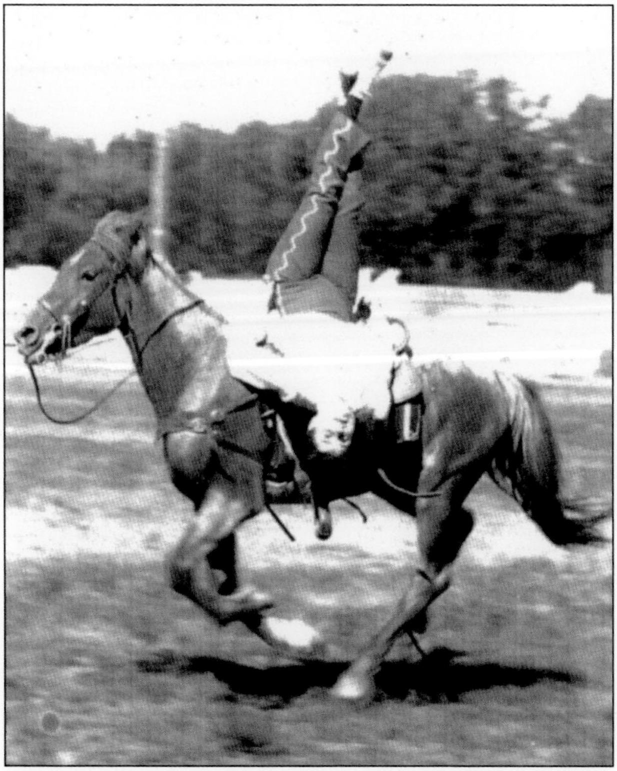

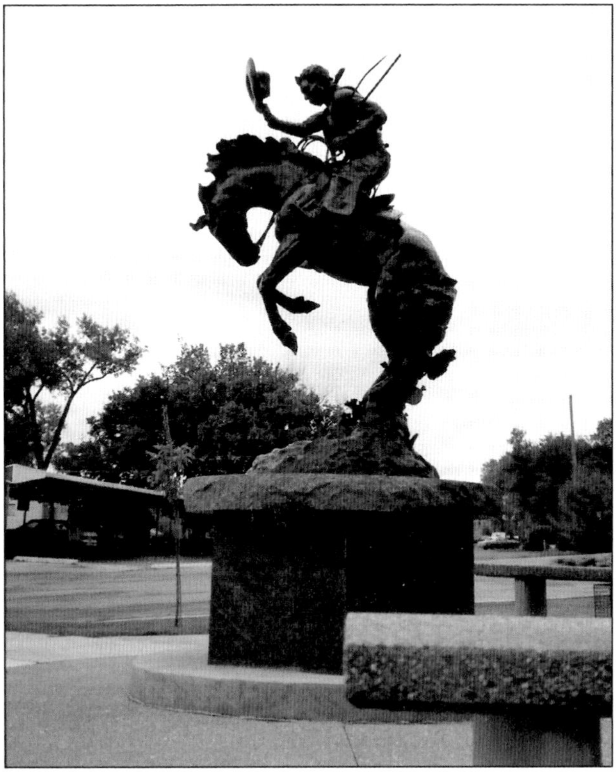

Belle Fourche is home to modern-day world champions. Bronze statues of professional rodeo cowboys stand on Belle Fourche's main street as a salute to their talents and to the recognition they have brought to the community. These top rodeo competitors Marvin (statue below) and Mark Garrett live in the area. Marvin is a four-time world bareback champion and was inducted into the Cowboy Hall of Fame in 1998. Mark won the National Finals Rodeo (NFR) World Bareback Championship in 1996. Belle Fourche's Cleve Schmidt is a recent NFR qualifier along with Scott Montague and many others. Birch's Khadafy Skoal, a quarter horse owned by rodeo stock contractor Powder River Productions, now fills Tipperary's shoes in the legend of rodeo broncs.

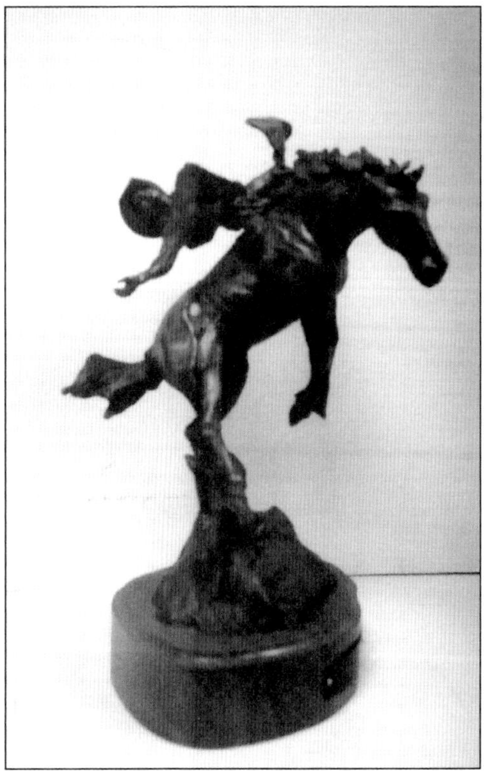

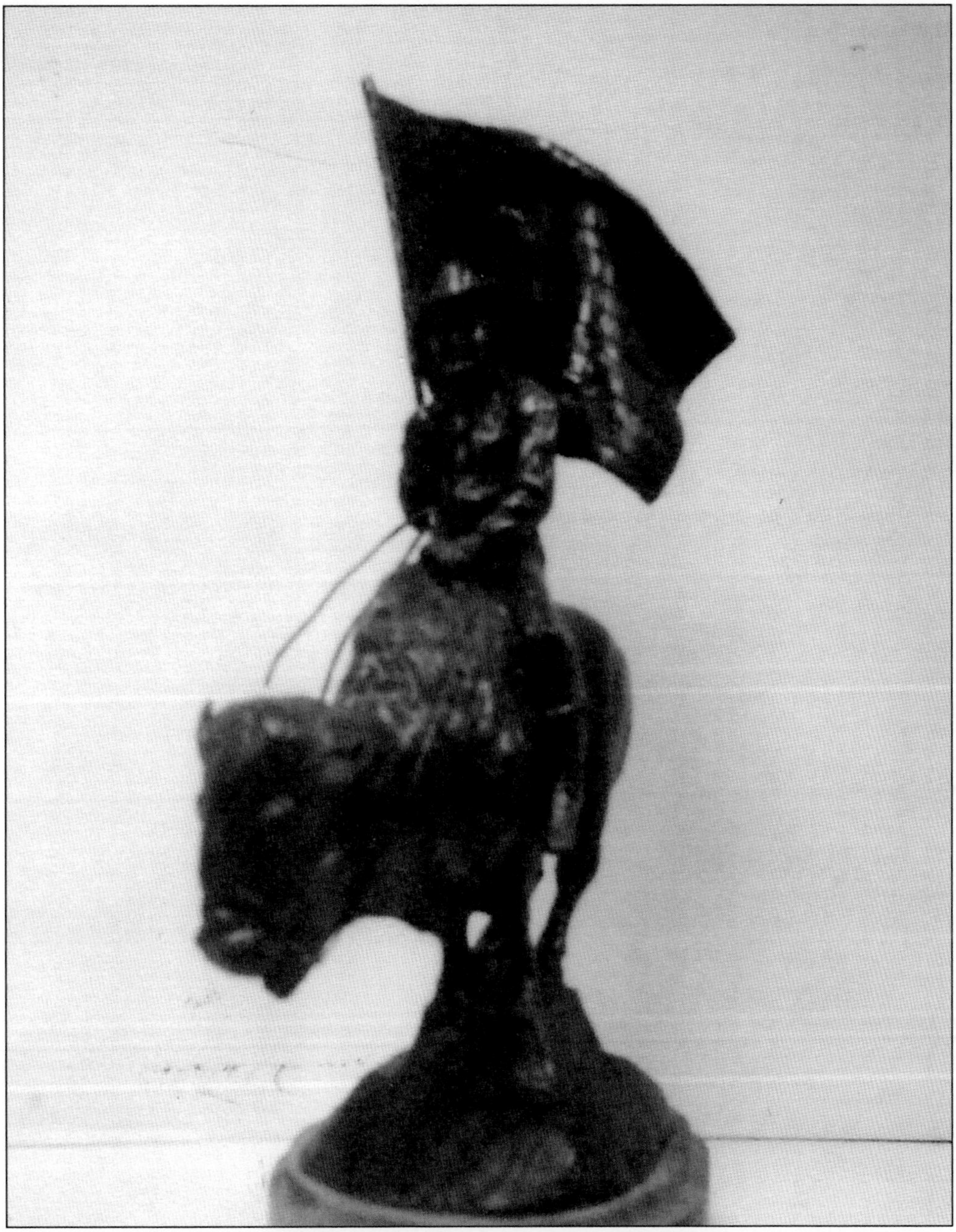

T. R. "Tony" Chytka from Belle Fourche is a cowboy artist whose art reflects his life experience. He is a rural South Dakota native, a rancher, and a former champion rodeo bull rider. His bronzes of the Belle Fourche bronc riders, Marvin and Mark Garrett, and buffalo trainer Jerry Olson sit on the main street of Belle Fourche. Chytka works his art from concept through casting and finishing his bronze sculpture. His story started as a would-be rodeo star who broke his leg twice before he decided to sculpt instead of ride. Chytka studied art at Black Hills University while he participated in the college rodeo. He later joined the NFR and remains a lifetime member. This statue of buffalo trainer and rodeo performer Jerry Olson is the third Chytka work of art on State Street in Belle Fourche.

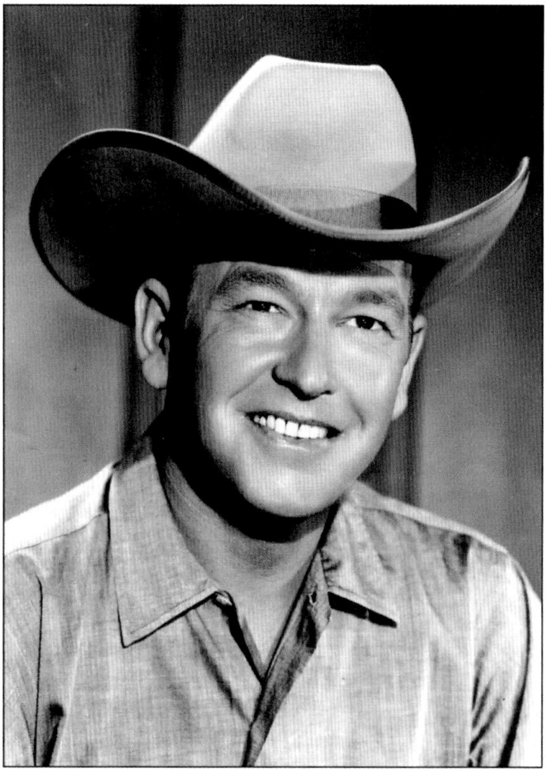

Rex Allen performed at the roundup during the 1950s. Allen was a Western singer and became a popular entertainer known as "the Arizona Cowboy." As a boy, he played guitar and sang at local functions with his fiddle-playing father until high school graduation, when he toured the Southwest as a rodeo rider. He got his start in show business on the East Coast as a vaudeville singer. Monkey acts were also included in the entertainment of the roundup. This monkey riding a border collie has been made popular by a modern-day advertisement campaign. The roundup committee still spends many hours interviewing and obtaining the best entertainment available, making the Black Hills Roundup a destination site for thousands of people. Officials from the livestock commission houses made annual trips to the celebration. The Chicago and North Western Railway put on special trains to deliver the guests to Belle Fourche for the Fourth of July event during the 1930s and 1940s.

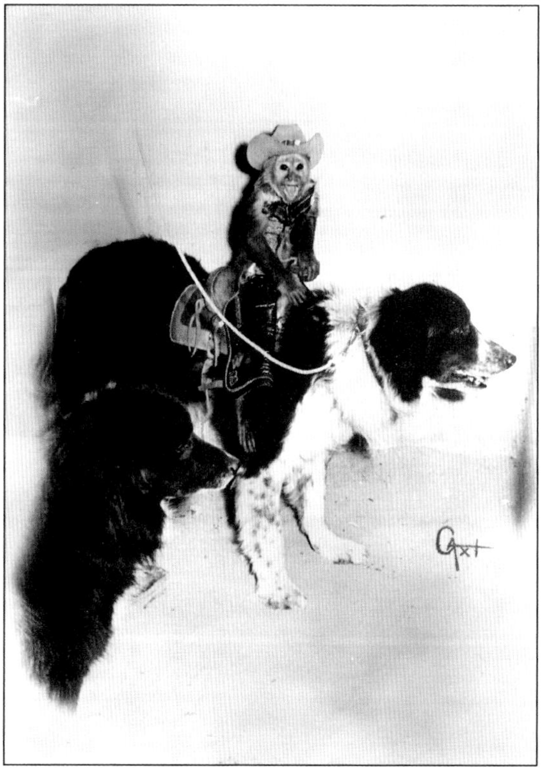

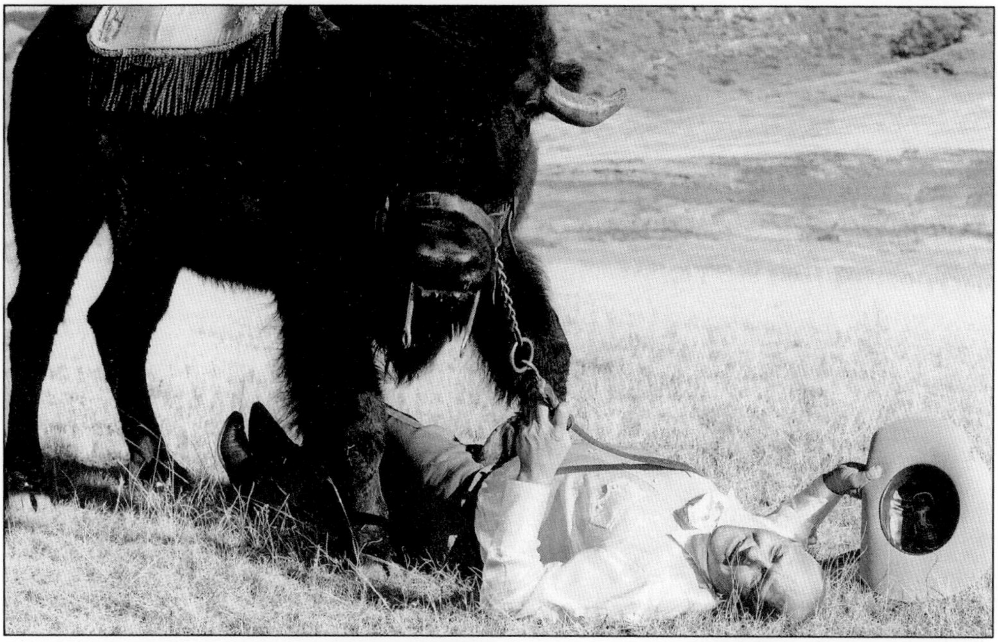

The Olsons produced a four-generation family of rodeo entertainers. LaRue Olson, the father, trained the first buffalo, Pat, which came from Rosander stock. The idea came from Pete Rosander, who advised LaRue to get a buffalo from Glenn Morgan in Alzada, Montana, and train it. LaRue toured rodeos throughout the United States. His son Jerry Olson followed the family trend with a rodeo act, riding Roman style on three black horses. His specialty was jumping these three horses into a moving truck. He also trained his buffalo Sam. He rode his buffalo around the arena doing tricks. He stood all four feet of the buffalo on a 12-inch pedestal, and as a finale, he rode him up a ramp to the top of his trailer and drove out of the arena. His grandson Jerry Wayne Olson and his wife, Judy, had a buffalo and have a horse and rope act. Great-grandson Jay Olson rides rough stock and has a bullwhip act. This is a true family of rodeo entertainers. Jerry Olson has been inducted into every rodeo and cowboy hall of fame known to the rodeo world.

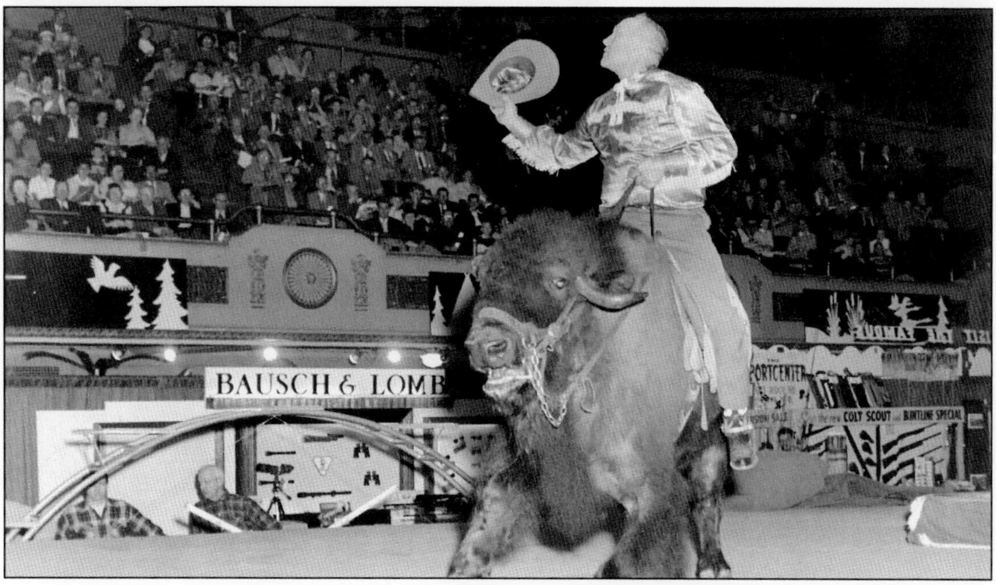

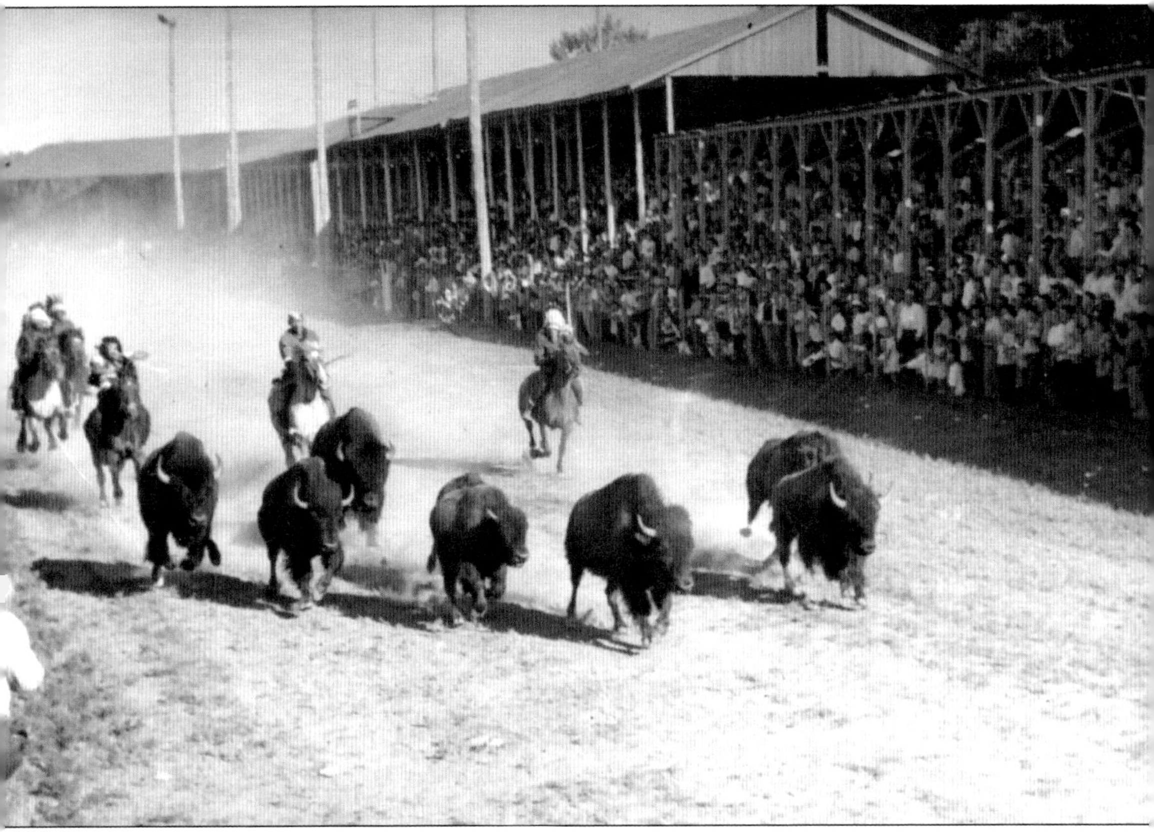

In the 1940s, 1950s, and early 1960s, Pete Rosander and his son Dick drove a small bunch of buffalo from their ranch north of Belle Fourche to the roundup grounds in Belle Fourche. During the rodeo, they dressed up as Native Americans and recruited a few of the Native Americans that were at the rodeo to chase the buffalo in a stampede. The buffalo stampeded on the track right in front of the crowd. The Rosanders ran their buffalo for 27 years, doing three performances yearly. The Rosanders crossbred the buffalo with Brahma cattle before artificial insemination was used.

Three

Industries and Growth

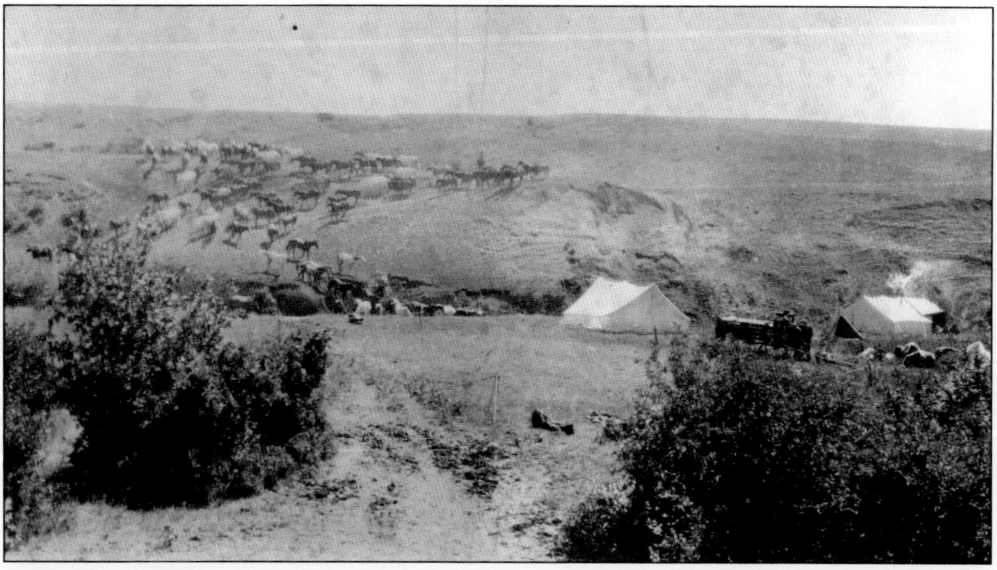

From 1876 to 1923, many cattle companies, such as Deffenbach, VVV, Turkey Track, Hash Knife, Driskill, Cross S, Flying V, CY, and many others were in the tristate area. They ran many thousands head of cattle on the open range. Cattle were rounded up twice a year. Stockmen realized that the nutrient of the short grass available in this area was perfect for raising cattle. However, they did not realize the possibility of the devastation of the northern winters. The winter of 1886–1887 dealt a crushing blow to the cattle companies. The cattle driven by blizzard after blizzard could not find shelter or feed. Thousands of cattle died, and losses ran as high as 90 percent. That winter broke many of the smaller companies and left the bigger companies in financial difficulties. Many of the cowboys stayed in the area, homesteading and continuing to raise cattle, horses, and sheep.

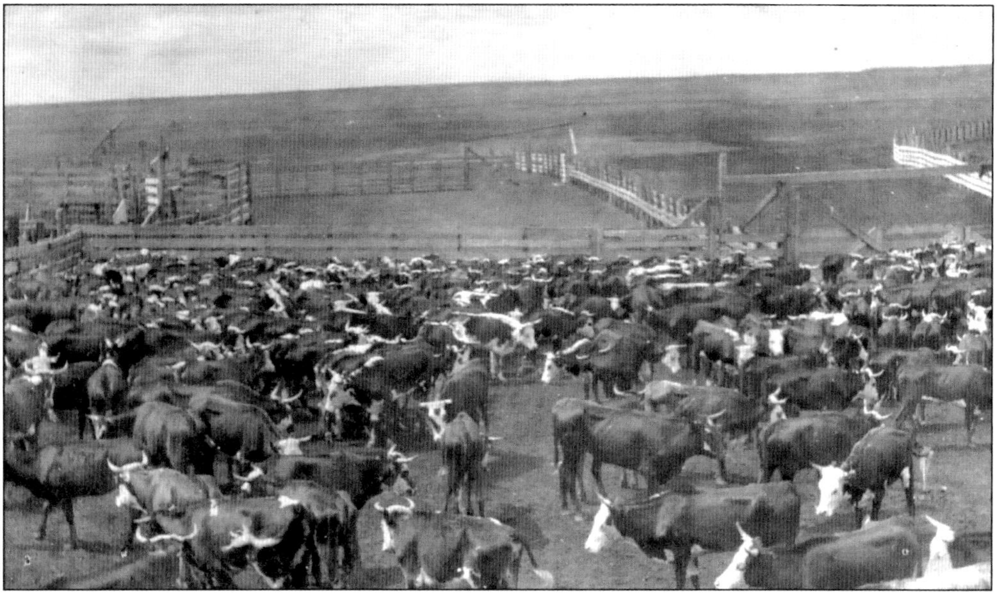

The last herd of longhorn cattle from Mexico owned by DZ outfit arrived at the dipping corral in 1914. Branding and roundup were part of the livestock industry; both horses and cattle were branded. The use of brands as a mark of identification dates back some 4,000 years. The American custom of cattle branding was adopted from Mexico; as the cattle industry moved northward into Texas, American ranchers accepted this method.

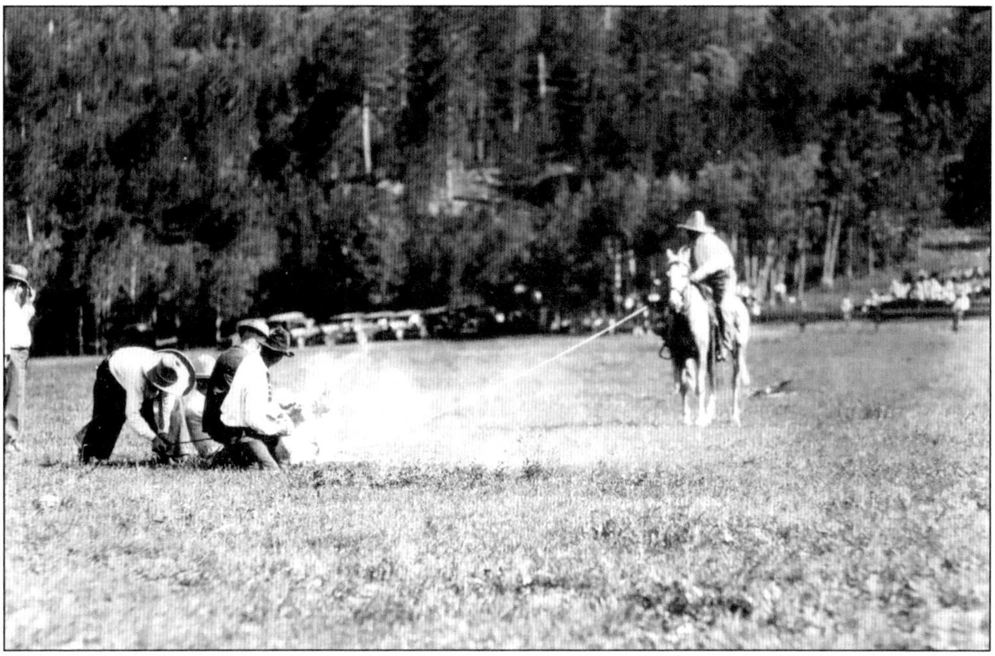

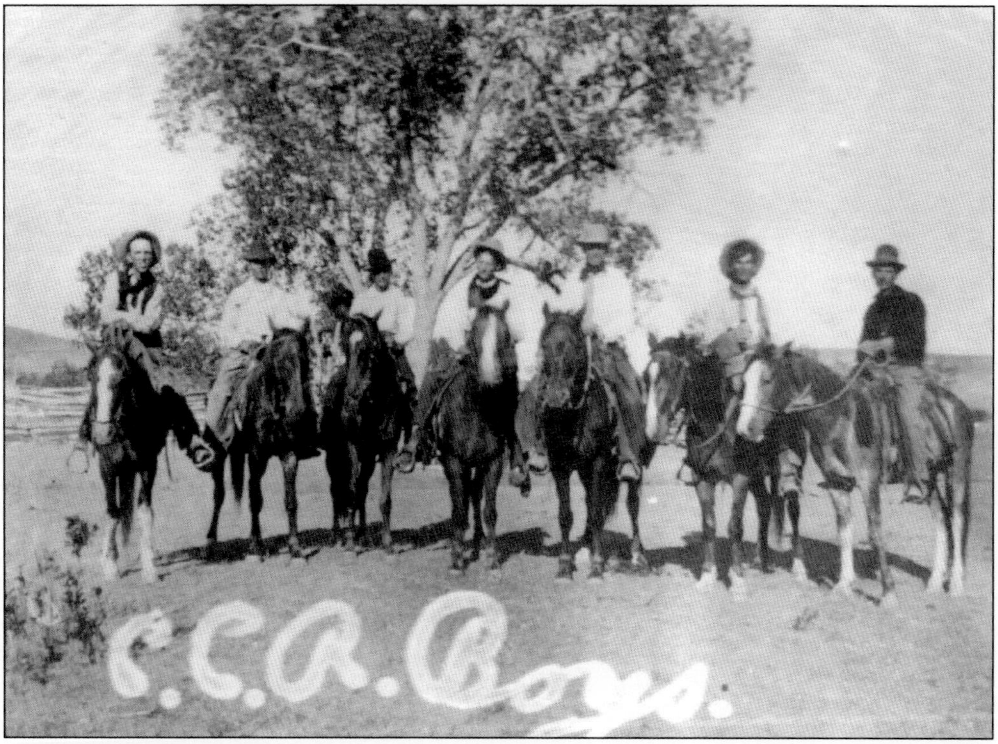

Cowboys riding for CCR outfit were Fred Brooks, Noble Rose, Dode Williams, Slim Mueller, Ben Guyer, John Dorman, and Honyocker Michels. Each company ran several "wagons." The bigger the company the more wagons it ran. A wagon consisted of a unit of men, horses, and equipment. Each was sent out on the range every spring to gather cattle that had drifted off during the winter. The group depended on the cook, who controlled the chuck wagon and fed the cowboys.

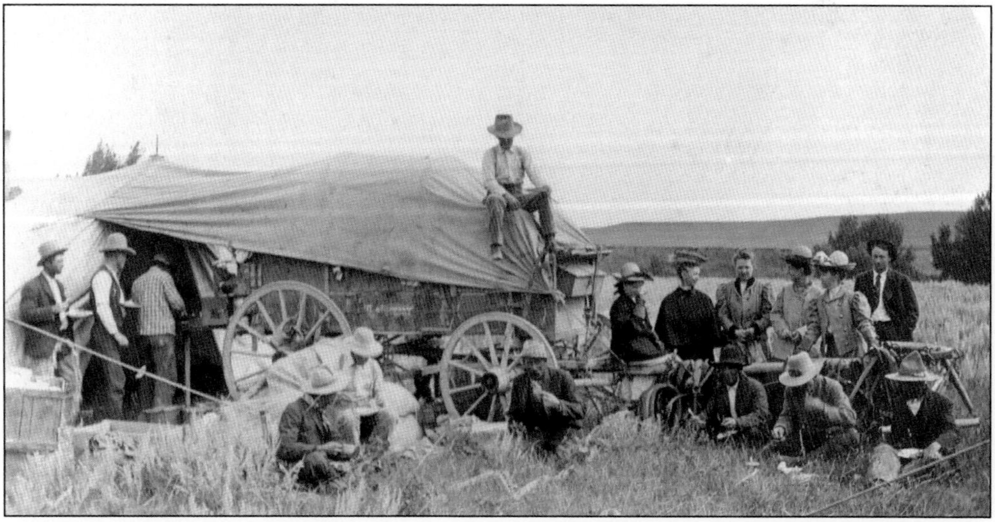

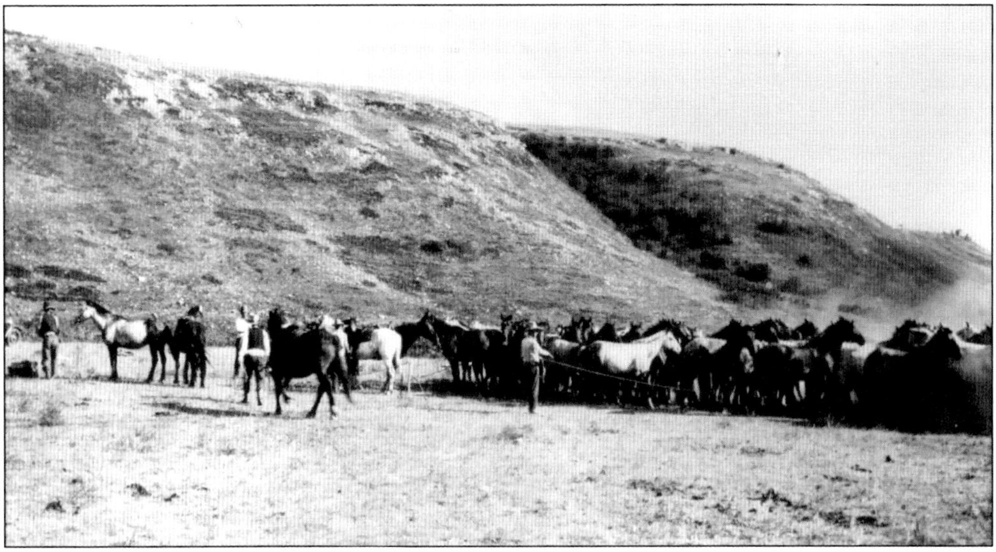

Horse production was part of the livestock industry in the tristate area. Seth Bullock, founder of Belle Fourche and good friend of Theodore Roosevelt, acquired a large tract of land in the foothills of the Black Hills at the junction of the Redwater and Belle Fourche Rivers. On this ranch, he and his partner, Sol Star, the mayor of Deadwood, bred standard-bred horses. Trotting and driving horses were also raised. The SB (Star and Bullock) brand of horses was known nationally. The Bullock family never lived on the farm, but Capt. Seth Bullock owned and operated it until 1916, when it was sold to the Great Western Sugar Company. Fred Fuller, below left, was their manager and trainer.

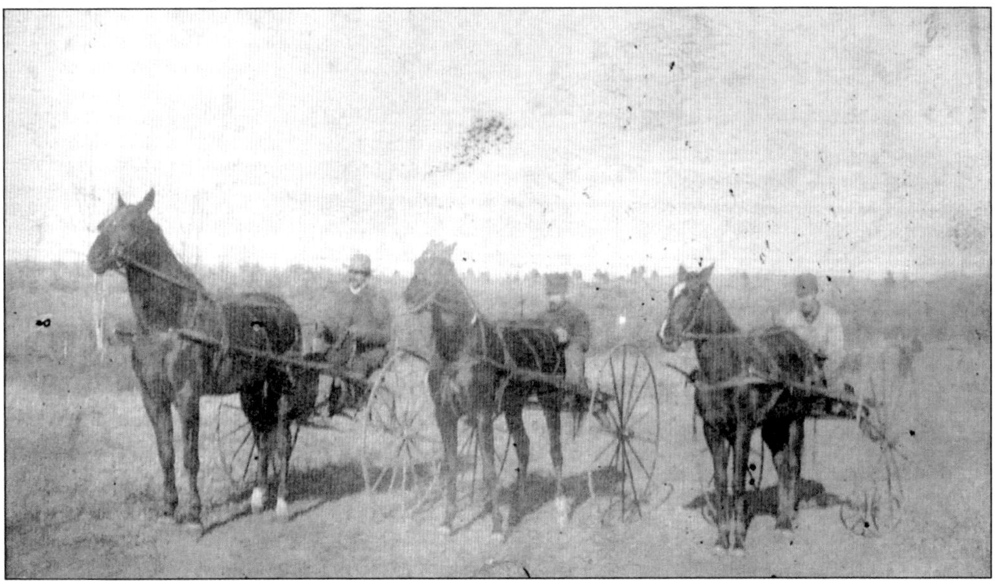

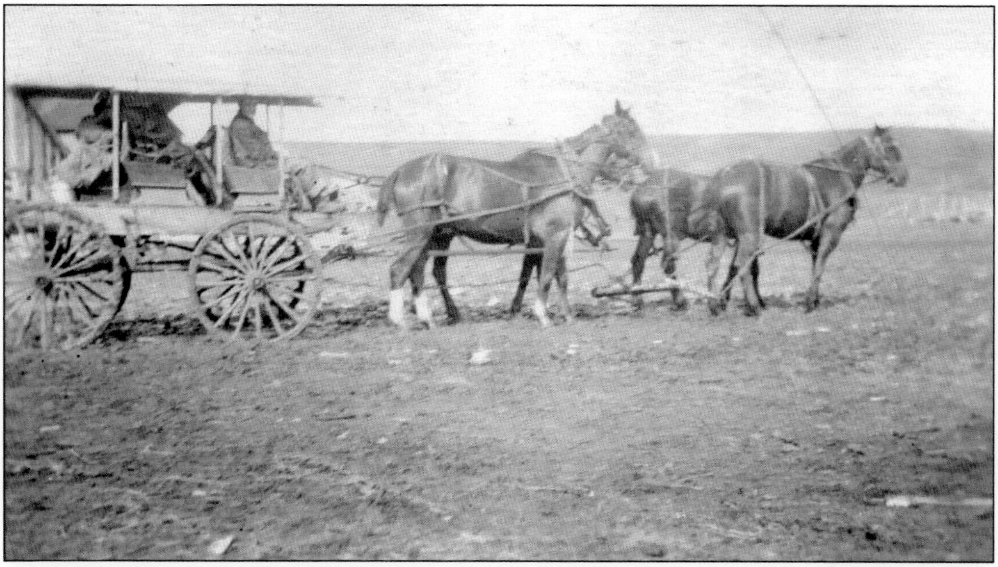

A four-horse-drawn stage served Camp Crook, a very early settlement on the Little Missouri River in the northern tristate area. The village was first called Wickhamville after Maj. Joseph Wickham, who hunted buffalo along the fertile Little Missouri Valley.

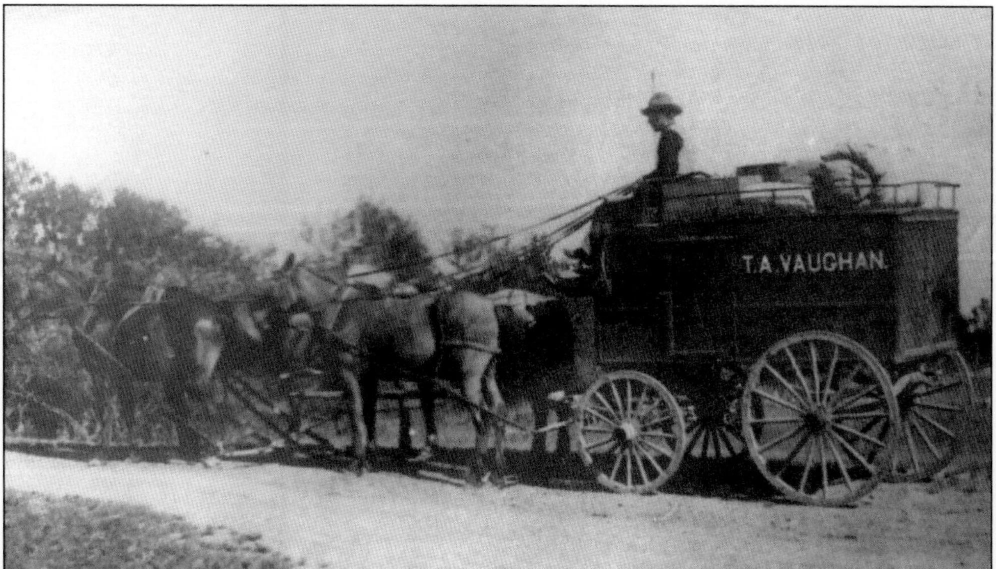

T. A. Vaughan's bandwagon carried supplies such as boots, jeans, underwear, and hats out to the roundup camps in 1897. The need for horses continued into the 20th century; area ranchers supplied horses to Fort Meade and the army during World War I.

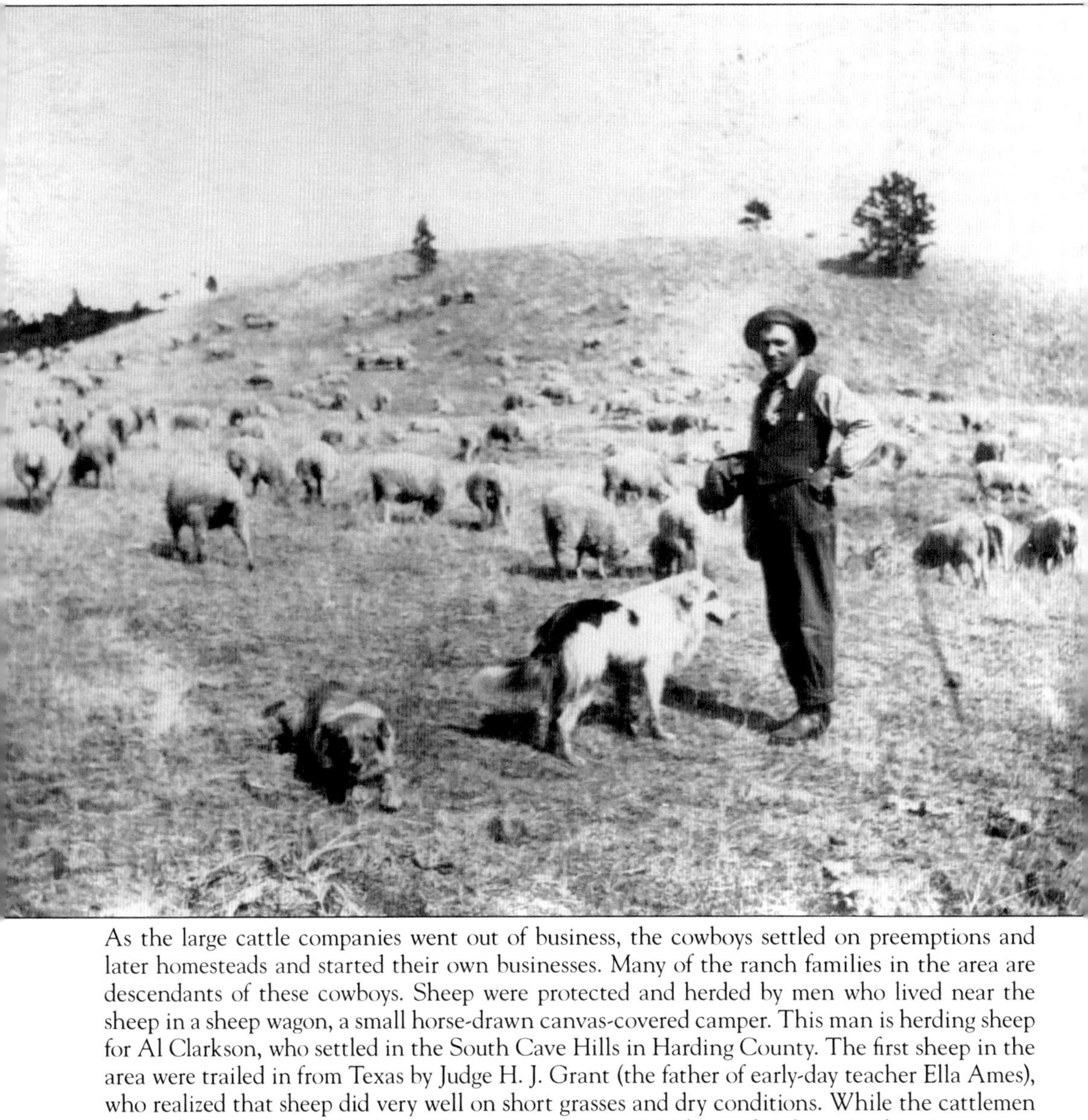

As the large cattle companies went out of business, the cowboys settled on preemptions and later homesteads and started their own businesses. Many of the ranch families in the area are descendants of these cowboys. Sheep were protected and herded by men who lived near the sheep in a sheep wagon, a small horse-drawn canvas-covered camper. This man is herding sheep for Al Clarkson, who settled in the South Cave Hills in Harding County. The first sheep in the area were trailed in from Texas by Judge H. J. Grant (the father of early-day teacher Ella Ames), who realized that sheep did very well on short grasses and dry conditions. While the cattlemen resented the coming of the sheep, there were never any incidents of violence in the tristate area. Eventually these same ranchers realized the income from sheep was double because of the wool and meat crop, and many of them started raising both sheep and cattle. Cattle only had one income, and calves were not ready for market for about three years.

Meta McClure is pictured at right with her pets, bum lambs. Sometimes the mother ewes (female sheep) did not have milk enough to feed their babies, especially if there were twins. Many ranch wives bottle raised these extras and used the income as their own personal money. Shearing was done in the spring or early summer. All shearing was done by hand in the early days; this crew is shearing at Guy Gilbert's place in 1907. The crew included George Lewis, Eert Lewis, Al Kerk, Thurlow ?, Perry Davis, Irwin Scouten, Lon Lewis, Bud Sprague, and Laren Hoskin. Each shearer had a pen of sheep, which usually averaged 100 to 125 in an eight-hour day. As the sheep were shorn, the wool was tied and thrown into a long wool sack that was suspended from a tall stand. As the wool was thrown in the bag, a person called the "stomper" jumped in and stomped it down as tightly as he could.

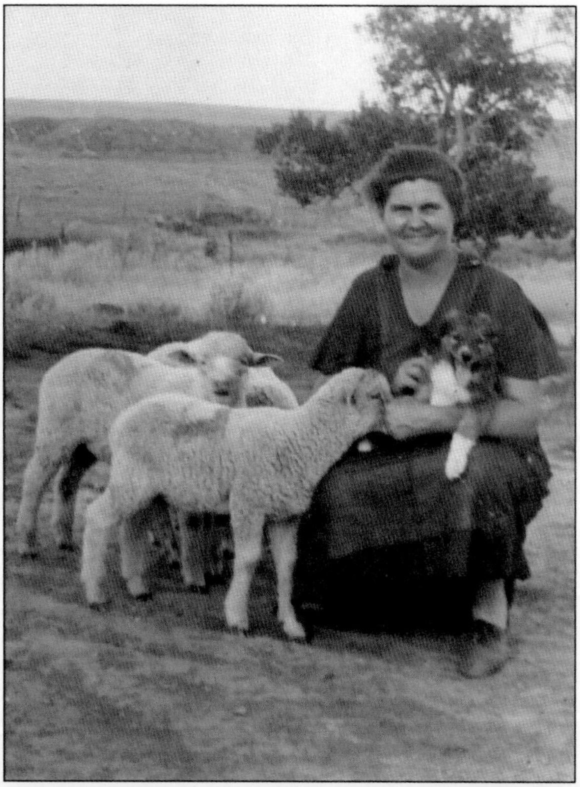

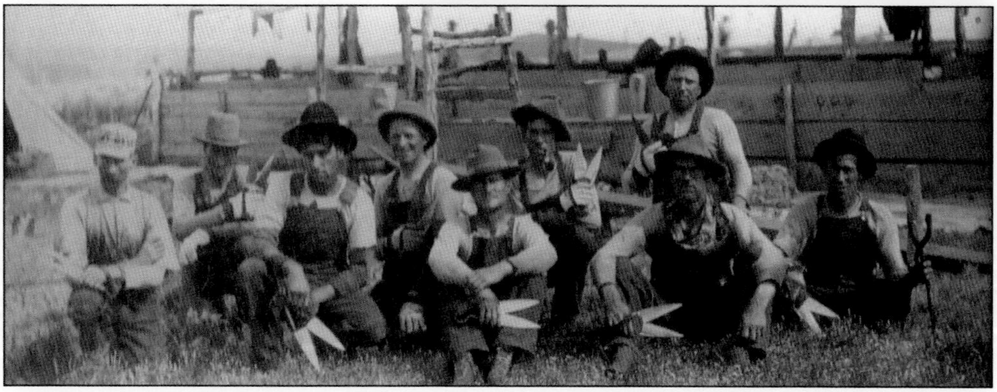

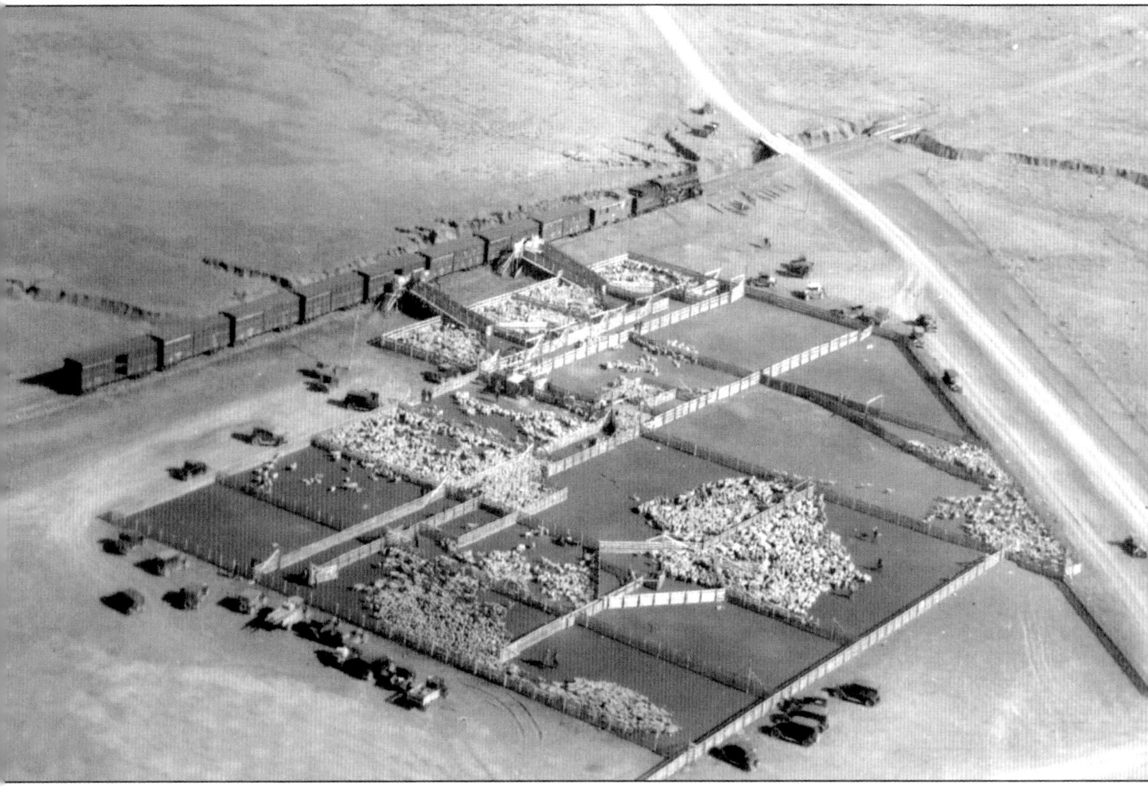

Livestock shipping was big business for the railroad. Back in 1900, Belle Fourche was called the biggest shipping point for range cattle in the West. The Freemont, Elkhorn and Missouri Valley Railroad shipped 3,000 cars of cattle to market from Belle Fourche in the fall of 1895. This shipment amounted to over 60,000 head, estimated at $2.75 million in value. One of the reasons the railroad chose Belle Fourche for the location of its depot was because the livestock market and loading yards were on Middle Creek north of the Belle Fourche River. The cattlemen and the railroad managers knew the cattle would be much easier to handle away from any farms or population centers. As early as 1894, the railroad company made deals to reserve grass and watering sites along the stock trails. Stock was trailed in from over 100 miles to be shipped. Sheep and cattle were shipped to the markets in Chicago, St. Louis, and South Omaha, Nebraska. Horses were shipped to St. Louis and Kansas City, Missouri.

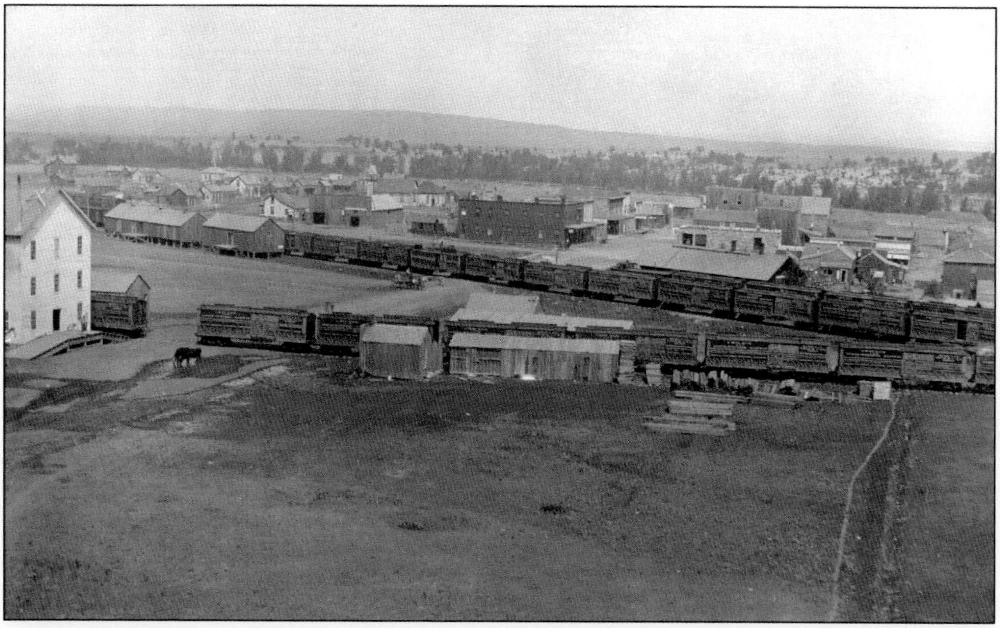

This early Belle Fourche photograph, taken before the big fire in 1895, shows the depot behind the train, the tall flour mill on the left, and the Belle Hotel and the Belle Fourche River in the background. The town was created because the Freemont, Elkhorn and Missouri Valley Railroad, a division of the Chicago and North Western Railway, agreed to accept Seth Bullock's offer and established both the livestock yards on Middle Creek and a depot south of the Belle Fourche River.

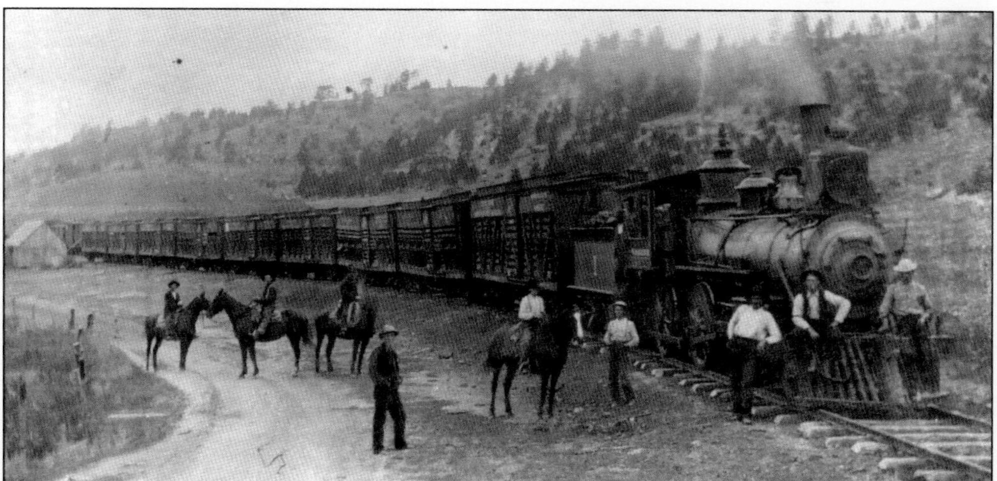

Cars of livestock are loaded and shipped into Belle Fourche from Aladdin, Wyoming, a small community 17 miles west of Belle Fourche on Hay Creek. The Wyoming and Missouri River Railroad operated between Aladdin and Belle Fourche, transporting people, livestock, agricultural products, and coal. Coal was being mined in several locations in the Wyoming community.

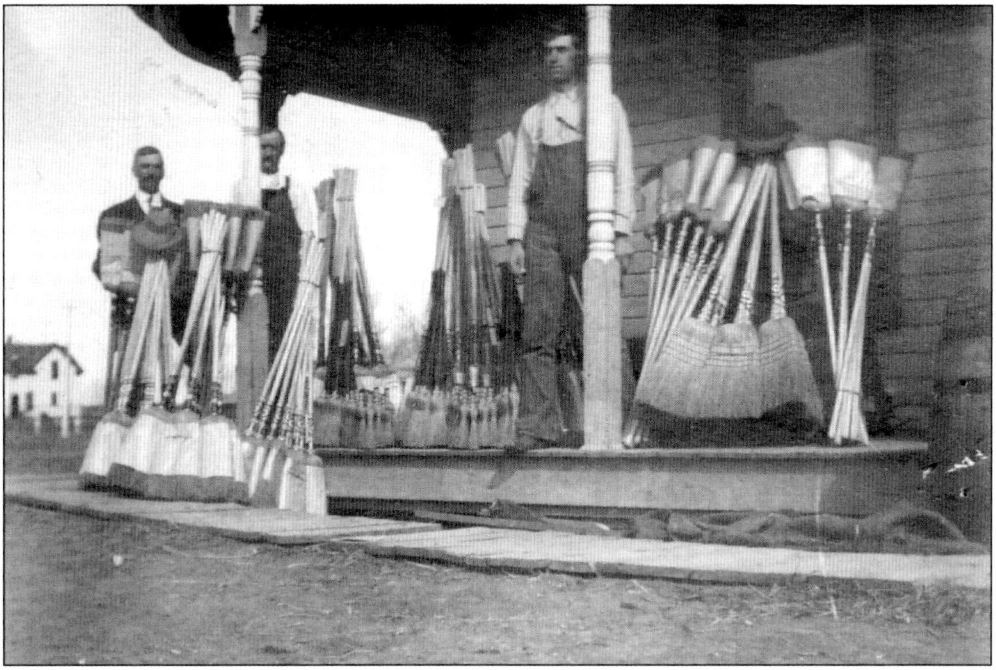

One of Belle Fourche's early-day industries was the manufacture of brooms. A broom factory was the talk of the town in 1911. E. E. Linch launched this enterprise. Brooms were loaded in wagons and shipped for sales throughout the Black Hills. It was located on Elkhorn Street on the east end of town near the Redwater River.

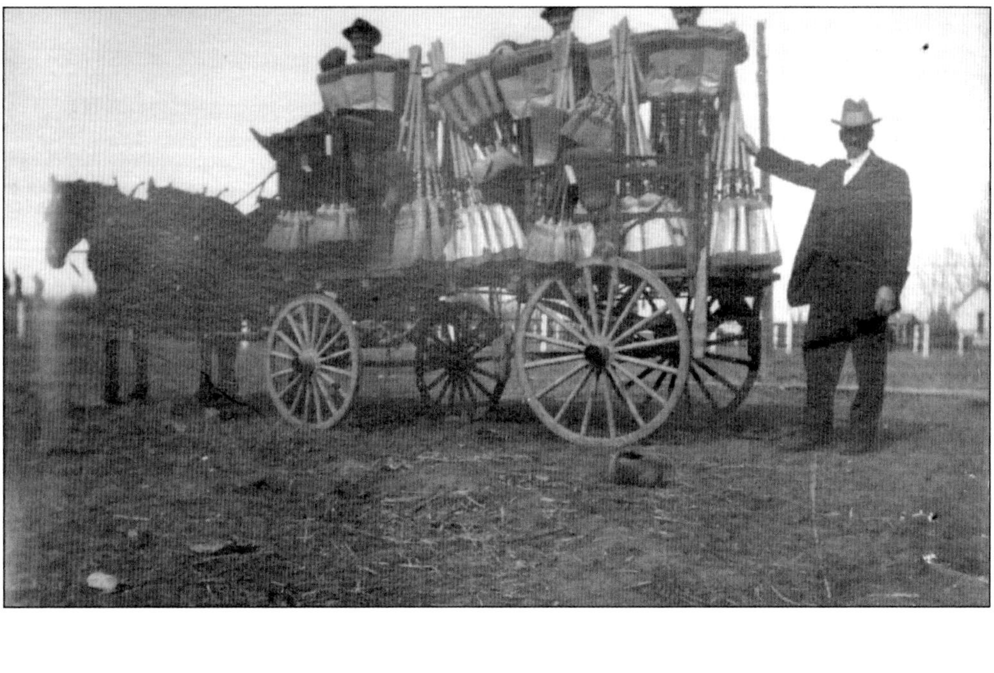

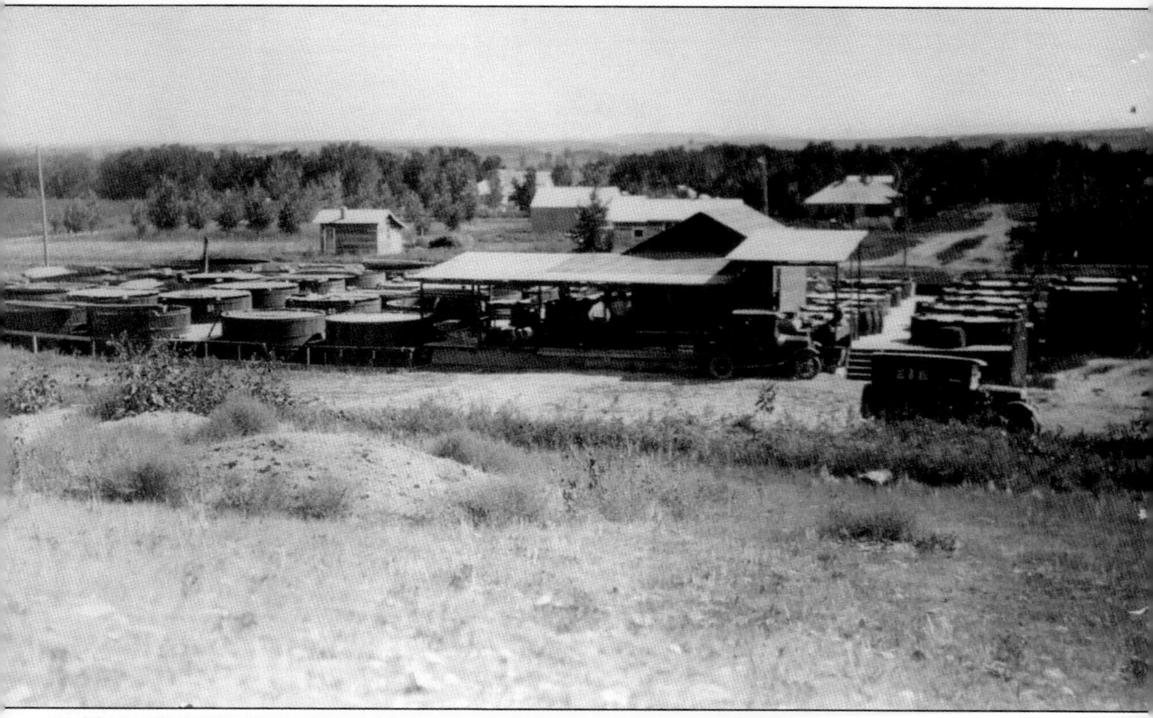

Pickle production seems unusual for an area where rain averages 10 to 12 inches per year. Once the area was developed for irrigation and the huge Orman Dam was built in 1912, the Squire Dingee Company sent out free cucumber seeds, and salting vats were set up in Belle Fourche, Nisland, Newell, Fruitdale, and Vale. In October 1925, the first carload (900 bushels) of salted pickles was shipped from Nisland to the cannery in Chicago. In December 1926, nine carloads were shipped from Belle Fourche and Nisland. Fifteen more vats were installed in Nisland, making a total of 60 tanks, the largest station of this kind in the United States. The production continued with great success until the drought of the 1930s. Business picked up during World War II as the army supplied the troops with pickles, trying to balance their diets. There was a World War II prisoner of war camp located near Orman Dam, and the German prisoners were used as cucumber pickers.

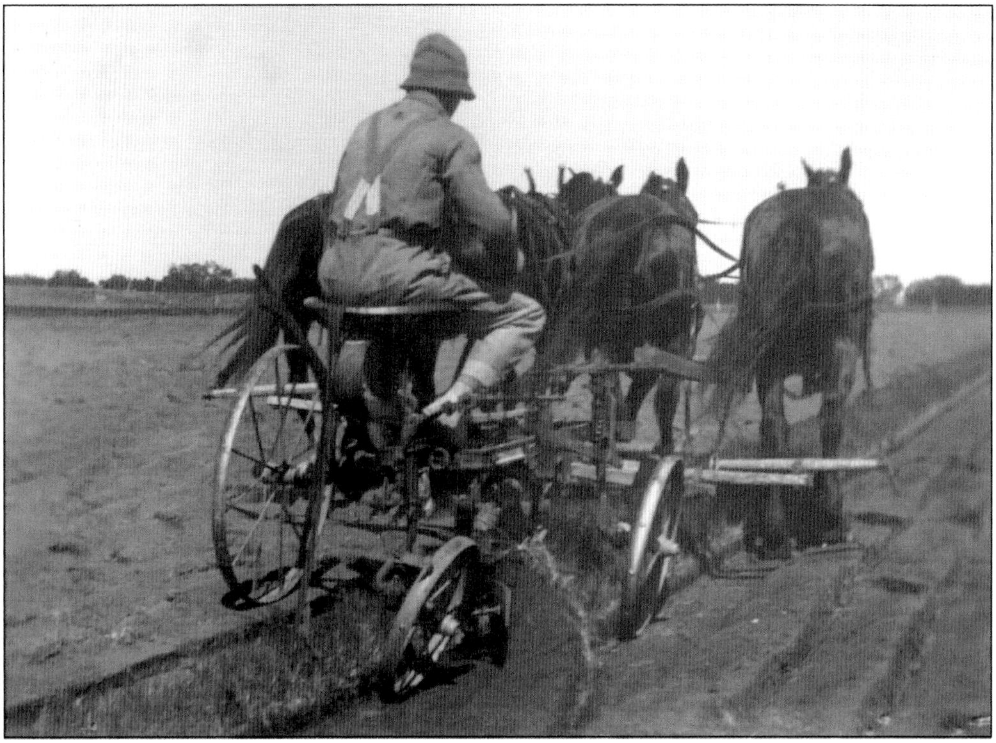

As soon as the gold rush into the Black Hills started, there was a need for food for both the gold seekers and their livestock. Early hunter and guide Johnny Spaulding decided that hunting gold was not for him. During his hunting excursions, he realized that the fertile ground that grew such great grass was perfect for farming. He settled just north of the Black Hills on the Redwater River. He was involved with other early settlers to develop an irrigation project—one that is still in use today. He plowed and planted oats to supply feed for the horses and mules used in the various mines. Breaking up virgin grasslands with horse-drawn plows was extremely difficult. The Homestead Act of 1862 asked the filers to put only 20 acres under cultivation out of the 160 acres of entitlement.

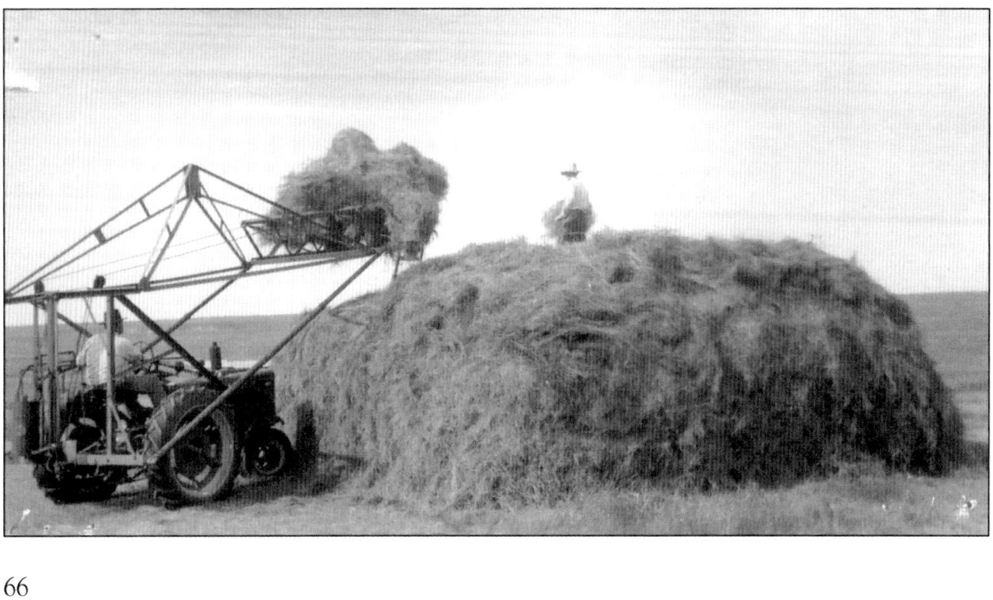

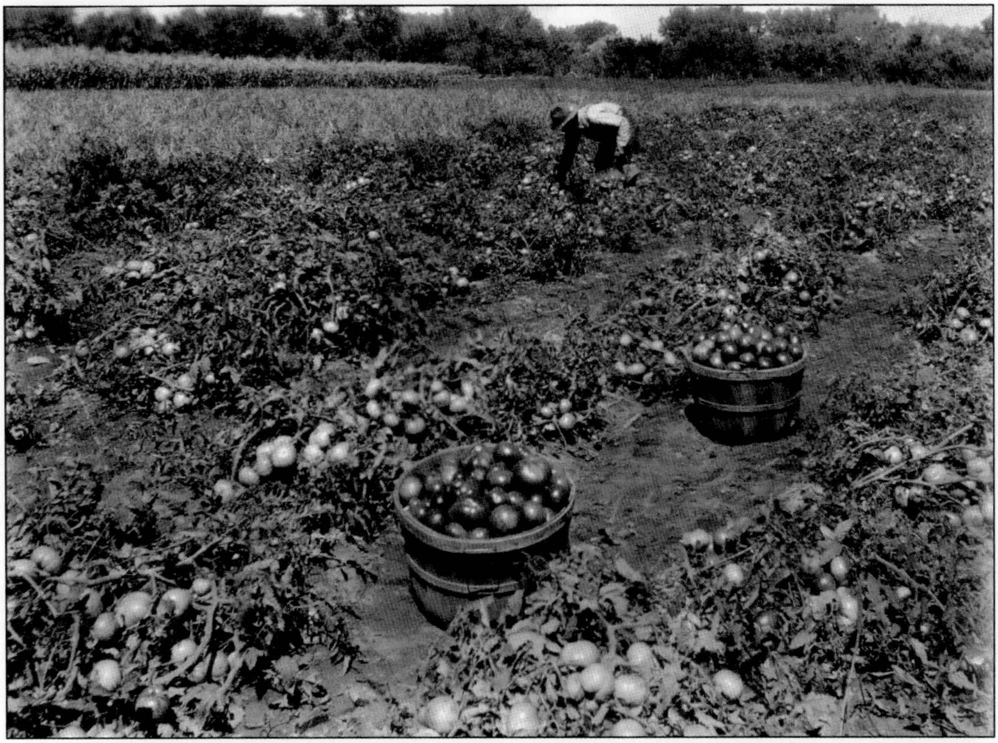

Truck farms include fields of vegetables. Louis Sturis and George Higashi grew vegetables: tomatoes, cabbages, cucumbers, and beans. Settlers in the Belle Fourche and Redwater valleys planted both hay and produce to supply area towns and miners. Many early-day farmers traveled once a week to Deadwood and the mining communities in the Black Hills, delivering their produce by horse and wagon.

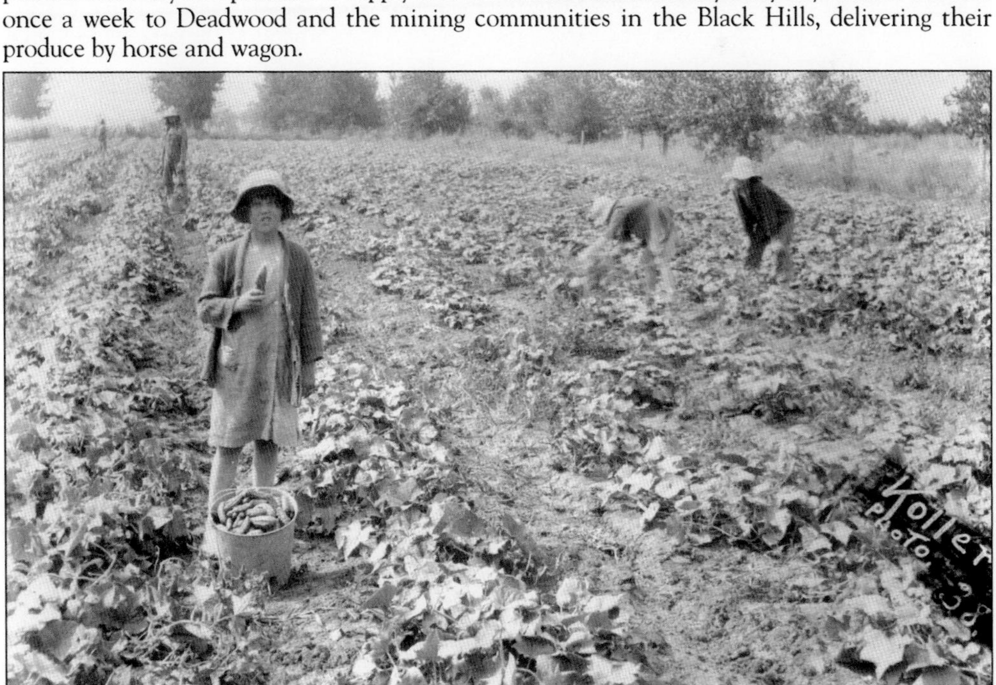

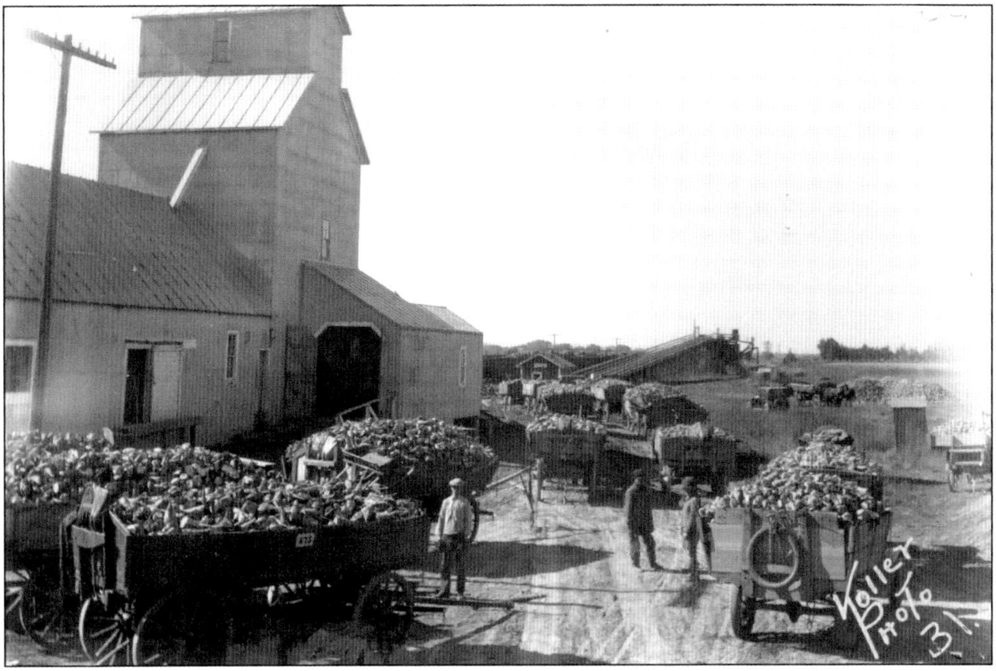

The sugar industry started through Seth Bullock's friendship with Pres. Theodore Roosevelt. In the January 29, 1904, *Northwest Post*, Bullock suggested the erection of a sugar beet factory here "particularly if the big ditch project should become a fact." In 1887, P. P. Vallery planted the first beets in the valley. The Belle Fourche irrigation project did indeed become a fact, and Bullock sold his property to the Great Western Sugar Company as a factory site. The dam was completed in 1910. The irrigators were given beet seeds to experiment growing sugar beets. The company established five large beet dumps when the growers pledged 8,000 acres of sugar beets would be planted. Sugar beets were shipped to the Great Western Sugar Company factory at Scottsbluff, Nebraska, in October 1917. Great Western sold out to the Utah-Idaho Sugar Company in 1927, and finally the factory became a reality.

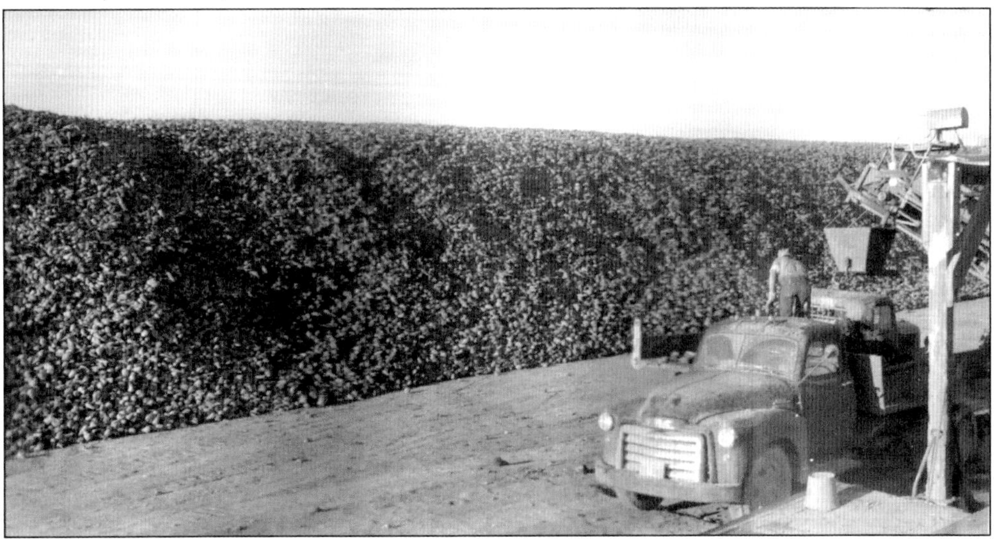

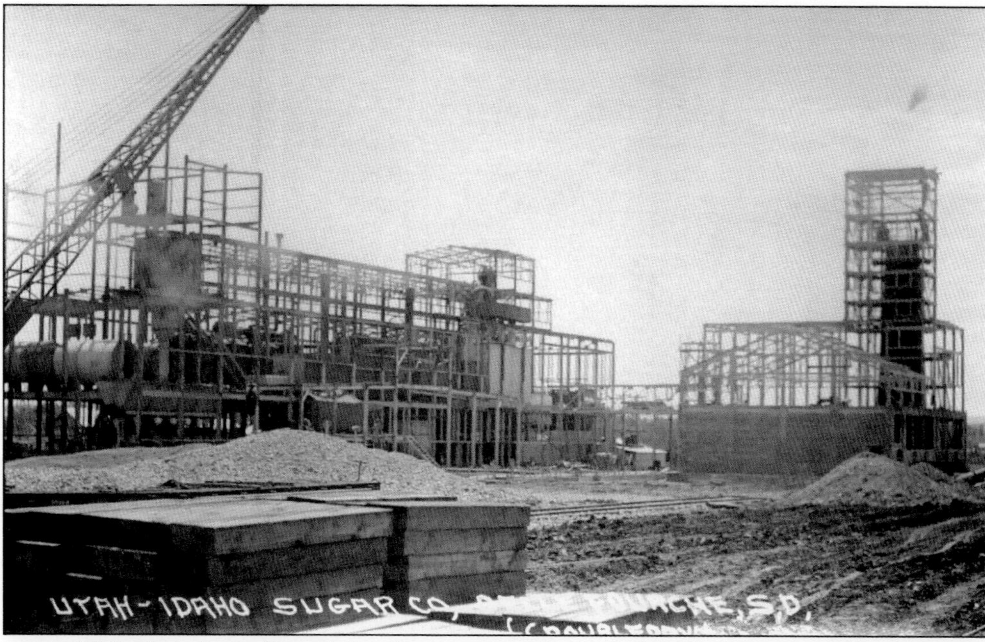

It was 1927 when the million-dollar dream was realized. Utah-Idaho Sugar Company moved a dismantled sugar factory to Belle Fourche, and the sugar beet business started booming. Promoters of Belle Fourche had spent over 20 years promoting this idea. D. B. Pratt came to Belle Fourche as the superintendent and oversaw the reassembling of the factory. The project was started on January 18, 1927, and by October, the big plant was processing sugar. Sugar beets were grown in the irrigation district, and thousands of pounds of sugar were processed. However, by 1960, the company found itself between increasing costs and limited volume. In 1965, the plant was closed; the last sugar of the last campaign was processed on Tuesday, January 12, 1965.

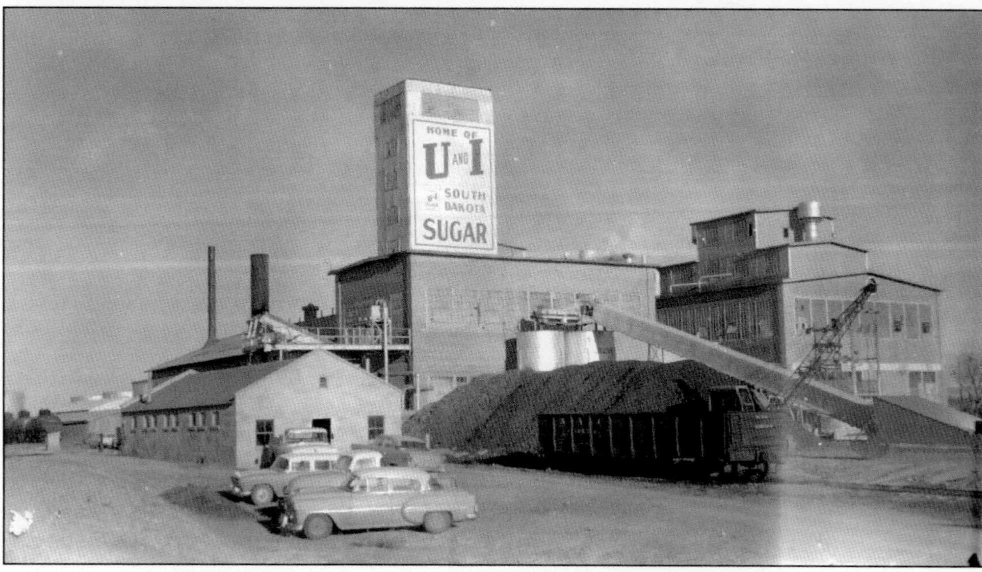

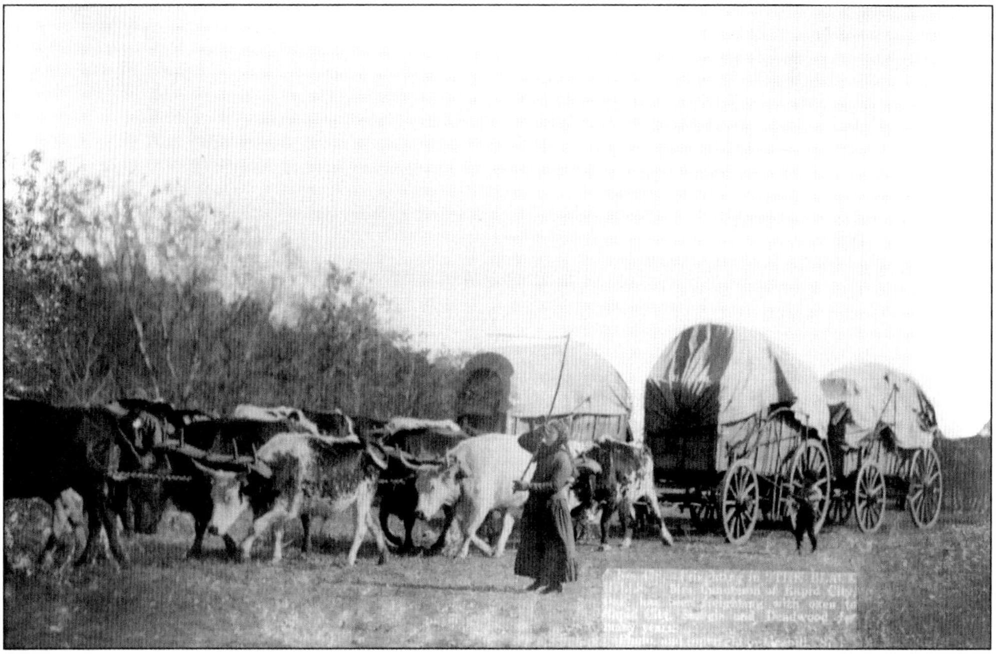

Freighting in the area was reported by Lydia Barr, who arrived in the Black Hills area in 1888 with her parents, Mr. and Mrs. John Barr. "I will never forget the trip. The roads were muddy; we were traveling by covered wagon and overtook this Mrs. Canutison with this same outfit as in the picture." Wool and other commodities also were freighted from the ranches to the railhead. When there was rain on the prairie, wagons were hitched to two or six horses. There were two wool houses in Belle Fourche, O'Connor and Schuft and O'Donnell Sheep and Wool. Nearly five million pounds of wool were sold each year from the warehouses in Belle Fourche.

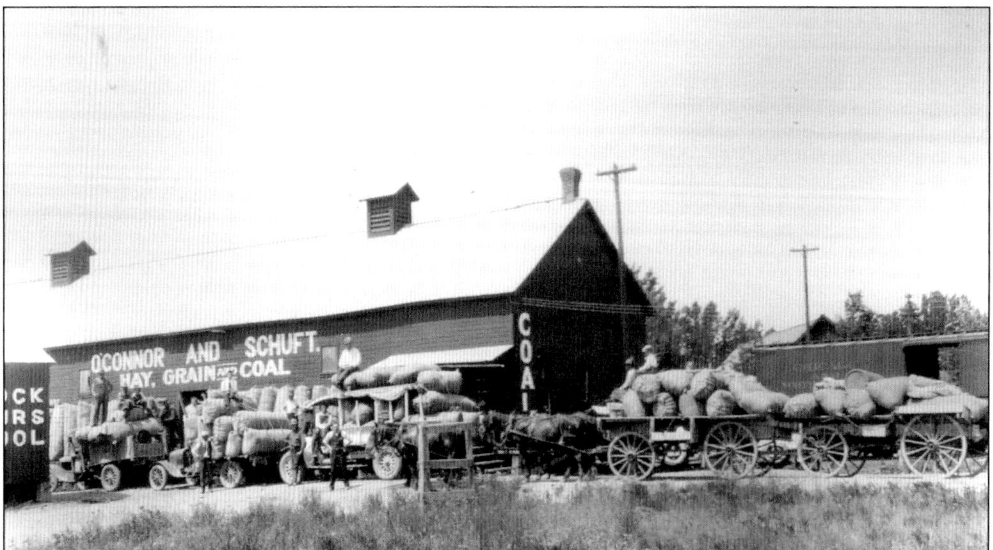

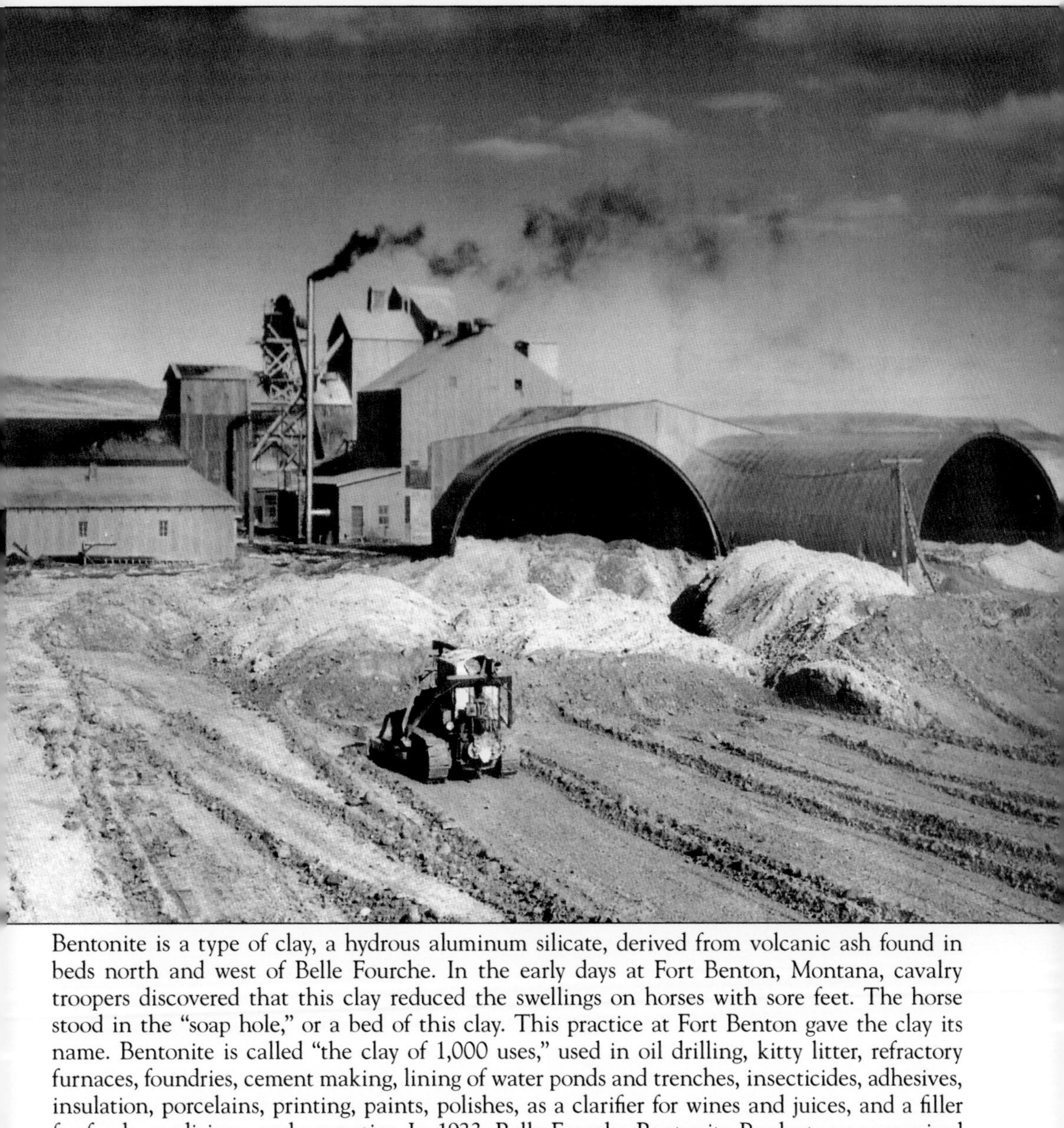

Bentonite is a type of clay, a hydrous aluminum silicate, derived from volcanic ash found in beds north and west of Belle Fourche. In the early days at Fort Benton, Montana, cavalry troopers discovered that this clay reduced the swellings on horses with sore feet. The horse stood in the "soap hole," or a bed of this clay. This practice at Fort Benton gave the clay its name. Bentonite is called "the clay of 1,000 uses," used in oil drilling, kitty litter, refractory furnaces, foundries, cement making, lining of water ponds and trenches, insecticides, adhesives, insulation, porcelains, printing, paints, polishes, as a clarifier for wines and juices, and a filler for foods, medicines, and cosmetics. In 1923, Belle Fourche Bentonite Products was organized with W. J. Smith as president. This local group was largely occupied with bentonite claims that were later to be sold to processing companies on a royalty basis. The first commercial milling occurred about 1935 and was developed by F. E. Schundler Bentonite Company of Illinois, later sold to Bariod Sales Company. Another company that developed a mill and drying plant was American Colloid, whose first plant was on the west edge of Belle Fourche near the livestock siding on Middle Creek.

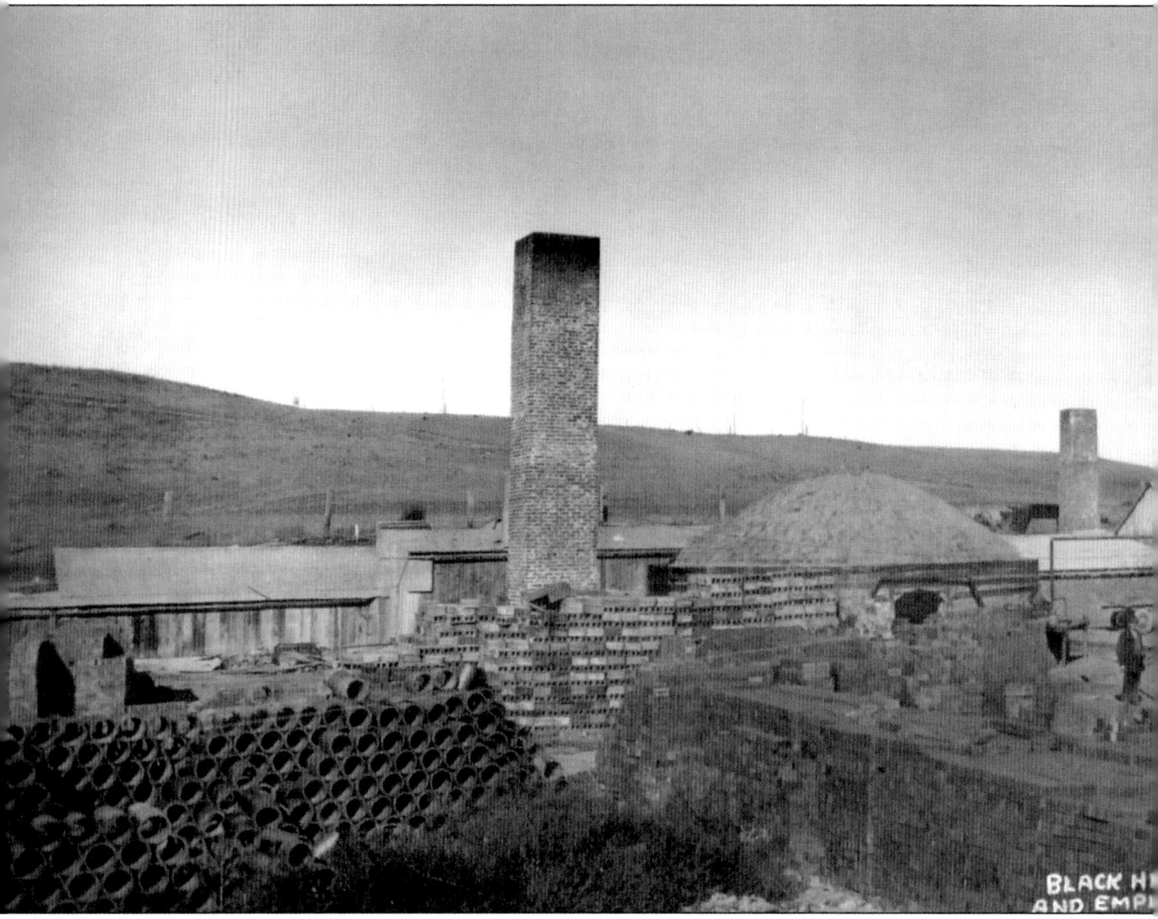

While excavating the canal for the power plant for the Tri-State Milling Company, Hans Quarnberg discovered a bed of exceptionally good clay suitable for making the finest building brick. In 1927, the Utah-Idaho Sugar Company was interested in locating in Belle Fourche. Quarnberg agreed to build a brick plant and to supply the bricks for the erection of their facilities. From this beginning, Black Hills Clay Products grew. In the late 1930s, five downdraft-

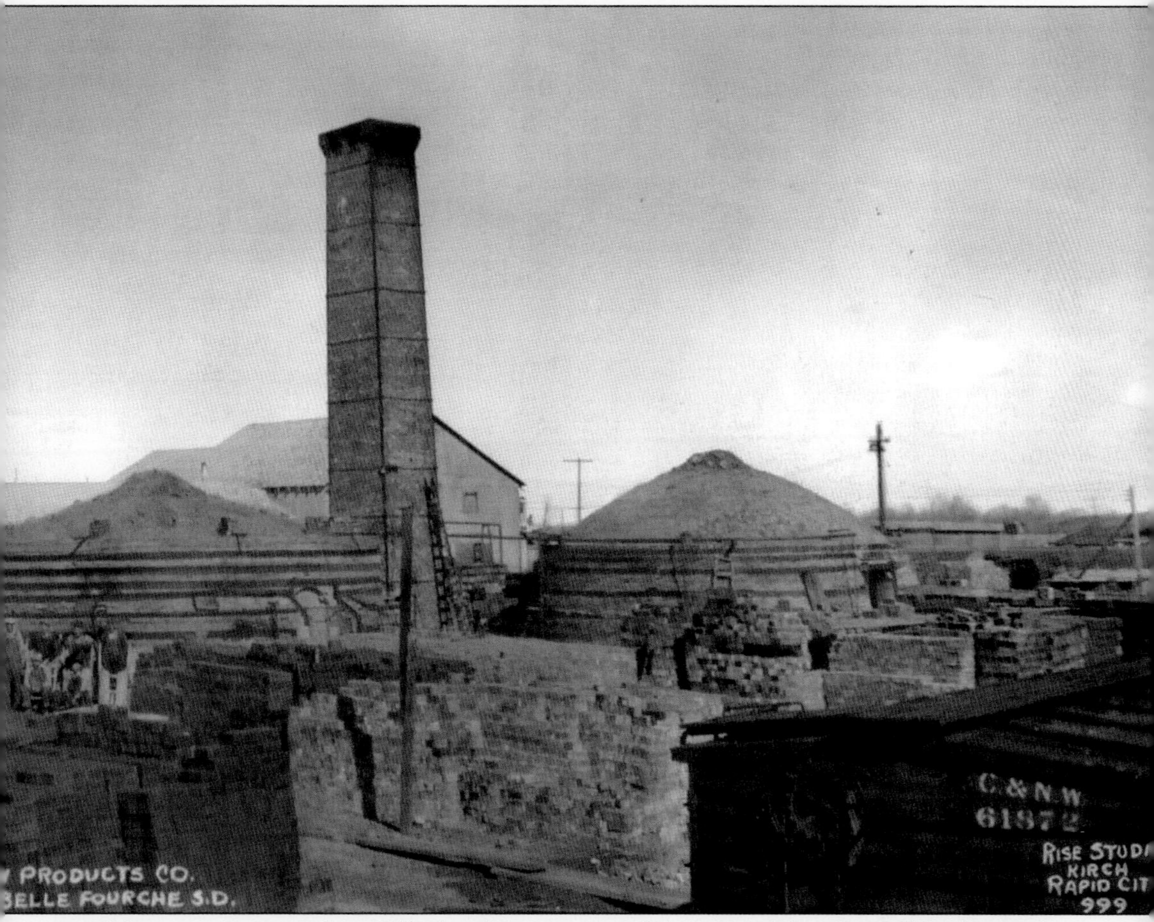

type kilns were in use, and in 1945, the plant was extended to seven kilns. Beautiful colors and top-quality materials and service helped Black Hills Clay Products grow from a small industry serving its local area to a company that served five states. Black Hills Clay Products was sold to a North Dakota company during the early 1970s and was later discontinued.

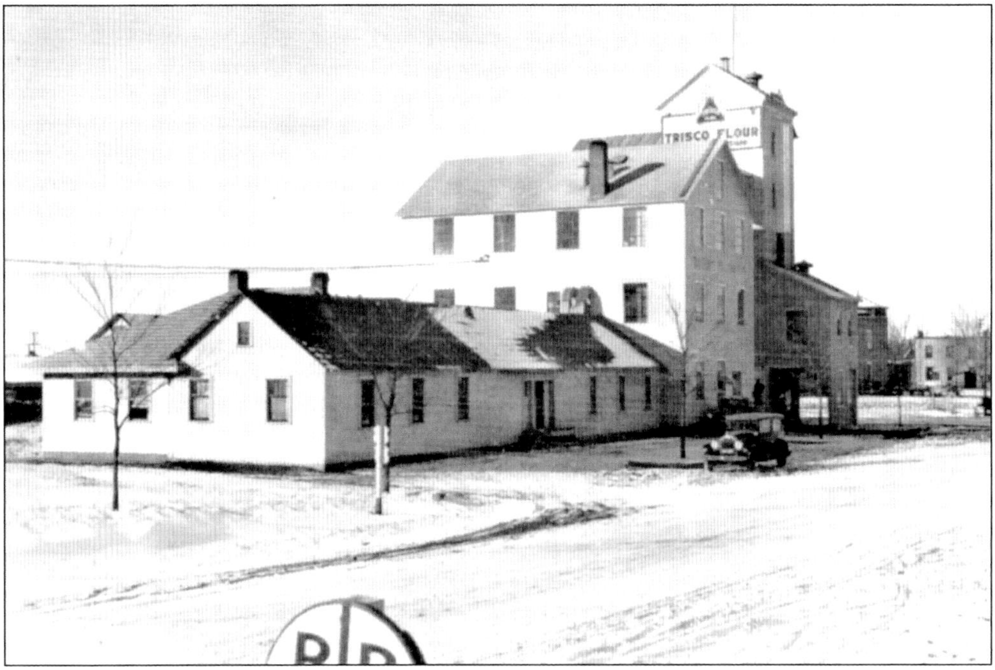

Tri-State Mill observed its golden anniversary in 1963. The name behind the mills, Quarnberg had been in the flour milling business for 150 years. Hans Quarnberg purchased the mill in Belle Fourche in 1913. Business was good in Belle Fourche and led to building three new mills in 1915. By 1926, Tri-State Mills owned 16 county elevators in western South Dakota. All pioneer mills owned prior to the Belle Fourche plant were operated by waterpower. The Belle Fourche mill was the first to use electric power. The Tri-State Milling Company was sold to the Hubbard Milling Company of Mankato, Minnesota, in 1970.

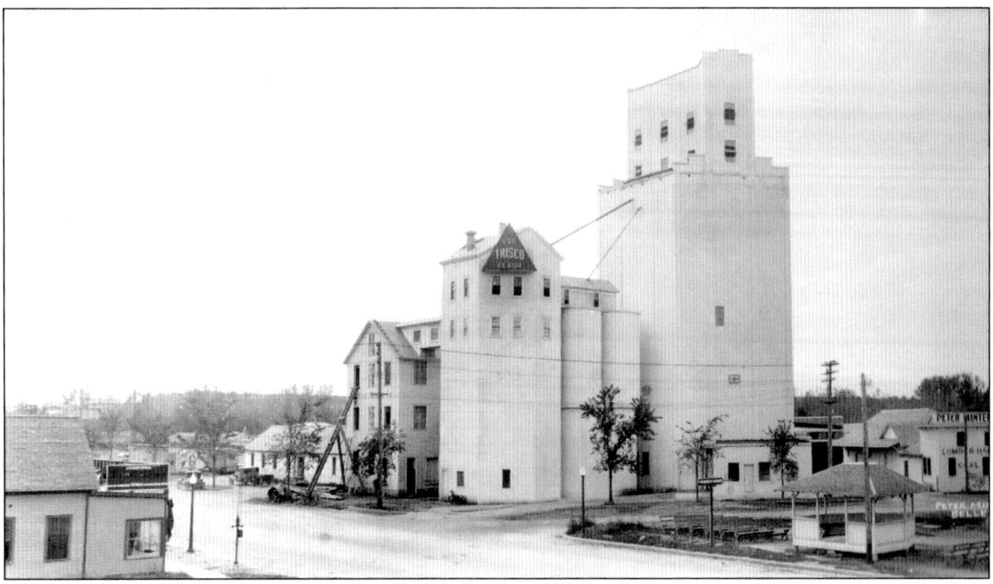

Four

TAMING THE LAND

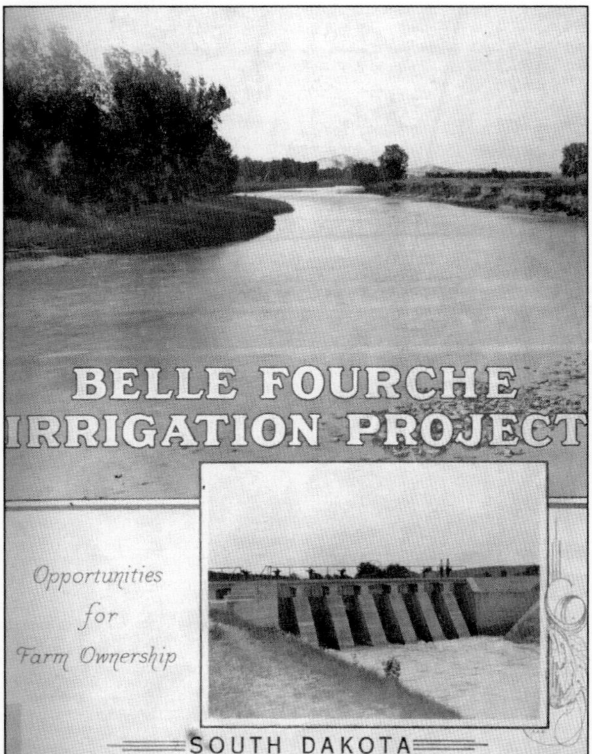

Belle Fourche Irrigation Project, one of the first projects authorized under the Reclamation Act, now includes more than 55,000 acres under irrigation. The district is owned by landowners and operated by an elected board of directors that maintains the 185,000 acre-feet water capacity Belle Fourche Reservoir, locally known as Orman Dam, and delivers water to users through more than 500 miles of canal and laterals from the dam. The Belle Fourche Irrigation Project remains a monument to the nation's earliest attempts at turning low-moisture areas into fertile cropland. Principal crops are alfalfa, corn, oats, and irrigated pastures. Sheep and lambs are fed on the fields of the project, and there are also many dairies, cattle-feeding, and hog-producing units as well as bee apiaries. Orman Dam was for many years the largest earthen dam in America and the second largest in the world.

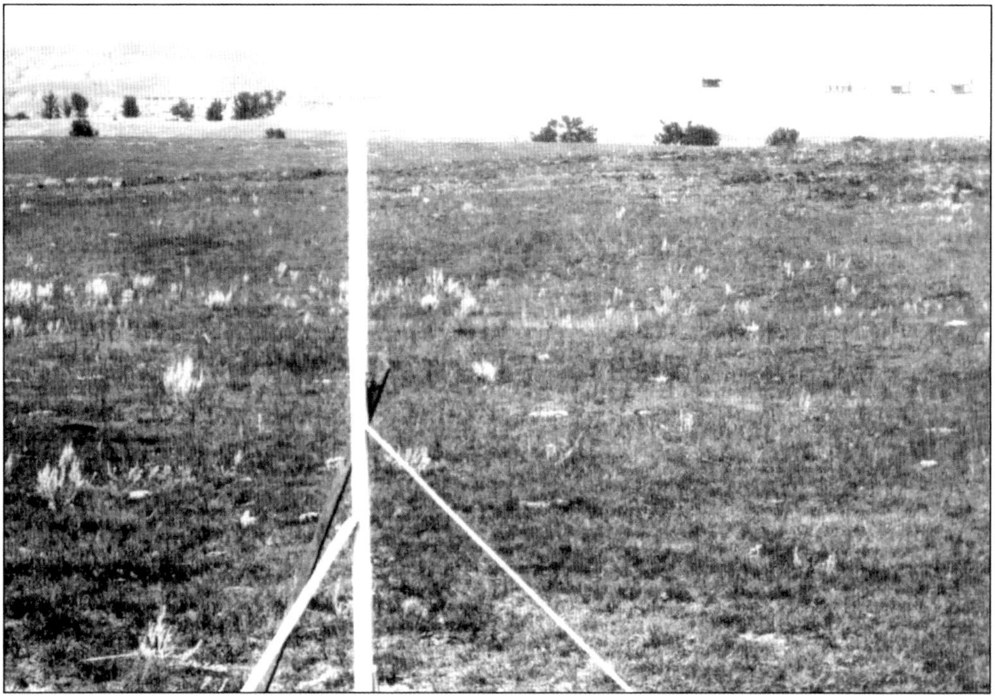

In 1903, Raymond F. Walters from the U.S. Geological Survey explained the general plan, "A diversion dam could be put across the Belle Fourche river a mile below town to elevate the water about twenty feet, at that level it would flow in a big intake canal that would carry it by gravity flow a distance of ten miles in northeasterly direction to the Owl Creek basin for storage."

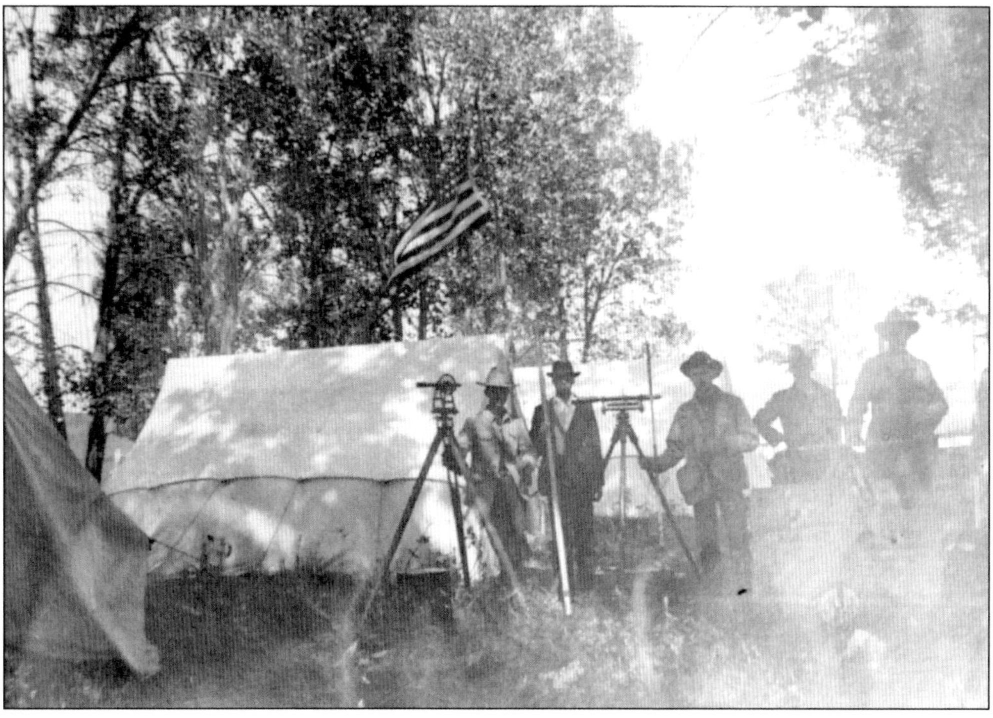

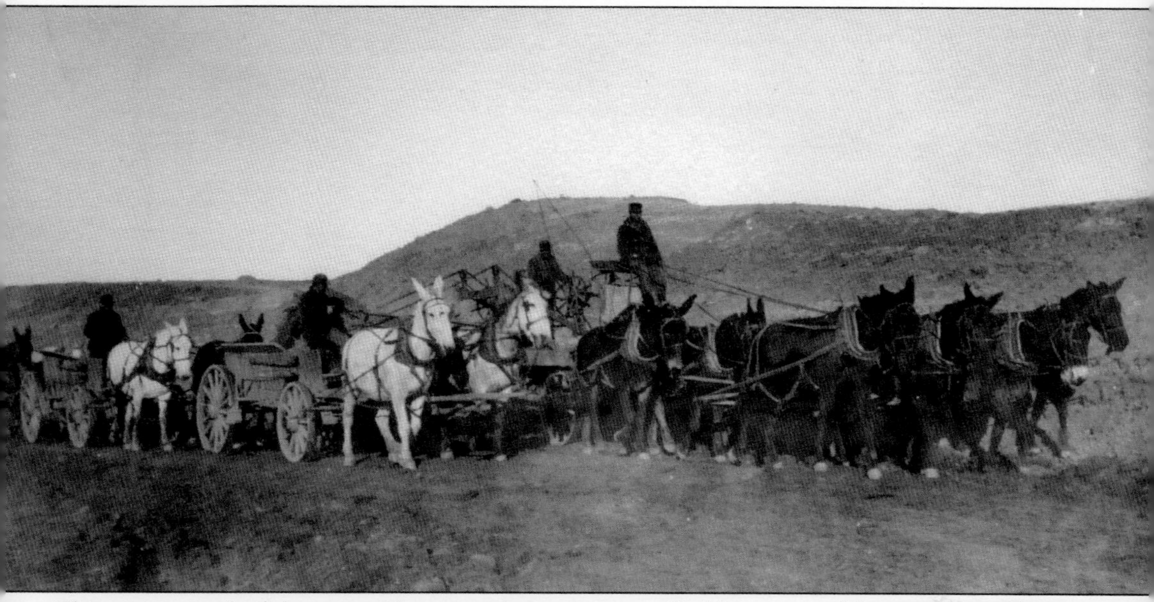

This project was built by men with teams, plows, scrapers called frescoes, and dump wagons. The big dam is a piled-up dike of hard-packed dirt and faced with slabs of thick concrete. Theodore Roosevelt ranched in the Dakota Territory as a young man when this area was called "the Great American Desert." Roosevelt's program of conservation developed the Reclamation Act that called for the building of two test projects with government money to demonstrate the value of water on unproductive lands. One dam was assigned to California and the other to South Dakota. Roosevelt was a friend of Seth Bullock from his early ranching days, and Bullock and Sol Star, businessmen from Deadwood, owned a horse ranch along the Belle Fourche River where Belle Fourche is now located. That friendship might have played a part in the location of this huge project. However, the available water and the perfect basin for the reservoir surely influenced the final decision.

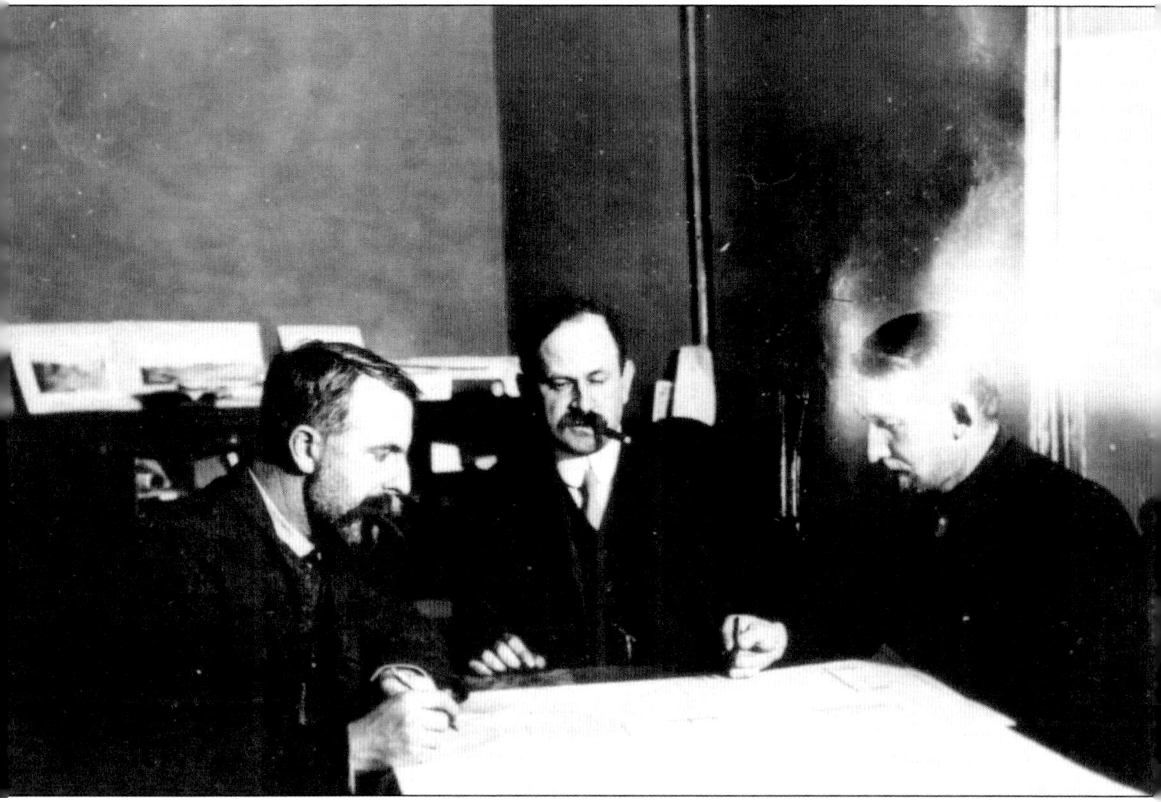

Reclamation Bureau offices were set up in Belle Fourche one door east of the Butte County Bank (presently the Wells Fargo Bank) for supervising engineers Charles E. Wells and C. H. Fitch, project engineer R. F. Walters, resident engineer W. W. Patch, and assistant engineers A. W. Walker and A. B. Cleaveland. Problems arose with such a large undertaking. On January 18, 1908, with progress not being satisfactory and the diversion dam contractor (Widdell, Finley, and Company) insolvent, the contract on the Belle Fourche Dam was suspended. That was resolved, and the government hired a new company to finish the diversion dam. It was found that much more fill on the dam was needed than was originally thought. New contracts for the reservoir dam and two main irrigation canals were let in November 1905 and awarded to Orman and Crooke, railroad contractors from Pueblo, Colorado, for $1,003,299.25. Their work camp was established below the dam site, and soon it also became the headquarters for the bureau's office, engineers, post office, camp store, and crew quarters.

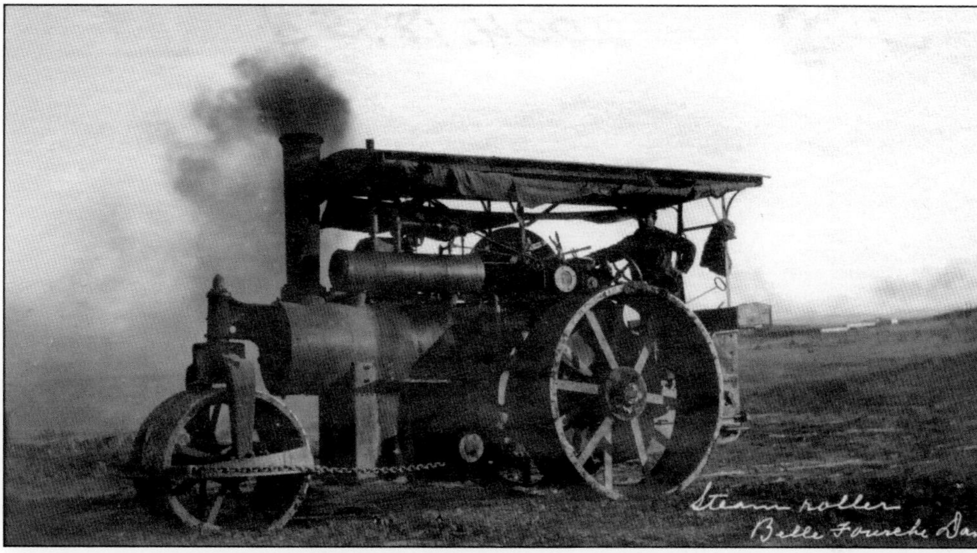

The dirt was spread in six-inch layers until the proper compaction was obtained. The dump wagon dirt delivered to the big dam was so powdery and dry that men and horses suffered from the choking dust. Water was brought from Owl Creek to wet down the dirt before it could be packed by the huge steamroller on the Inlet Canal.

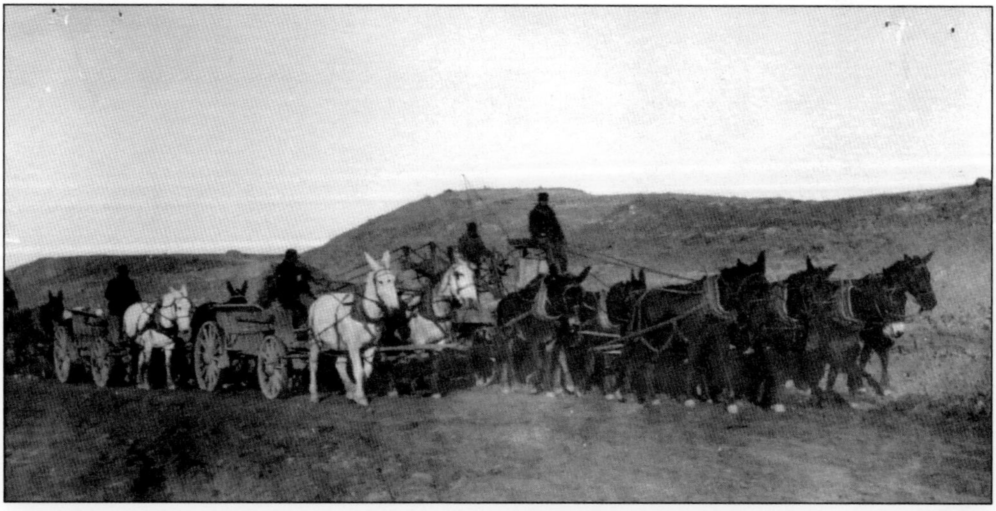
According to records kept by construction engineer W. W. Patch, there were many day-to-day problems in building the dam, including finding sufficient hay and oats for the nearly 1,000 horses used in the construction. Ralph Shaykett, a rancher from nearby, reported, "I have seen as many as four circles of fresnoes and wheel scrapers with two hundred or two hundred and fifty teams in a circle all going at once."

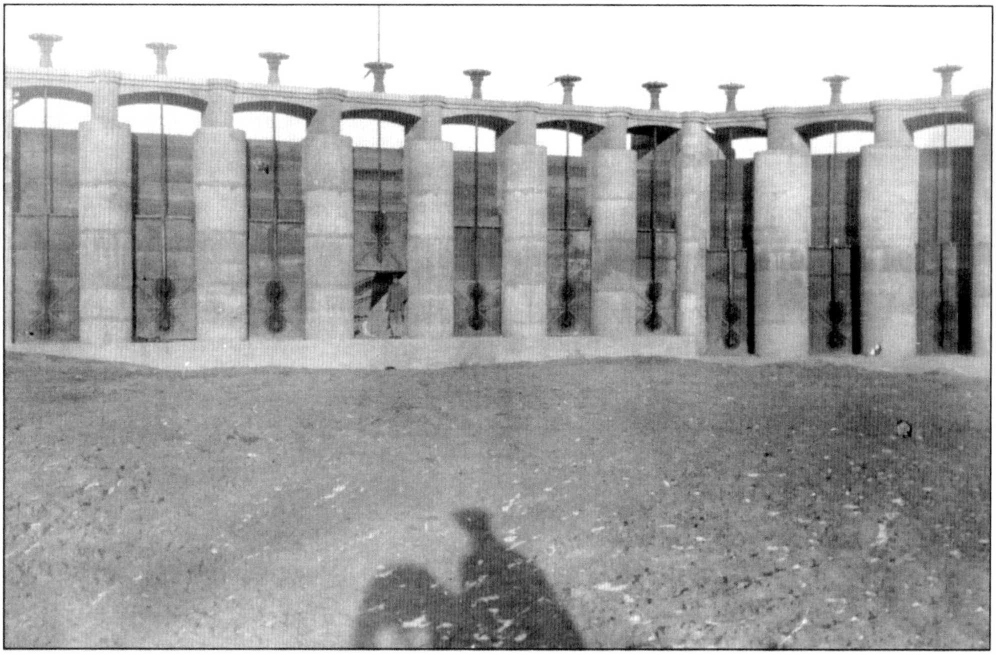

Constructing the Inlet Canal made months of work for men and teams. This ditch, about 20 feet deep and 40 feet wide, ran for 10 or more miles to the reservoir basin. The canal's head was fitted with massive concrete headgates that could be opened to receive or closed to let the flow continue down the river over the diversion dam. Water storage limit is controlled because high winds run waves across the lake that dash against the cement facings of the dam. Building the 10 miles of canal was a challenging chore. In some areas, the ground was so hard that blasting crews had to dynamite the channel to loosen up the dirt.

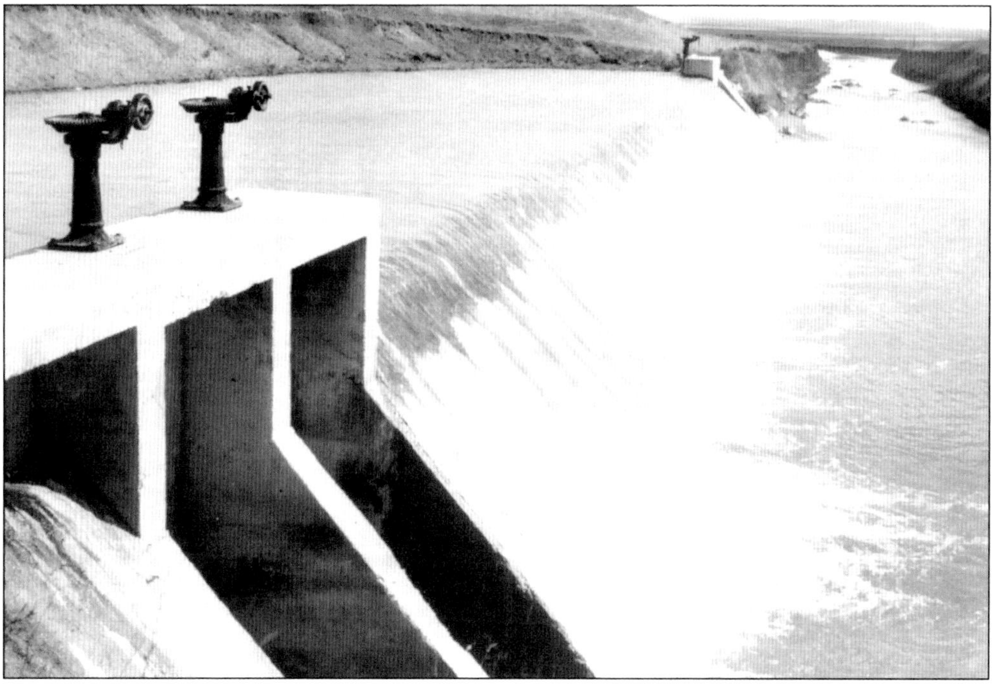

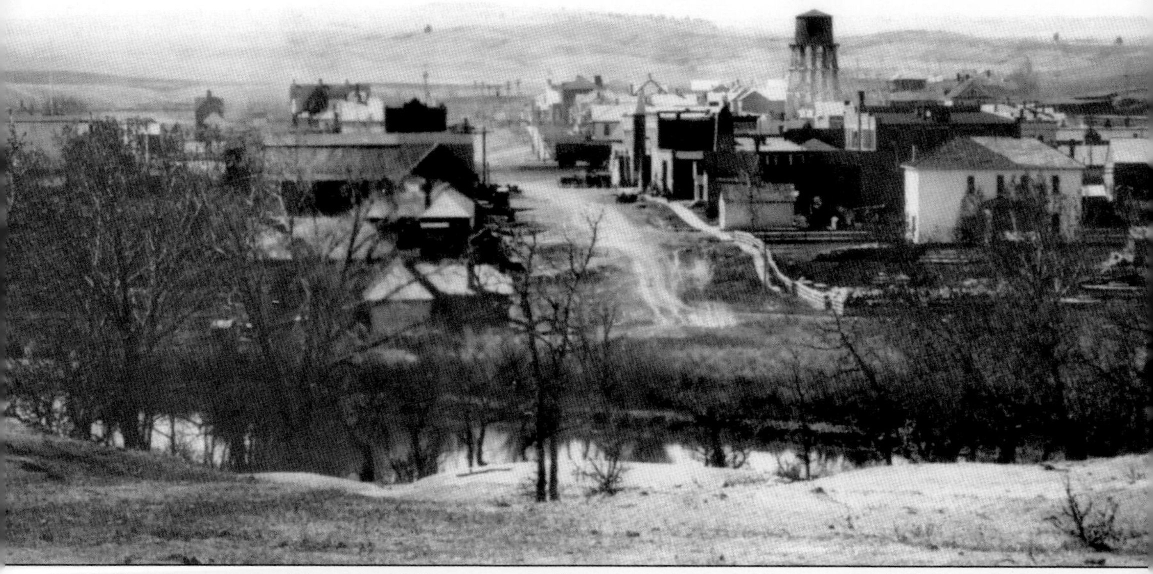

Belle Fourche, pictured here in 1905, was a small town with a population of only 700 and was located just north of the Black Hills. At the time, it was a well-known cattle-shipping point in the tristate trade territory. It was Butte County's only town, as Minnesela was already a ghost camp of earlier times, and there was no Fruitdale, Nisland, or Newell. On February 2, 1905, the old *Northwest Post* carried a headline that read, "All Doubt Removed: Government Formally Approves Belle Fourche Project." Irrigation was no speculation to Butte County. There were two irrigation systems in operation in nearby Redwater Valley and West Side Ditch. Plans and estimates for the project, to be completed near Belle Fourche, were completed during the winter of 1903 and 1904. These plans were then reviewed by a government board of engineers, which reported that it was feasible to irrigate an area of not less than 60,000 acres. The project was officially approved by Secretary of Interior Ethan A. Hitchcock on May 10, 1904, and $2.1 million was set. This seemed like a fabulous amount of money, and some people were opposed to the project. It took over five years to build the dam and ditch system and bring them into operation.

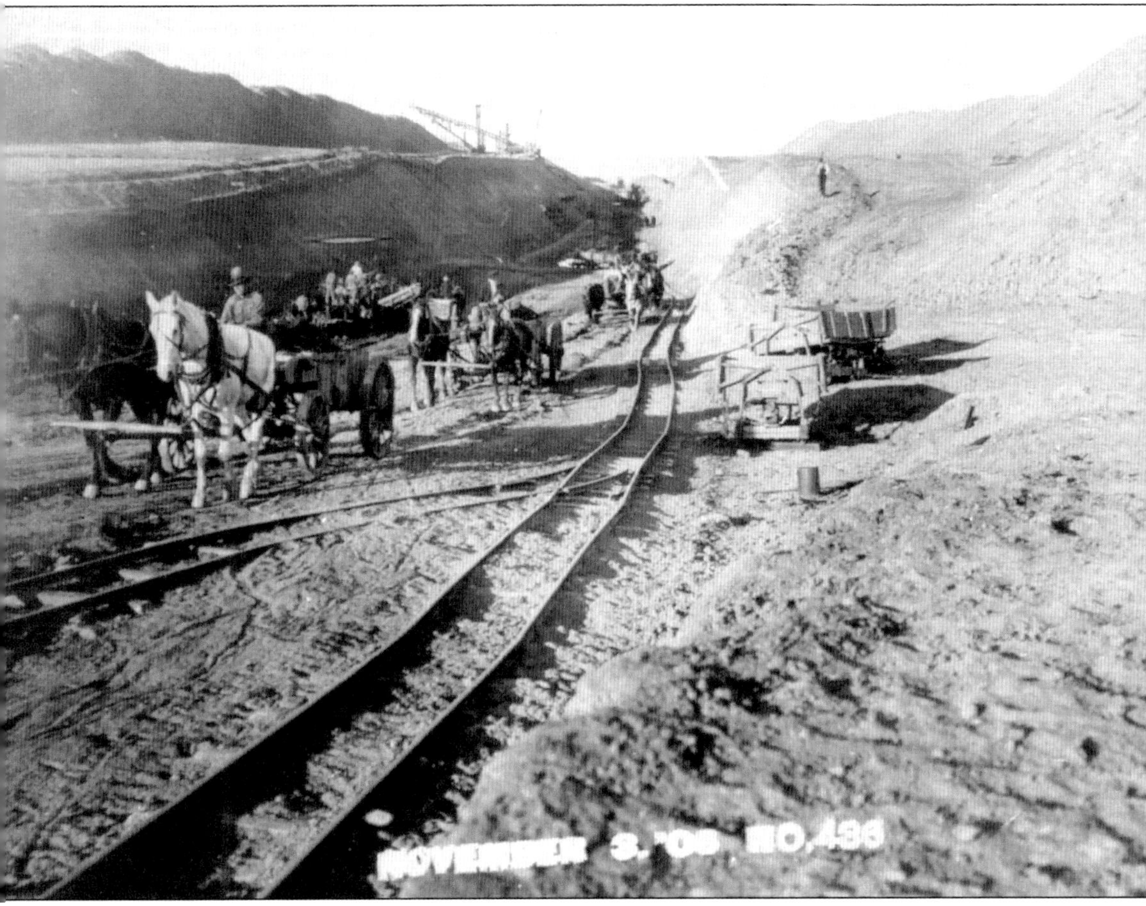

Orman and Crooke of Pueblo, Colorado, were well-known railroad grade builders. As the dam resembled a long, high fill of dirt often constructed for track beds, they thought they could move dirt to the site at 15¢ per yard. Orman and Crooke shipped in big construction outfits that included some power equipment. It was 13 miles east of Belle Fourche. Everything was freight hauled from town, the location of the closest railhead. They brought in two steam shovels using standard-width track. They were brought down the north side of the river from Middle Creek stock pens on short sections of track. They ran the length of one section and then pulled another section up with horses and moved to the front laying another section. When they got these machines to the dam, they brought in narrow-gauge engines and cars and laid a narrow-gauge track.

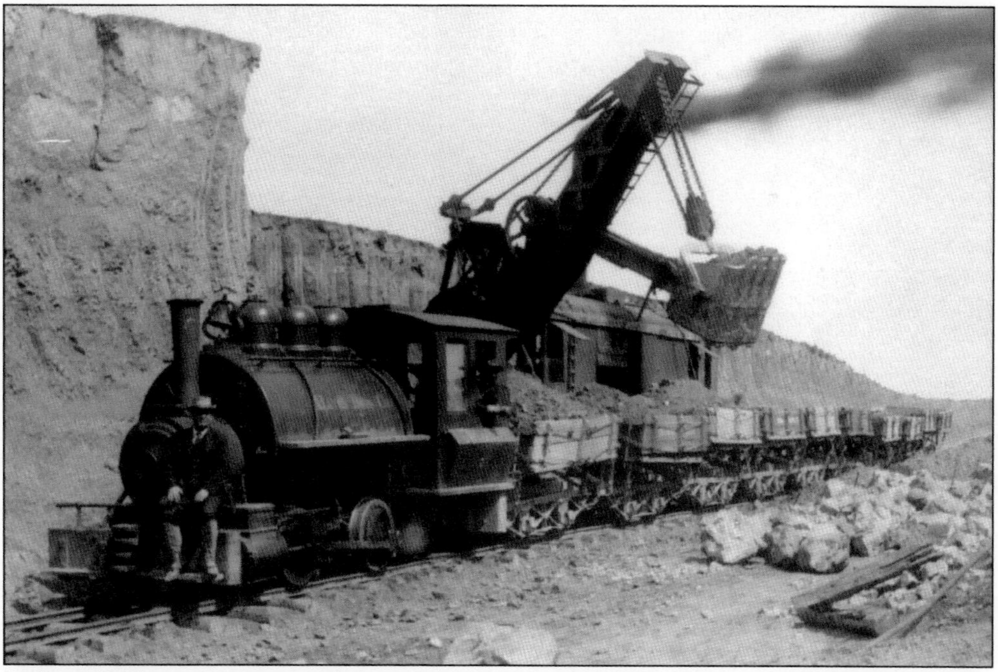

By June 1905, construction work was underway. The *Northwest Post* reported, "Canal work by Widell, Finley and Company is actually underway and the manner in which the big traction engine walks along with the elevator grader is a wonder. It takes but 10 seconds to load each of the numerous dump wagons which follow one another to and from the elevator to the adjoining banks." The narrow-gauge dinkey engines were used to move both loads of dirt to the face of the dam and the cement blocks from the river block plant. The two dinkeys were delivered by the standard-gauge engine.

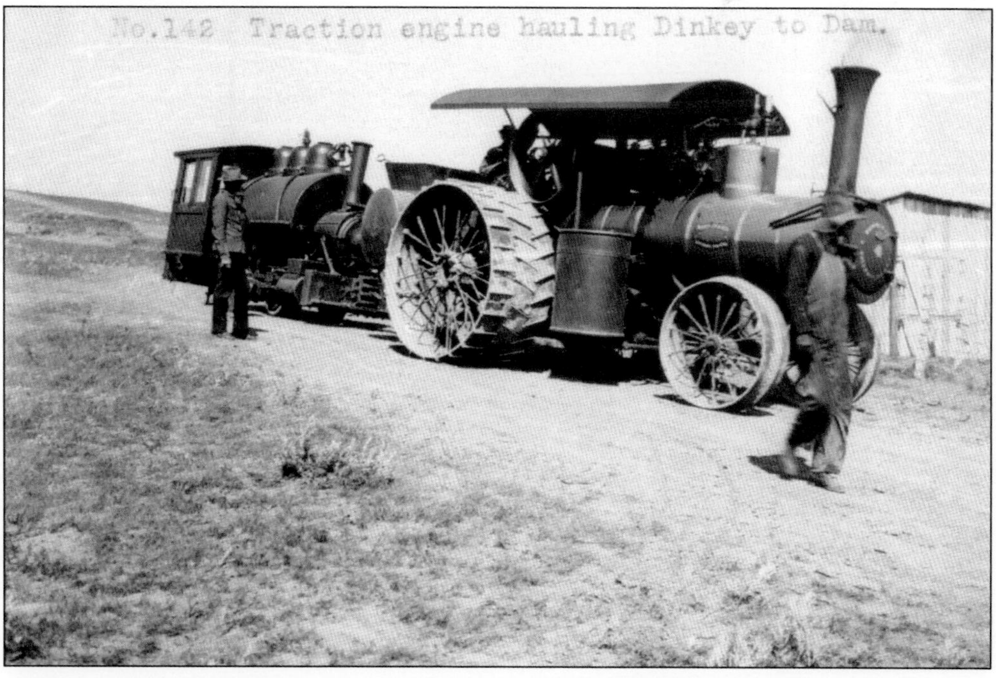

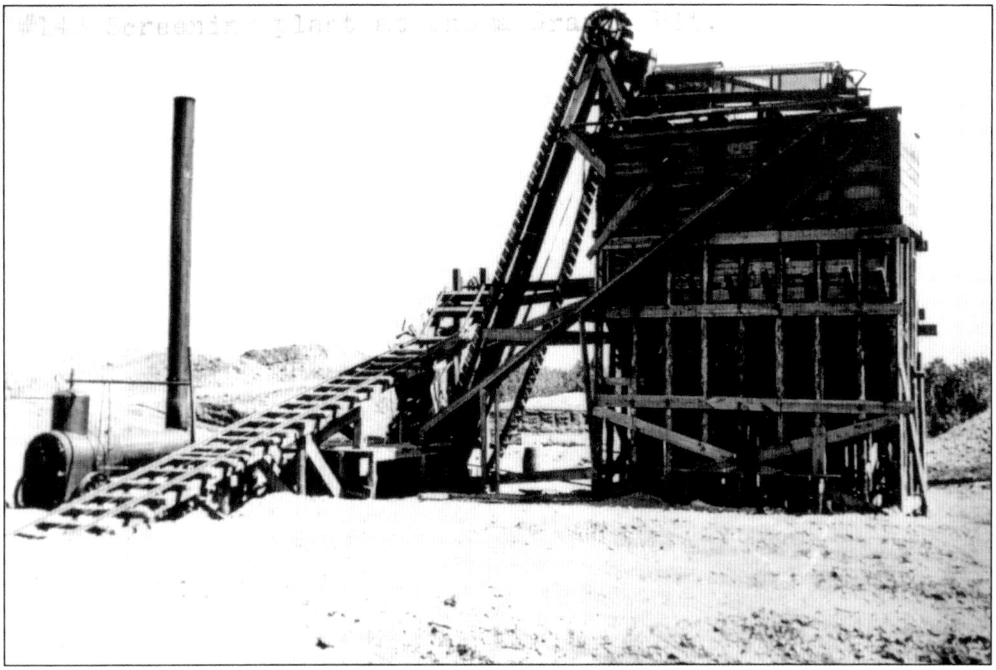

The cement blocks for the face of the dam were also hauled from the river about six miles south. This location was where the gravel was located near Snoma, a small pioneer town settled by Finnish homesteaders. All the cement was mixed with shovels and hauled to the forms with wheelbarrows. Each block was five by six feet and eight inches thick. Workers started making the blocks on May 6, 1907, and produced about 100 per day. The blocks were kept wet for 30 days to cure properly and were covered with earth to keep them from drying out. Acres and acres of blocks were poured before any were placed on the face of the dam.

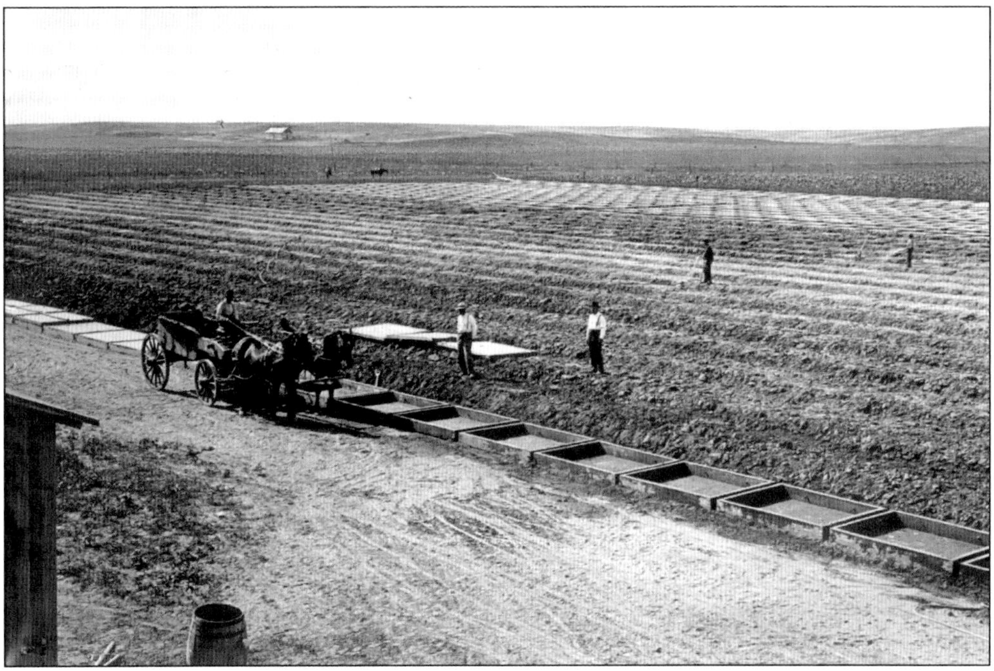

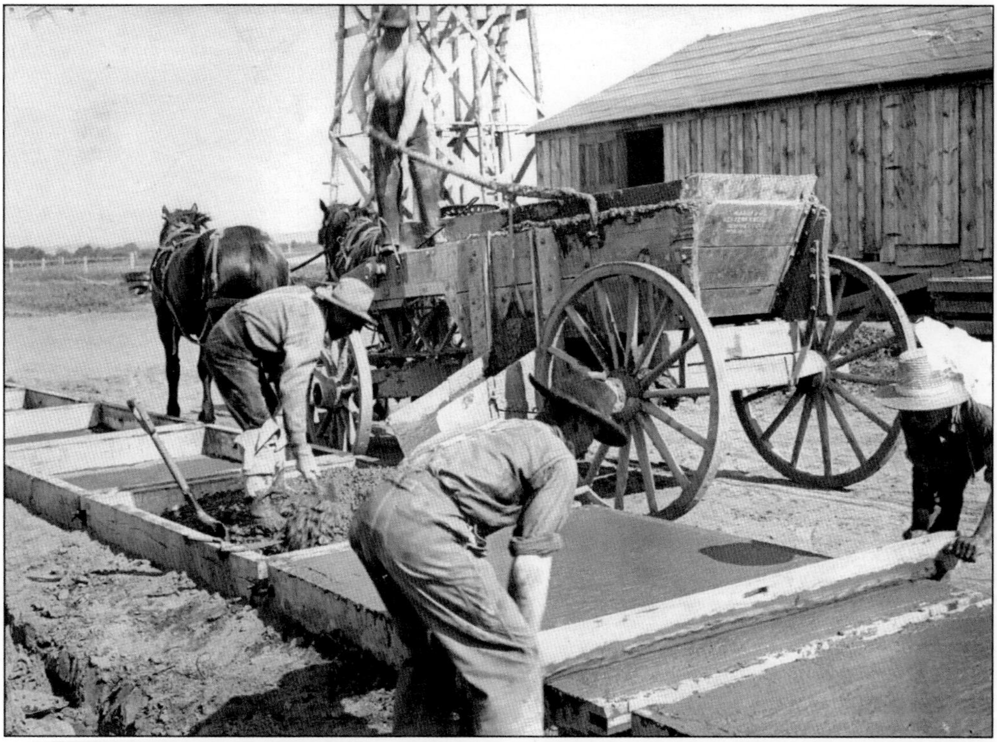

The blocks on the face of the dam were placed with dinkey engines and gin poles, with one on top of the dam and one at the bottom. A narrow-gauge rail track was built to haul the cement blocks from Snoma to the dam, a distance of five miles. Again dinkey engines were used, pulling 11 cars that hauled forty-four 3,000-pound blocks per trip. The total weight of a trainload of blocks was over 66 tons.

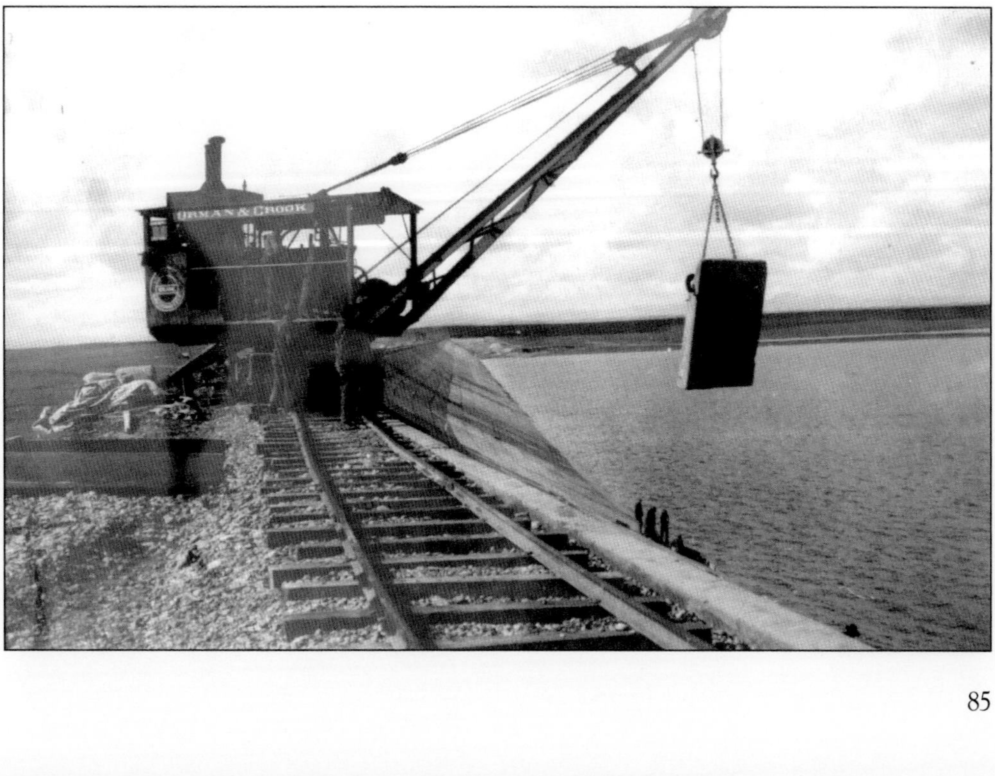

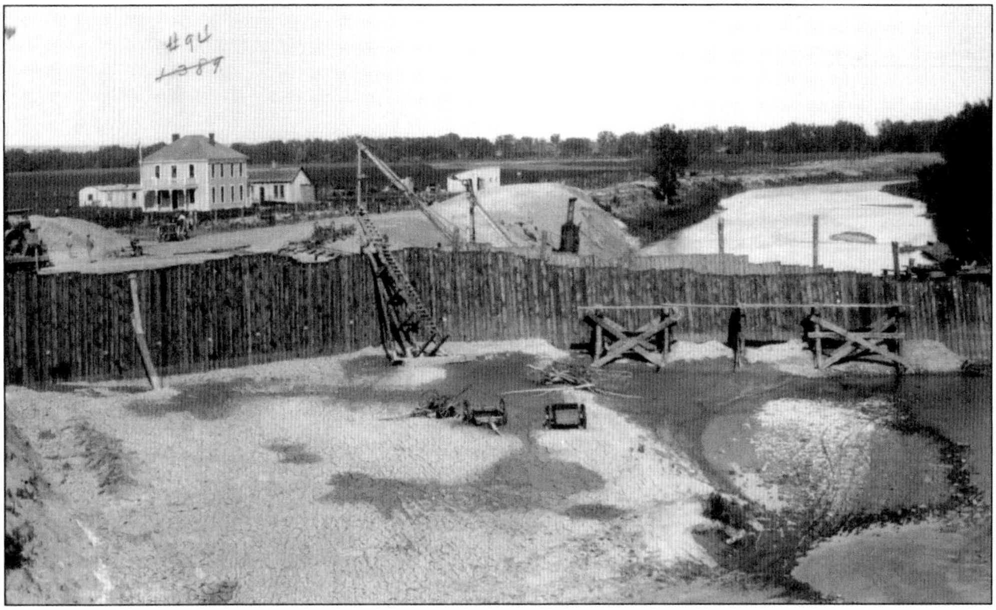

The Belle Fourche Project started with the diversion dam one mile north of Belle Fourche. The dam diverted the water from the Belle Fourche River, raised it up 20 feet, and channeled it into Owl Creek. The large Owl Creek basin, 12 miles east of Belle Fourche, was where the water is stored. The 290-mile Belle Fourche River starts in Wyoming. It flows east from Wyoming skirting the foothills of the Black Hills and eventually joins the Cheyenne River halfway between the Wyoming border and Missouri River. Major tributaries that come out of the Black Hills from the south include the Redwater River and Whitewood Creek. A compact with Wyoming and Keyhole Dam, another dam built on the Belle Fourche River, has greatly affected the capacity of the Belle Fourche Dam for irrigation. Ninety percent of the water in the river is guaranteed to the irrigators. The dam has been repaired and refaced several times and continues to supply water to 57,068 acres, as well as furnishing recreation. The primary recreation activity at Belle Fourche Reservoir is fishing, with limited boating and water-skiing.

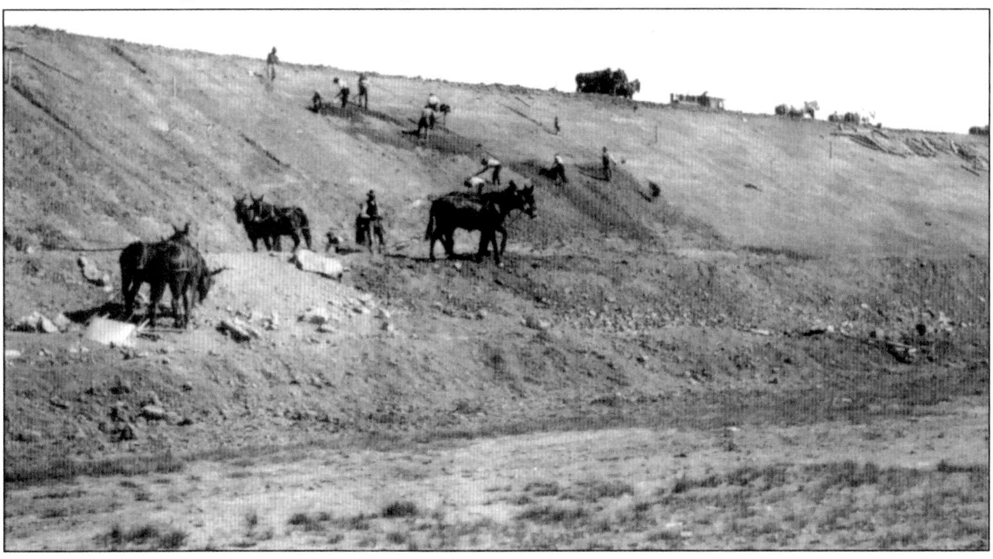

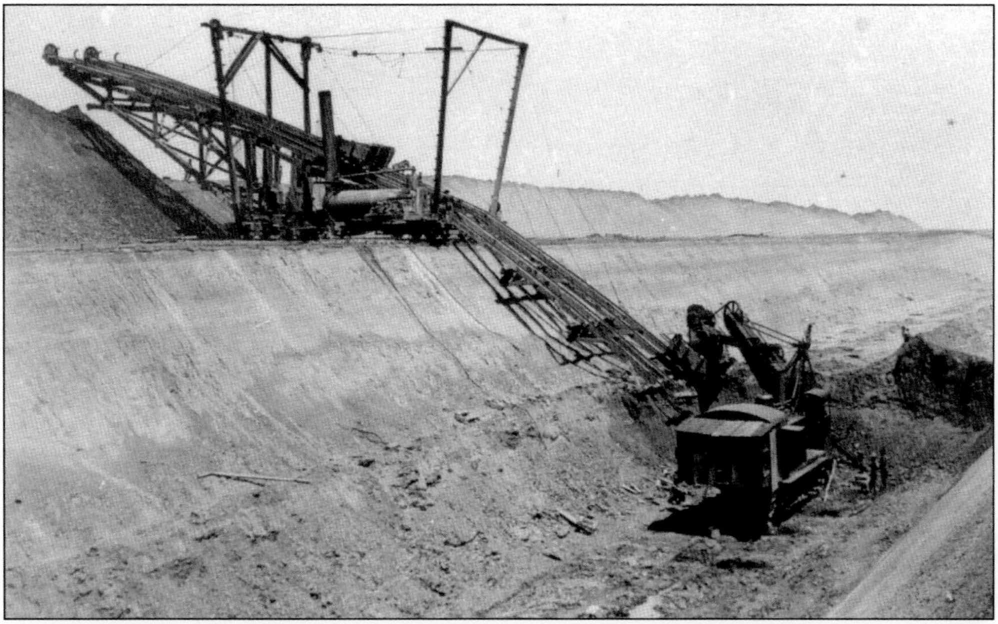

In the summer of 1909, workers filled Owl Creek Gap, signaling the near completion of the project. Owl Creek was the basin on which Orman Dam was being constructed, and a V-shaped gap had been left in the middle of the dam, allowing creek water to pass downstream. After three years of construction work on the dam, the first water from the reservoir was turned into the ditches for a test run to some of the farms. Besides the intake canal flow from the diversion dam, the flood runoff of Owl Creek flows directly into the lake. The big dam was not completed to the satisfaction of the reclamation bureau until 1917, although it was in operation long before that date. It takes two years of normal river flow to fill the reservoir, and when it is filled, there is a two-year supply of water impounded for project irrigation.

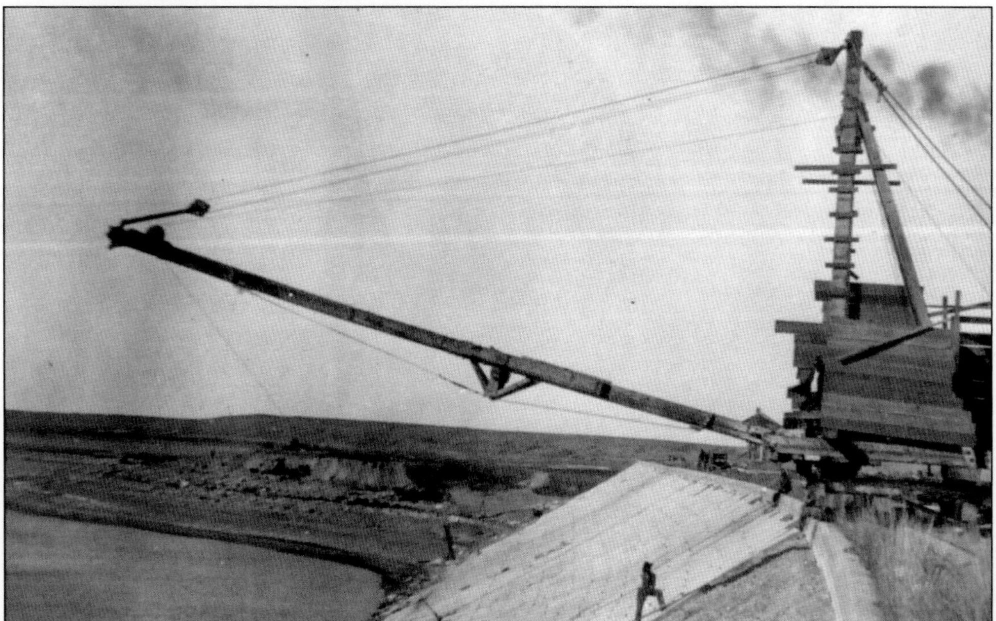

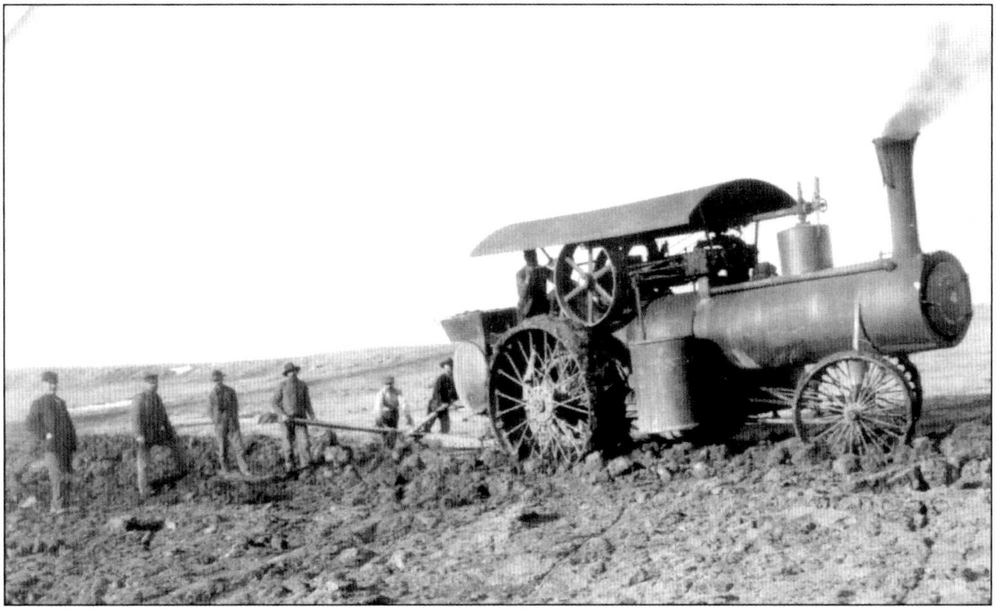

Despite recurring financial and weather problems, progress on the dam continued. The amount of manpower and horsepower needed was a great boom to the whole area. New homesteaders used the employment at the dam to supplement their meager income from ranching and farming. However, there were constant financial problems. Paychecks failed to arrive shortly after Orman and Crooke went out of business. Later area banks refused to honor paychecks. Several times the laborers organized strikes for higher pay. Unfavorable weather washed out the diversion dam and equipment, which no matter how large became mired in the heavy clay gumbo. In 1905, flood after flood came down the rivers. The diversion dam, despite the coffer dam, filled up with water time after time. It was a heartbreaking and business-breaking setback that involved repeated starts at great expense. Construction of the facilities for the Belle Fourche Project began in 1905 and had progressed sufficiently by 1908 to permit the delivery of irrigation water to 12,000 acres. The original project was completed in 1914.

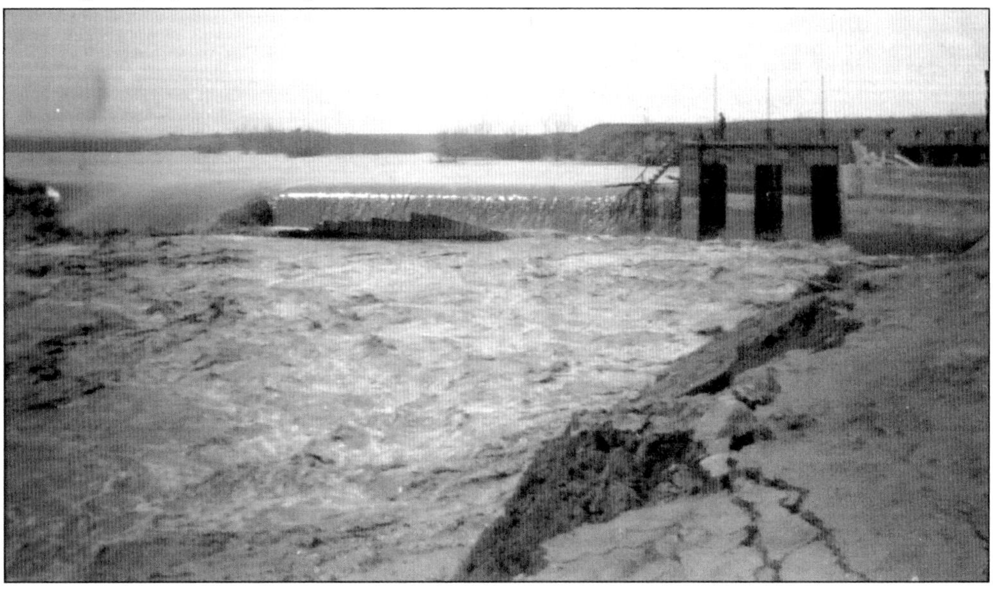

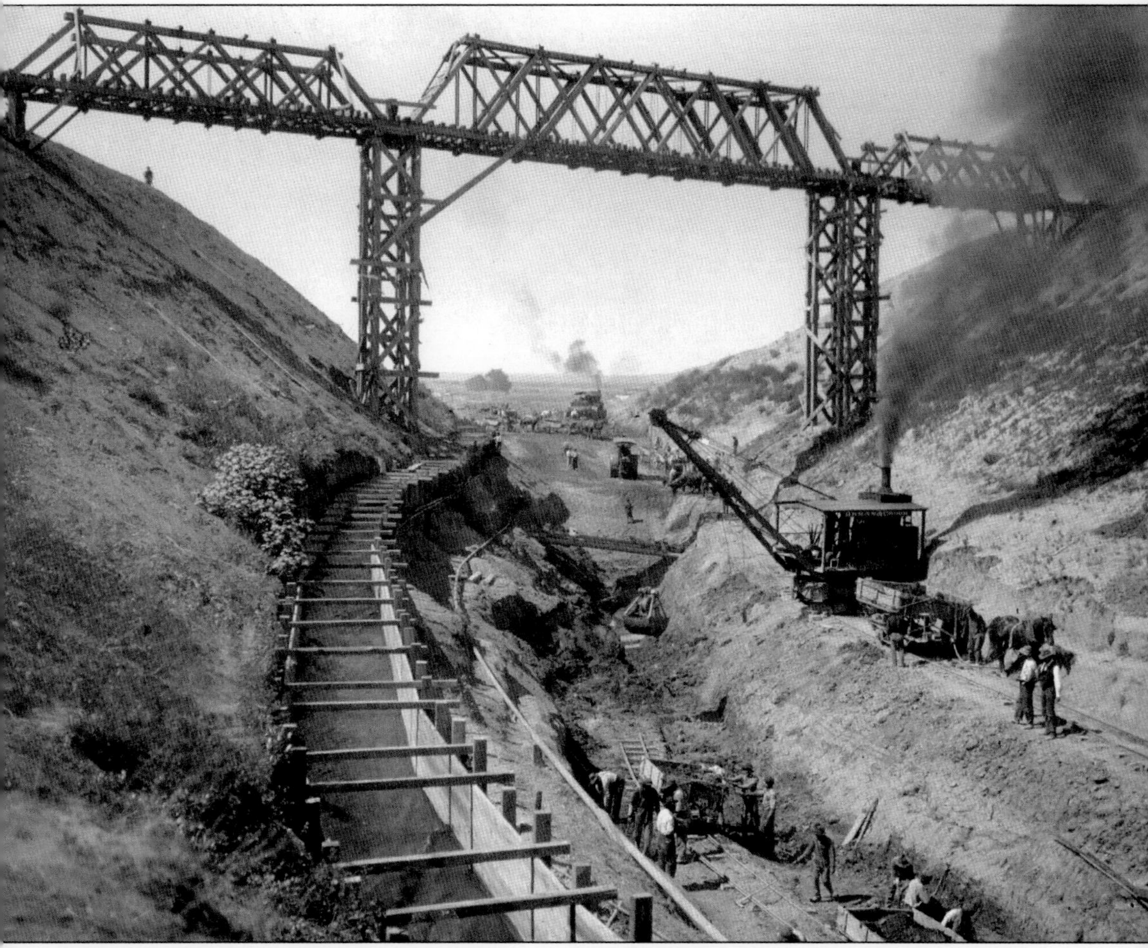

"Work on the gigantic Belle Fourche project, owing to the exceptionally rainy weather, is not so far along as was expected and hoped that it would be at this time. However, the contractors have not been idle . . . Machinery galore has been received," reported the *Northwest Post*. "Among the various machines already on the ground is a large 20 ton cable way engine, to be used in transporting material back and forth across the river, and for handing the steel sheet piling, heavy timbers and concrete. Two other powerful engines will be used for moving small cars, loaded with gravel and concrete, up the incline track. A large 40 horsepower boiler will be utilized to furnish steam for pumping water to the various engines and also the huge crusher and concrete mixer." The first unit of the project was completed, and water was turned on on April 14, 1908; the second unit was opened in March 1910.

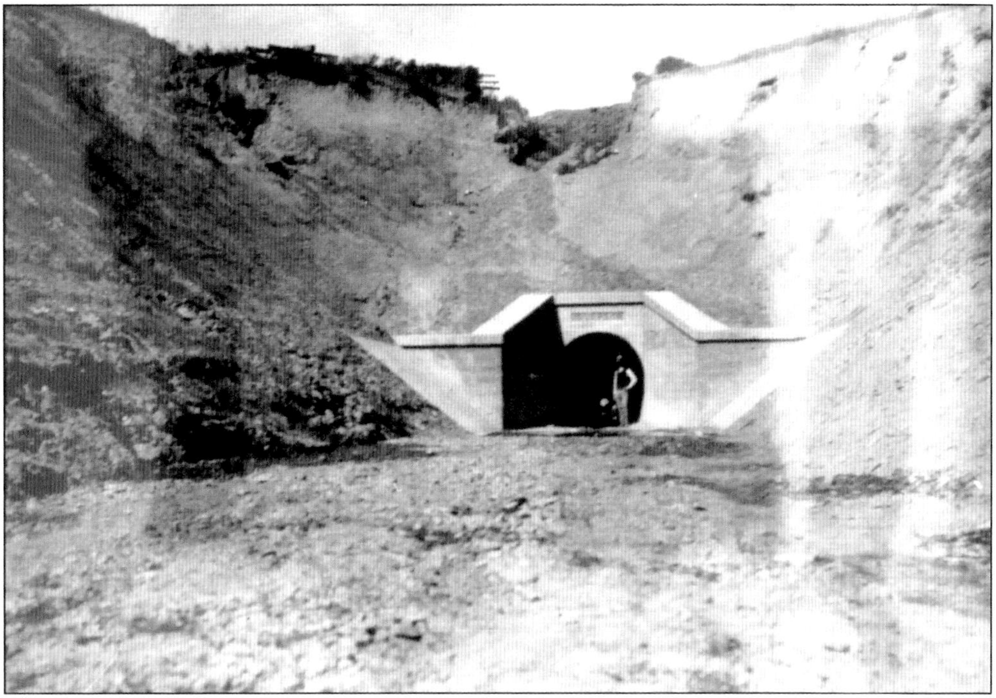

The outlet canals were serviced by concrete tunnels under the dam. Both tunnels were fitted with regulatory valves that can be opened and closed from the spillway housing on top of the dam. The South Side Canal pictured was about 40 feet wide and 20 feet deep. The North Side Canal that serviced a bigger area was about 50 feet wide and 30 feet deep at its spillway behind the dam. Dozens of smaller canals called laterals carry the water.

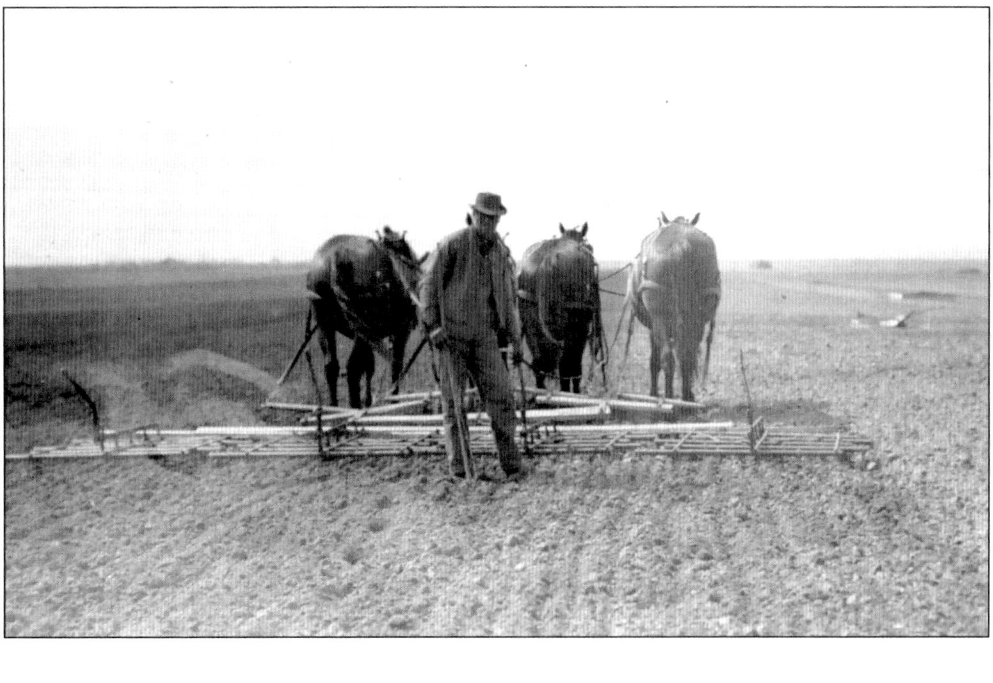

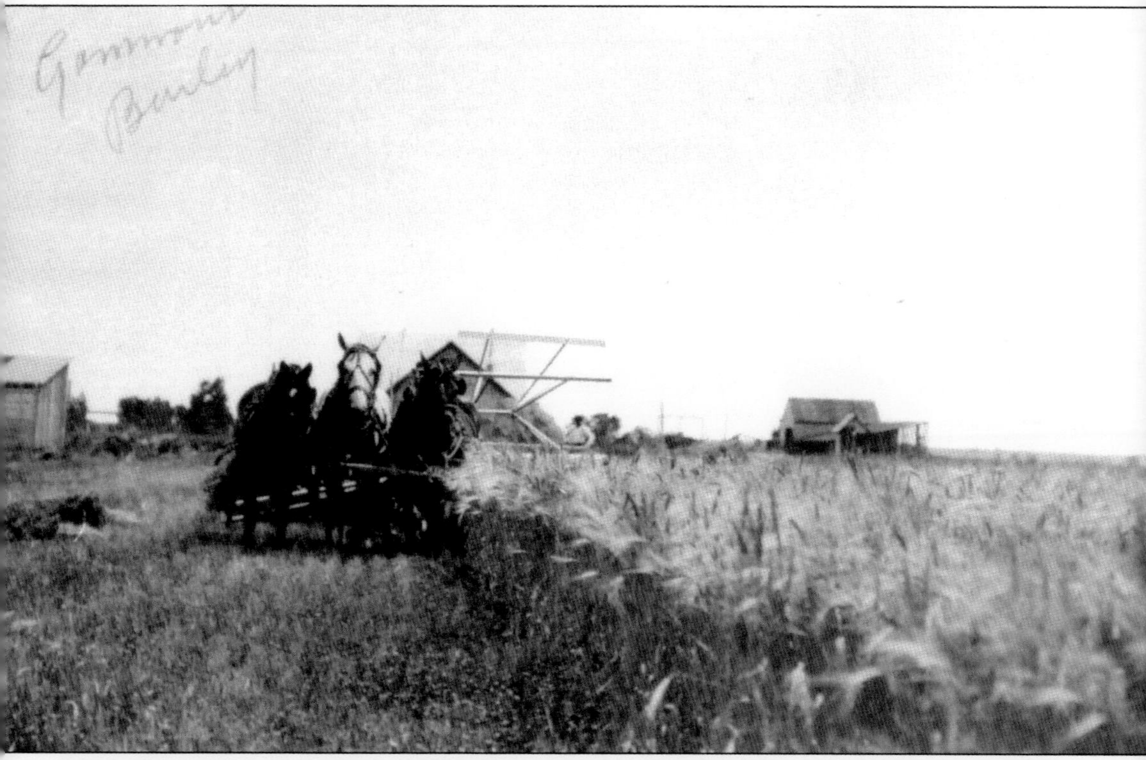

Orman Dam and the water it supplied proved to be a boon to Belle Fourche and the surrounding area. Land in the irrigation project sold for $25 and up, an amazing price to pay back in 1910. This irrigated acreage produced abundant crops of hay, grain, and corn, far beyond the wildest dreams of these early settlers. Irrigation also introduced a myriad of new cash crops to western South Dakota, including cucumbers, sugar beets, onions, pinto beans, and even peanuts. A water users association was formed in June 1904. The first board of directors included Charles Blackwell, Nis Sorensen, W. S. Hamilton, Peter Edwards, H. C. Wilson, Andrew Erickson, James C. Young, William Holst, and A. Giles. The irrigated area under the ditch amounted to 57,182 acres. Some of this land lies northeast of the dam in the Arpan Flats area, and the balance is down the Belle Fourche Valley 25 miles east of Vale and Newell.

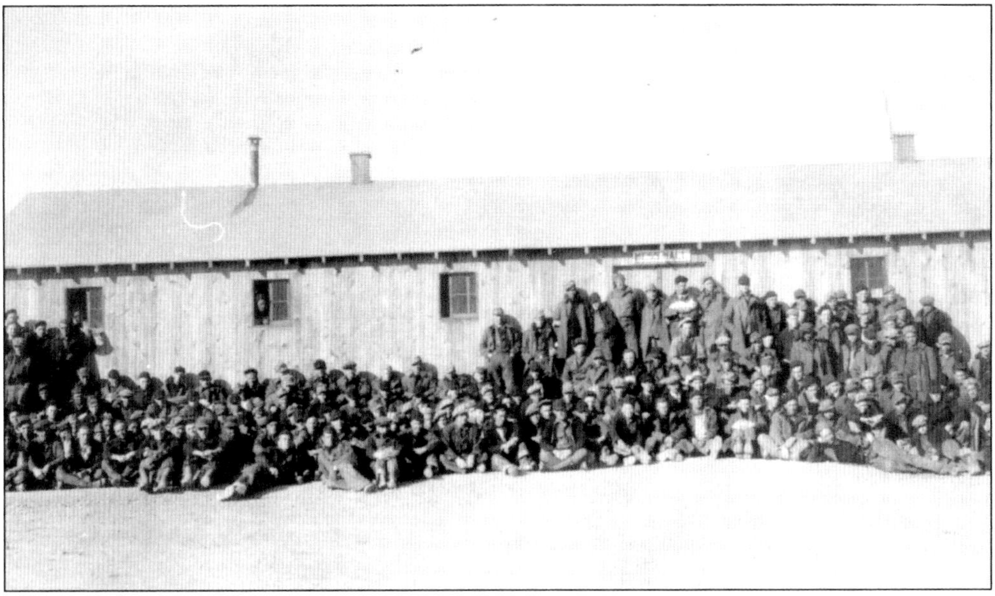

During the Depression of the 1930s, the federal government established the Civilian Conservation Corps (CCC) to give work to young men ages 17 to 24. One of these CCC camps was located near the face of Orman Dam. There were probably about 200 to 250 young men in camp 2750. Barracks were provided as well as food, clothing, and a wage. These workers repaired and maintained the dam and canals. Later this same camp was used for the World War II German prisoners of war. These men were used as farm laborers especially in the sugar beet fields. This situation worked well, as there were many area farmers who were first-generation Americans from Germany. Many of these farmers still spoke German.

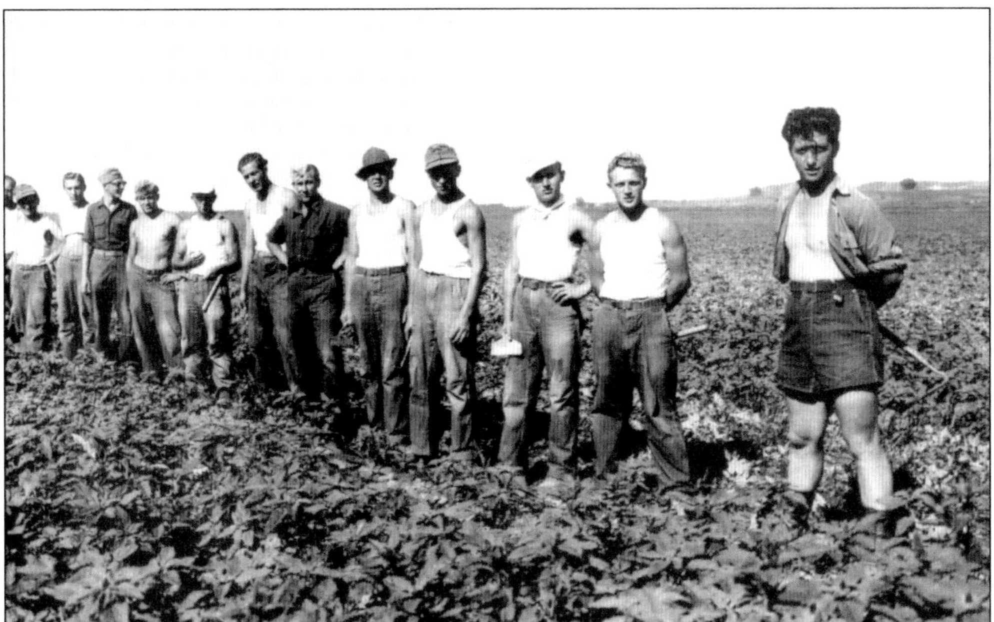

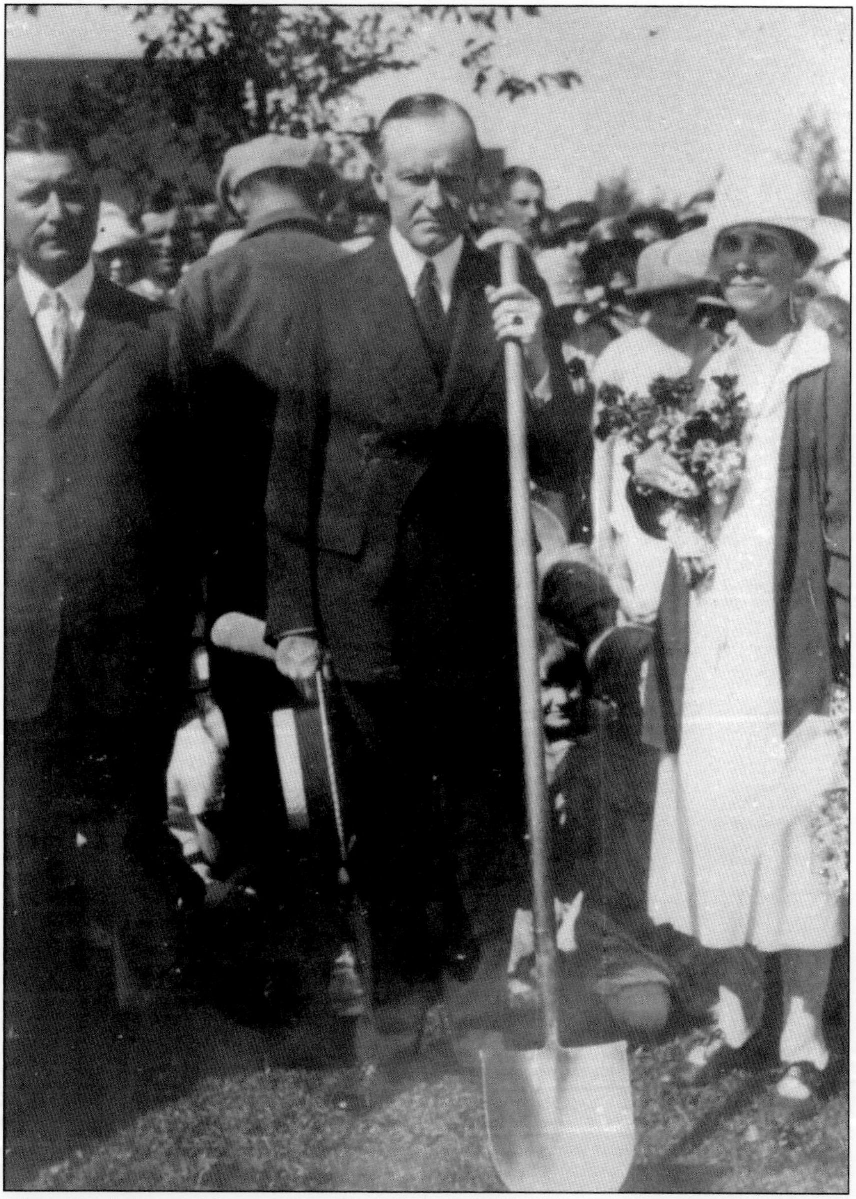

Pres. Calvin Coolidge and his wife made the Black Hills their summer home in the summer of 1927. They visited the Bureau of Reclamation office in Newell on September 1, 1927. This was a crucial period in the history of the Belle Fourche project as the secretary of interior had ordered that Orman Dam and the canal works be sold at auction to rid the government of what he called a white elephant that should never have been built. In 1928, the farmers of the valley signed a contract with the federal government stating they would operate and maintain the project. The manager directs the day-to-day activities of the district. Project water users have repaid the construction cost obligation of $3,558,807. The estimated federal tax collections attributable to the Belle Fourche project area in the years 1940 to 1959 amounted to more than $6 million, an amount far greater than the original cost. There were many other distinguished guests who visited the area during these years. Among them was Secretary of the Interior James Rudolph Garfield on July 24, 1908, and with his party was U.S. marshal Seth Bullock.

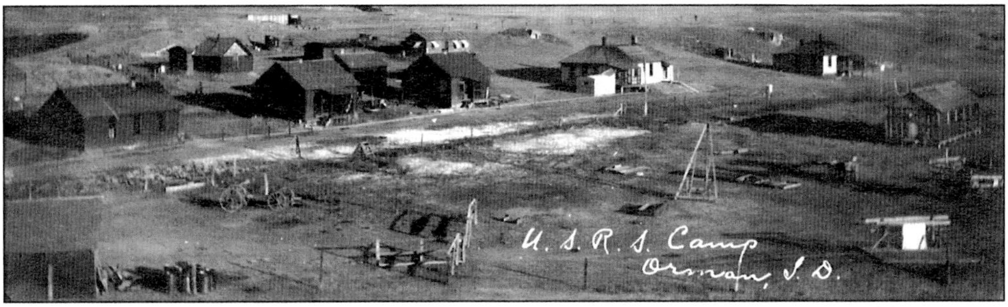

Orman, the headquarters for the construction team for the dam, was the second-largest city in the state during the project. It is located east of the face of the dam and remained a small town and post office until 1914. The large project required a large workforce. The men worked 8 to 10 hours each day, six days a week, for $1.75 a day. But they still had fun at events, such as dances, ball games, and hunting. The guys washing their clothes are (from left to right) Fred Schackleford, Joe Clarkson, and John Gilbert.

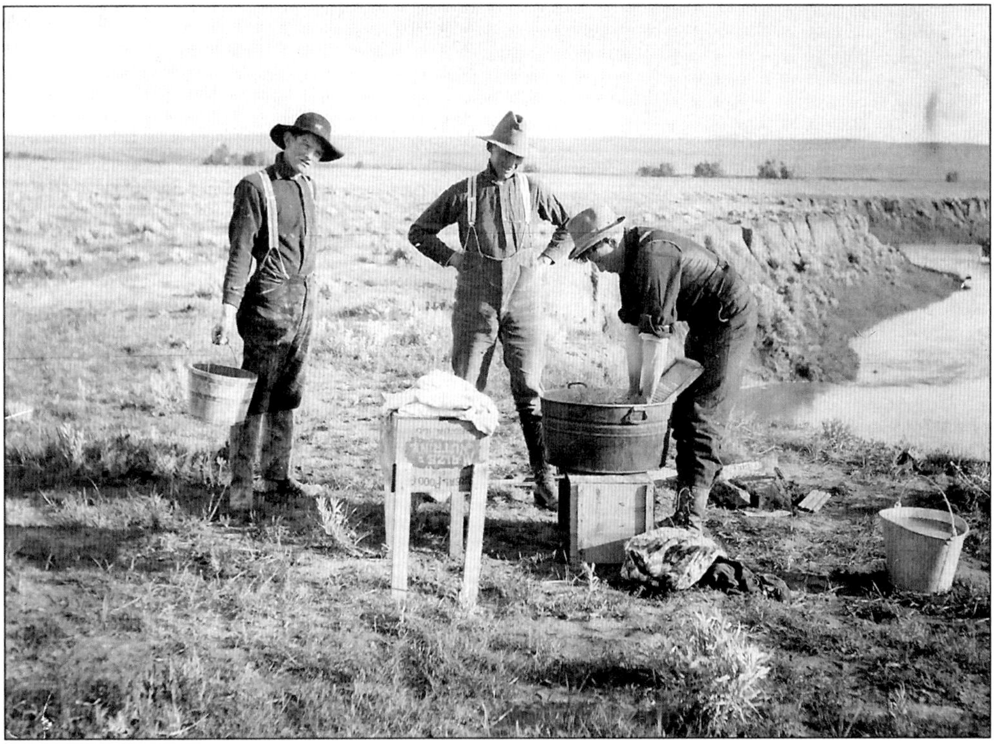

Five

Disaster Strikes

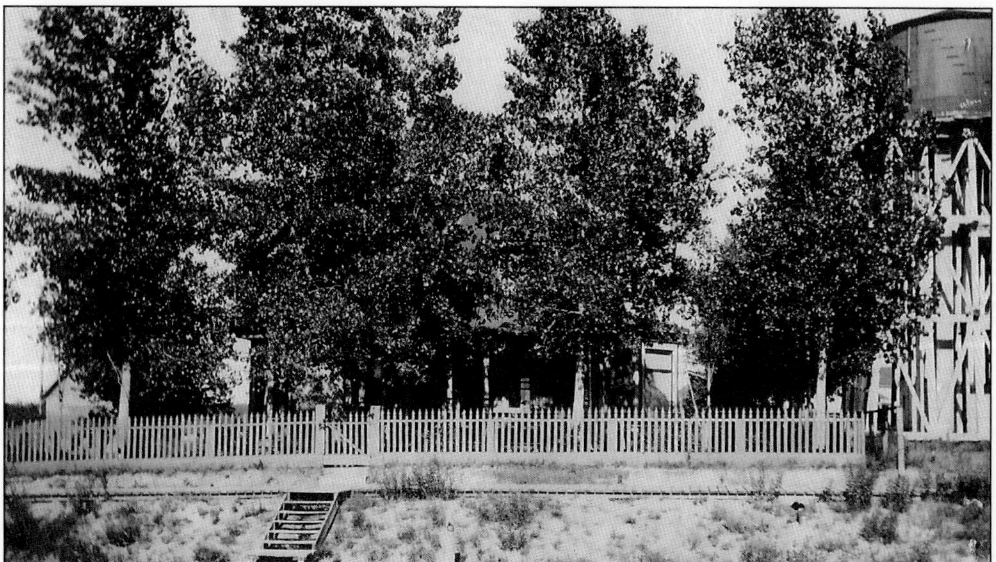

Following the great fire in 1895, of which there are no known photographs, concern over future fires was great within the town. Especially after spending so much money to rebuild downtown, citizens wanted to make sure that a fire of this proportion never happened again. Fire protection was a major topic, and the city was up to the challenge. This water tower was the first constructed solely for the purpose of protecting the town from fire. Since then, Belle Fourche has always had great protection from fire, and fires have never raged like they did in 1895.

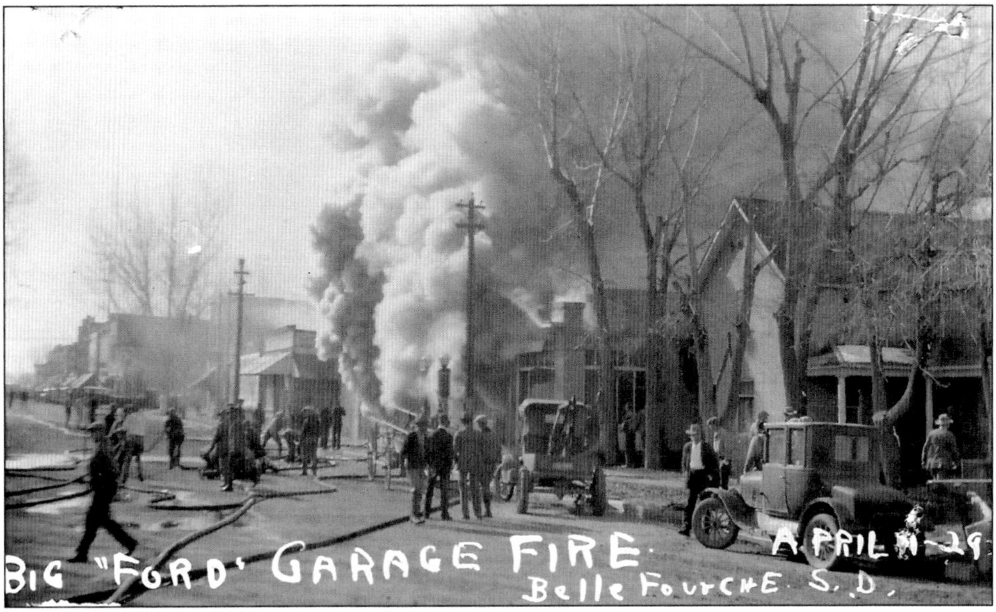

Fire was a major problem in many Western towns, especially in their early years when many of the buildings were still temporary and made of wood. Although Belle Fourche never experienced another fire quite as devastating as the fire that destroyed much of downtown in 1895, fire has broken out in the town on several other occasions.

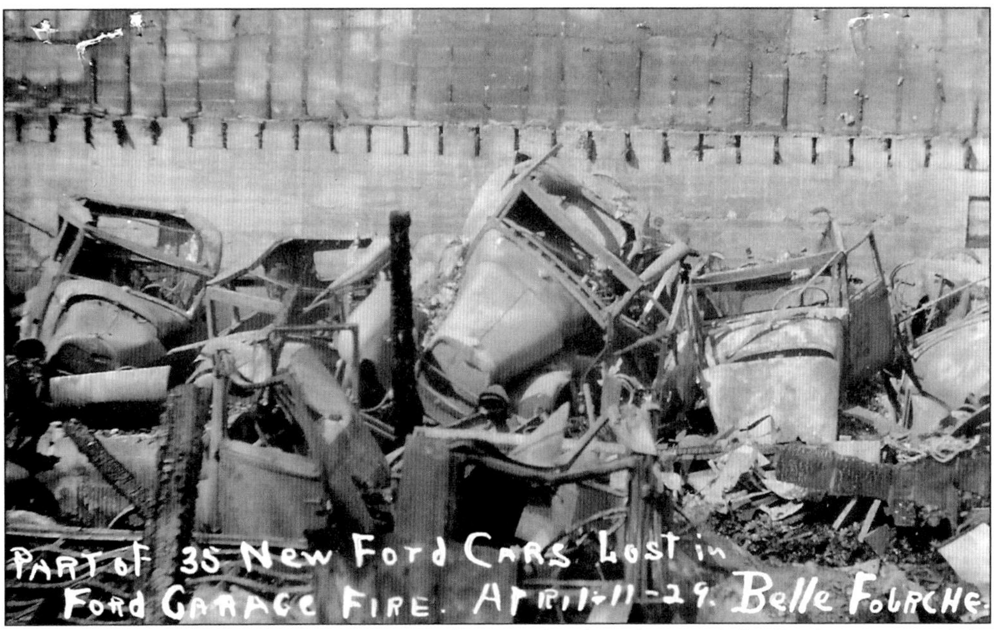

This photograph shows the 1929 fire in Belle Fourche that destroyed the Ford garage. Luckily, with the use of fire protection in the area, the fire was contained and did not spread to other parts of the town, even though there was a lot of gasoline to fuel the fire.

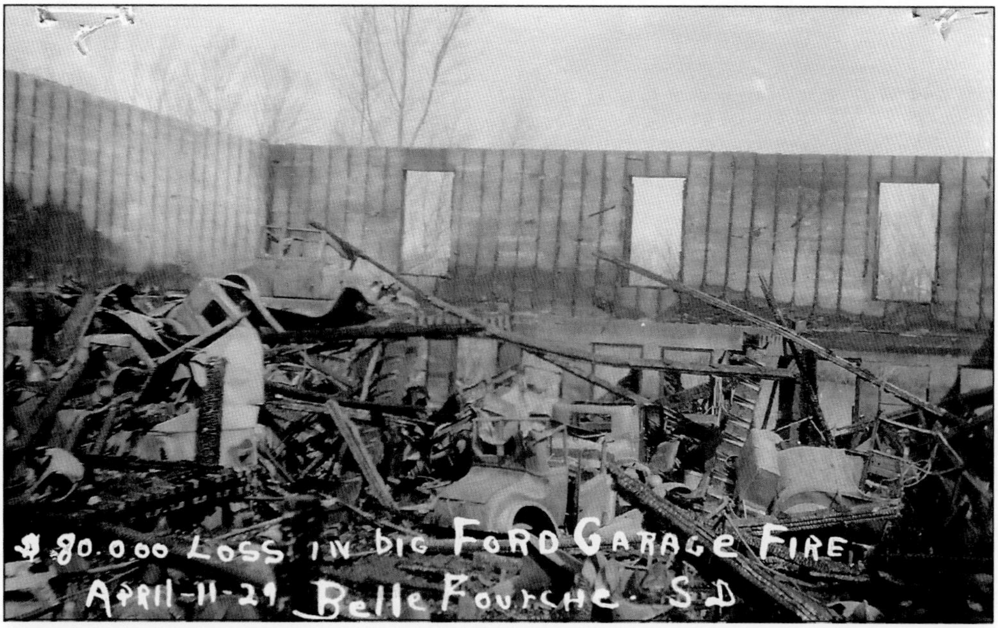

Even though this fire did not devastate the city, it was devastating to the Ford garage. About 35 new Ford cars were destroyed, and the total damage was over $80,000, a hefty sum in 1929.

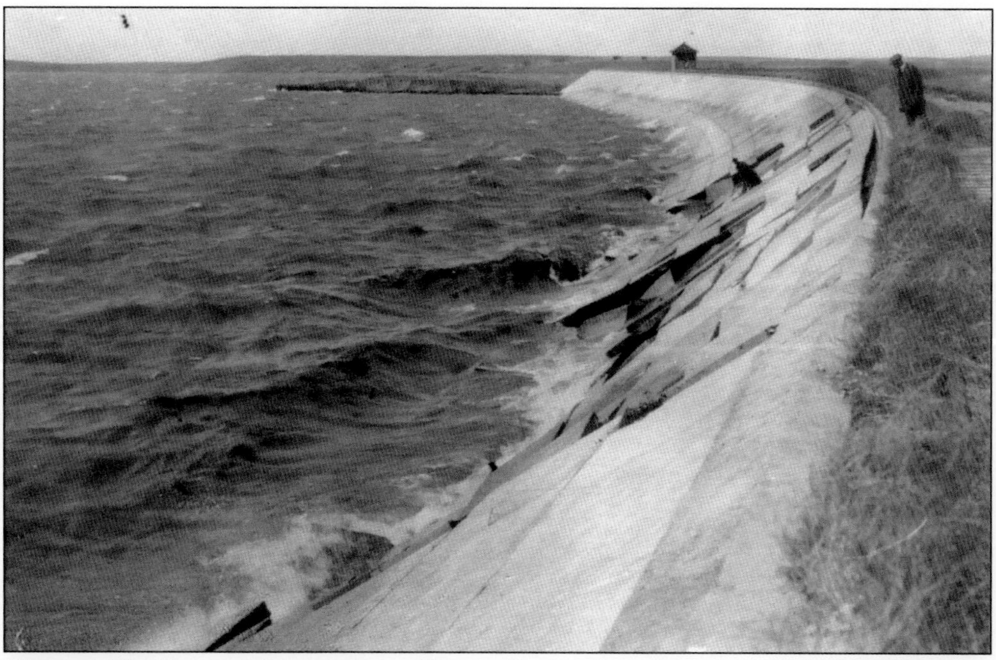
Water and flooding can have a major effect on Orman Dam. In order to help distribute water from the dam, two canals were dug. These canals were dug during the creation of the dam, but the last was not finished until 1916. The face of the dam has been washed away with high water and high winds.

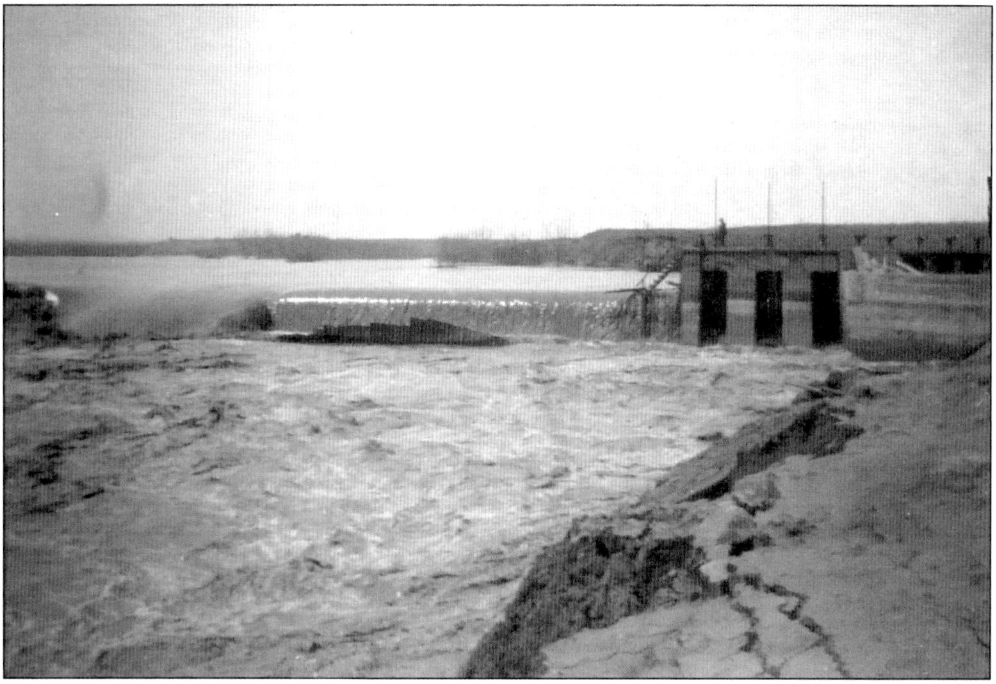

Based on the technology of the era, a project as large as Orman Dam was quite an enormous task. Along with the newer steam-powered technology and the use of railroads, horses were still important during this project's construction.

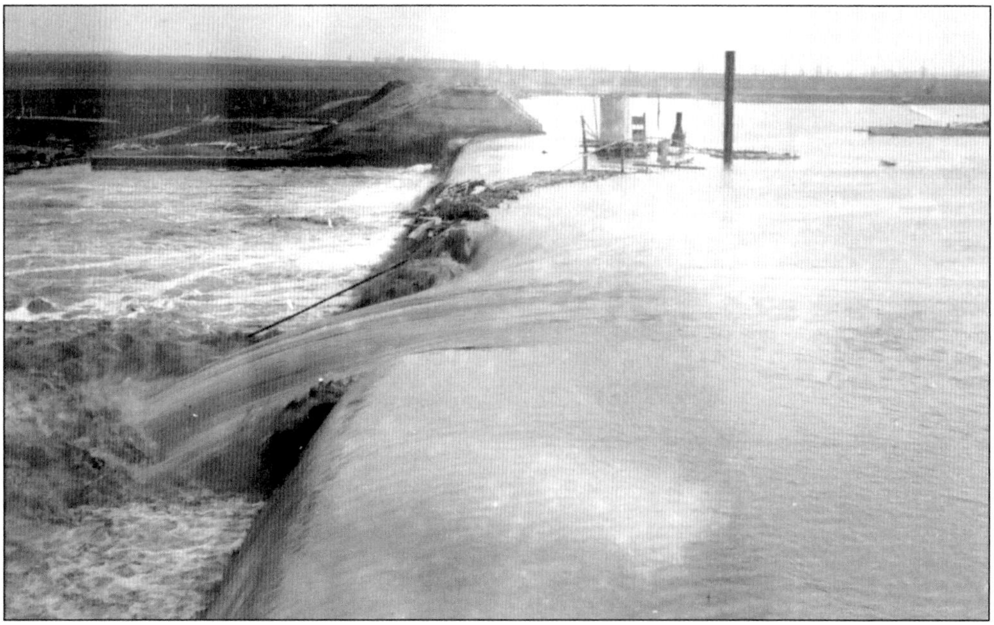

Earl Davis owned a ranch north of Belle Fourche. He was an accomplished horseman and broke wild horses as a way to earn some money. During the Orman Dam project, Davis contracted out the use of his horses to help with moving dirt. A flood that stopped work on the canal project also drown many of his horses and washed away much of his equipment. In the wake of this tragedy, Davis opened a meat market in Belle Fourche to make a living.

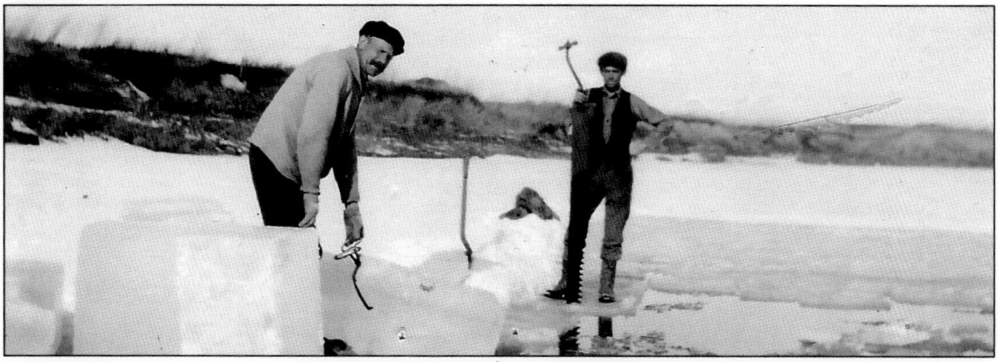

Winter in western South Dakota is often harsh and very cold. The rivers and creeks in the area freeze. In the early days of Belle Fourche, the ice was harvested and stored to be used throughout the year. This photograph shows two men harvesting ice from the Belle Fourche River.

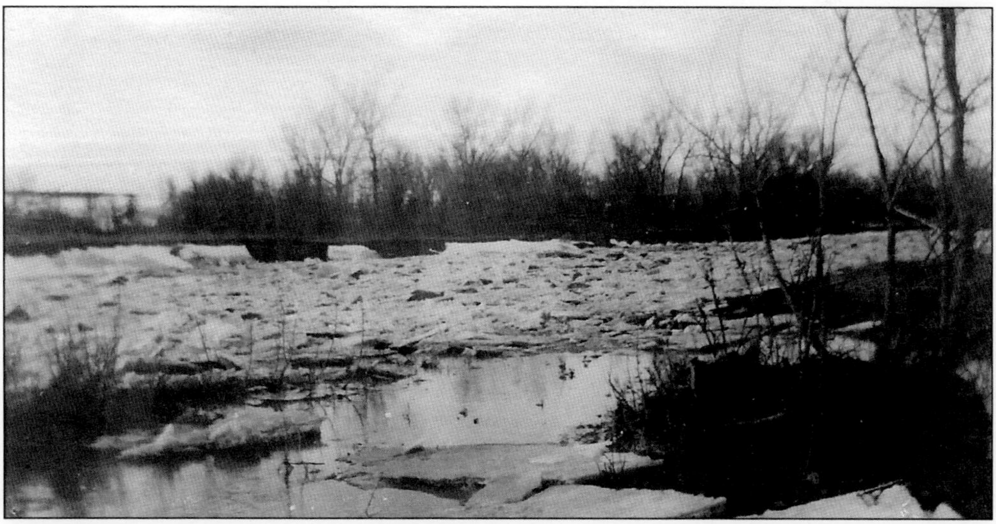

Although the ice from the rivers could be harvested and used, it also carried hazards. Here is an ice jam on the Belle Fourche River around 1917. Ice sometimes backed up for several miles and needed to be dynamited away. The ice also led to another hazard—floods.

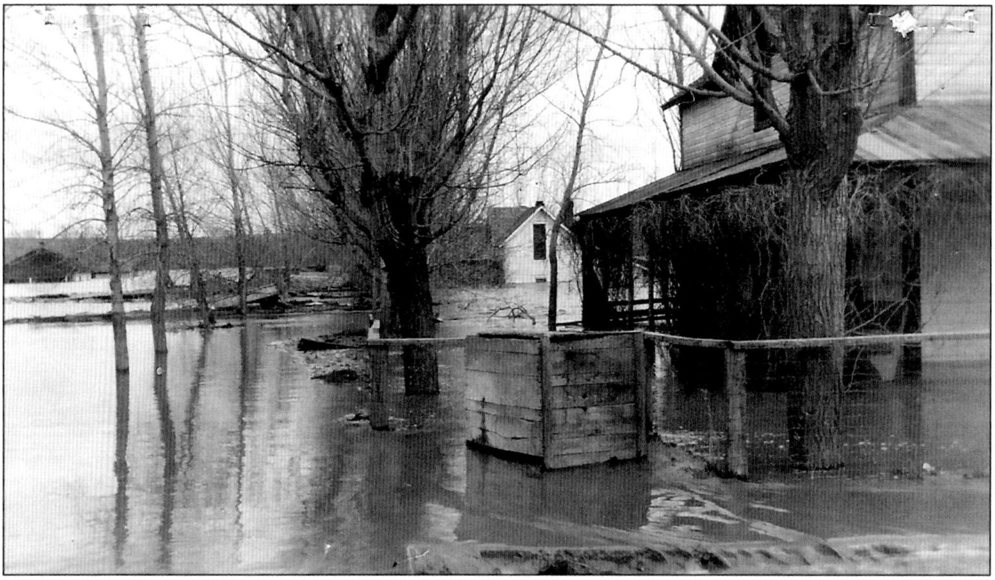

The ice that built up and jammed the river also helped to back up water on the river, which could not carry away the melting snow fast enough. The river flooded almost every year, but there were years when the floods were much worse than others.

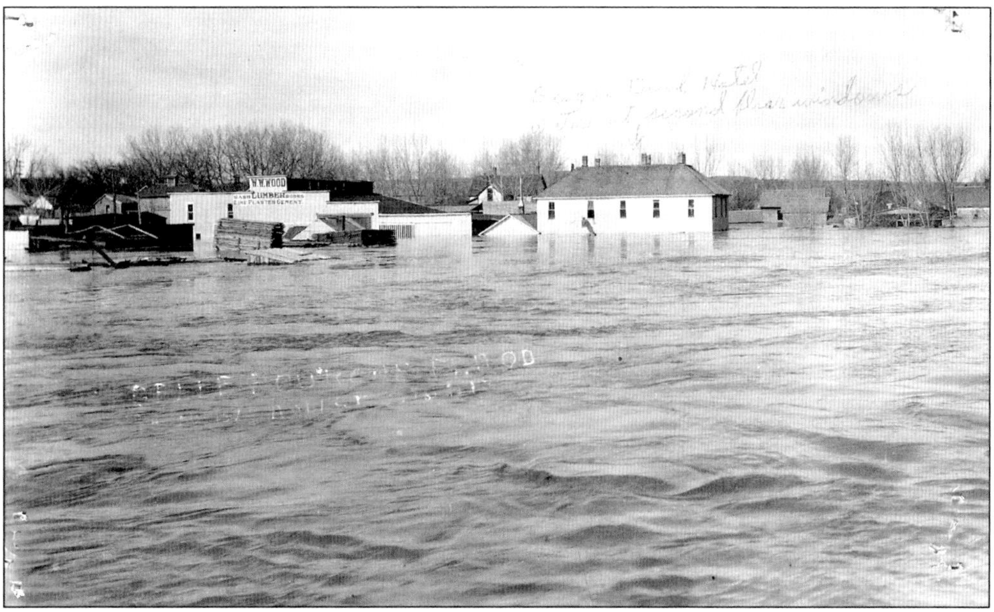

One of the worst floods on record in Belle Fourche took place in 1924. During this flood, over 50 houses were destroyed, and countless families were left homeless. As this view from Fifth Avenue shows, the floodwater engulfed everything.

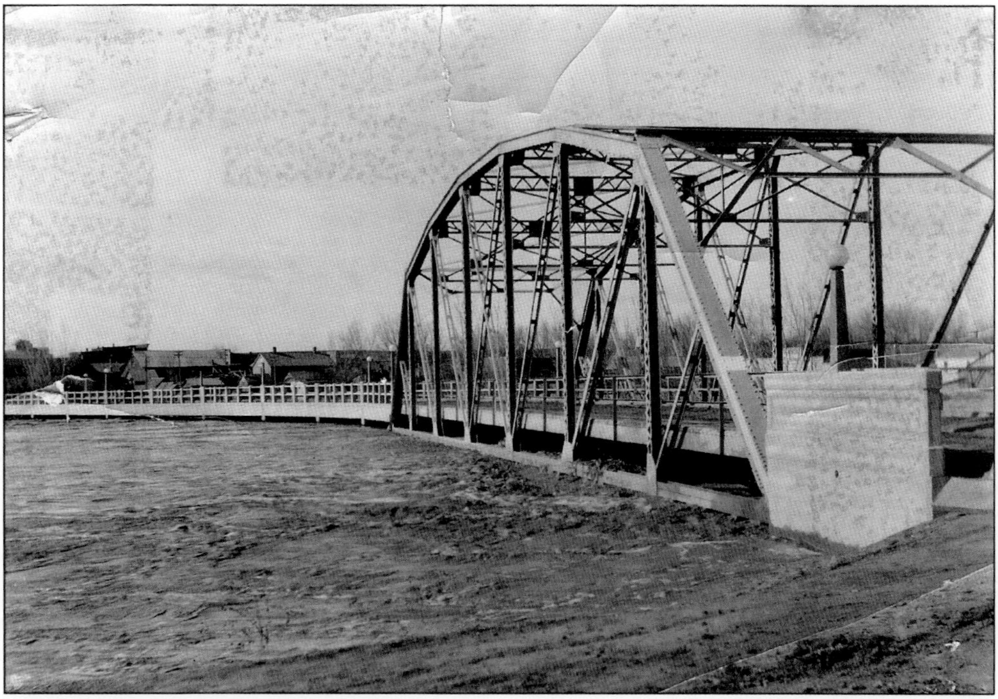

Water in the 1924 flood came right up to the roadbed of the Belle Fourche River bridge. The American Red Cross came to Belle Fourche from Wyoming to help the flood-stricken families and to help the community rebuild.

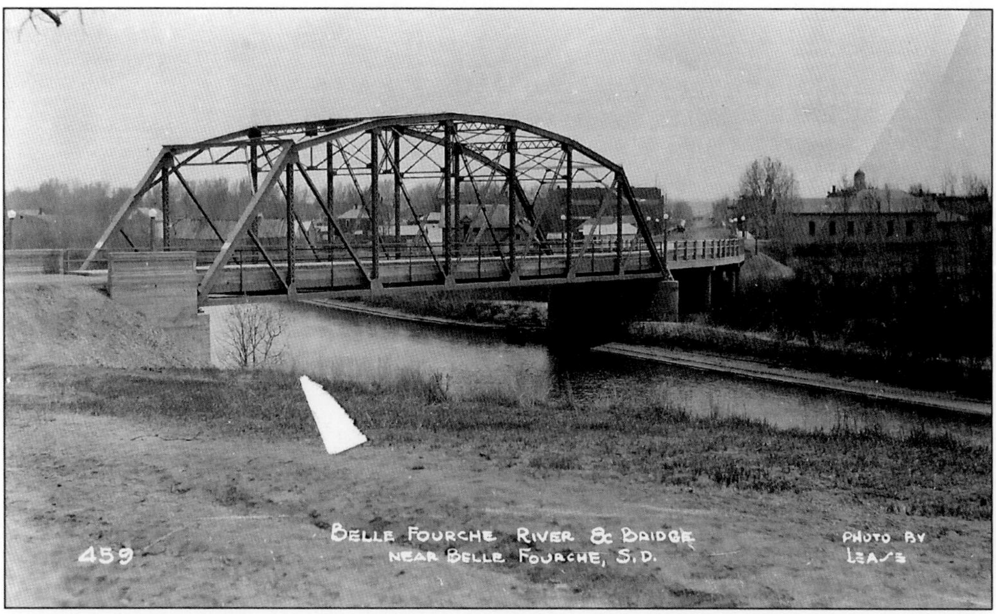

Here is the same bridge over the Belle Fourche River. Compared to the flood photograph, the water is much lower. The Belle Fourche River often dries up during the hot, dry summers, and water can slow to a trickle.

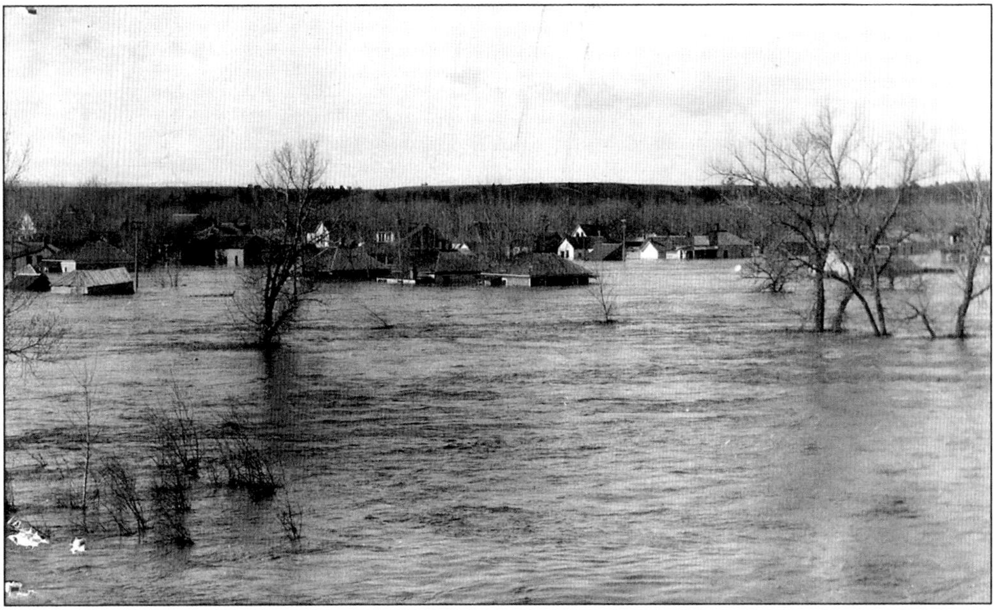

Here floodwaters almost reach the rooftops of some homes in Belle Fourche. The total damage was over $100,000 in Belle Fourche, and many more thousands of dollars in damage was done to croplands along the Belle Fourche River outside town.

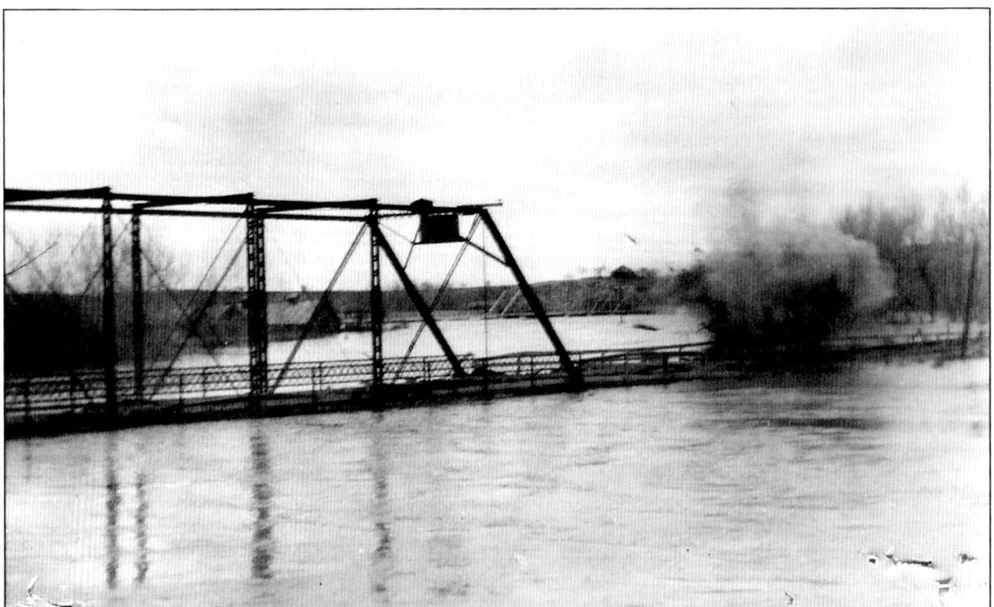

During the 1924 flood, the water backed up so far and got so high that people in town had to make a difficult decision. Water came up to the roadbed on this railroad bridge, which was causing drag and hindering the flow of water even more. Citizens of Belle Fourche decided to dynamite the bridge and let it float down the river so that water could flow more easily once again.

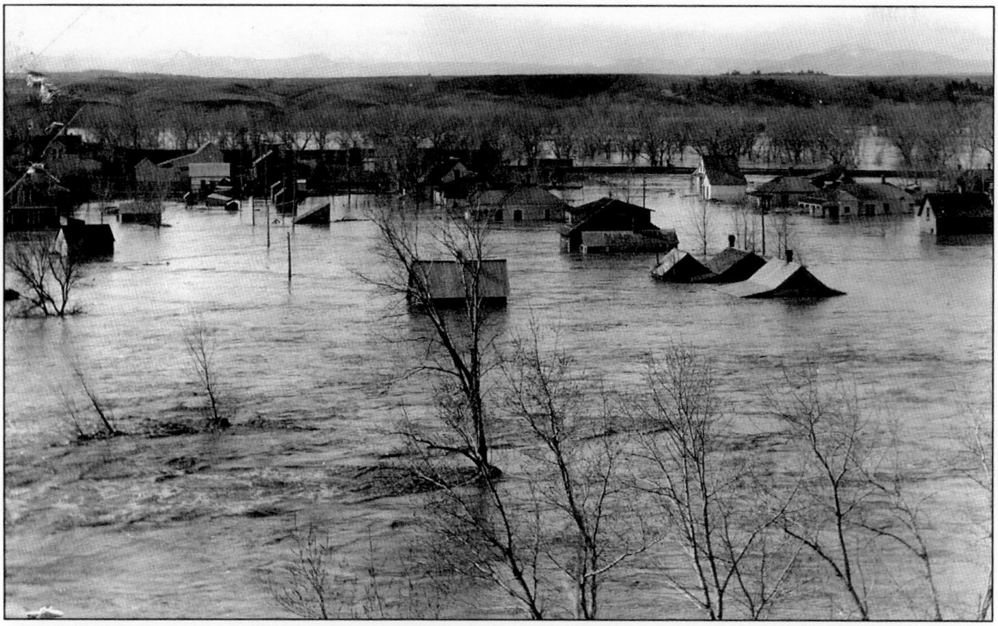

The terrible flood in 1924 and the damage that was caused brought about calls for better flood control in the city. Following the flood, a dike was built along the river that still protects the city from the rising water and has saved many buildings on several occasions.

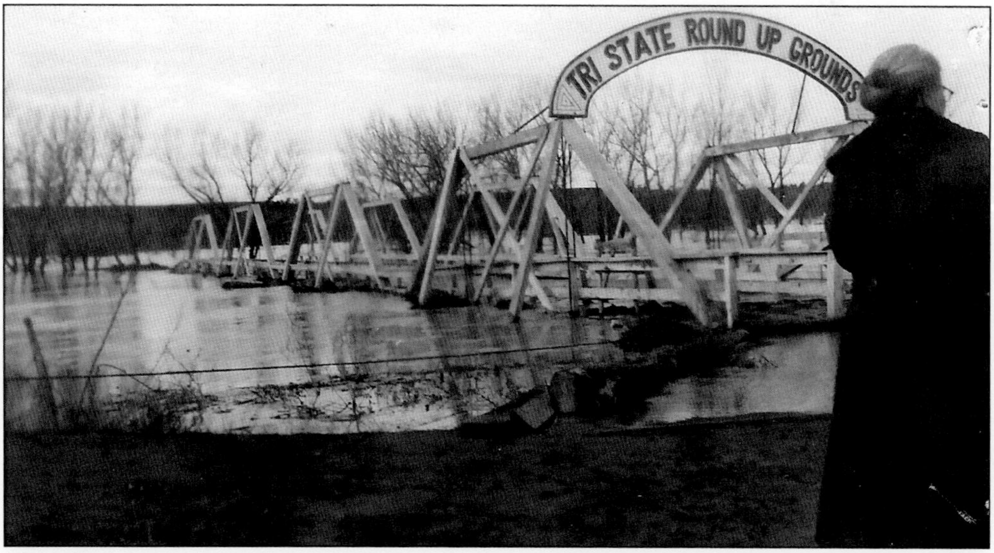

This photograph shows the entrance to the Tri-State Roundup grounds, now the Black Hills Roundup. It is a professional rodeo run every year over the Fourth of July. The area runs along the Belle Fourche River and has only one entrance, which is shown here underwater.

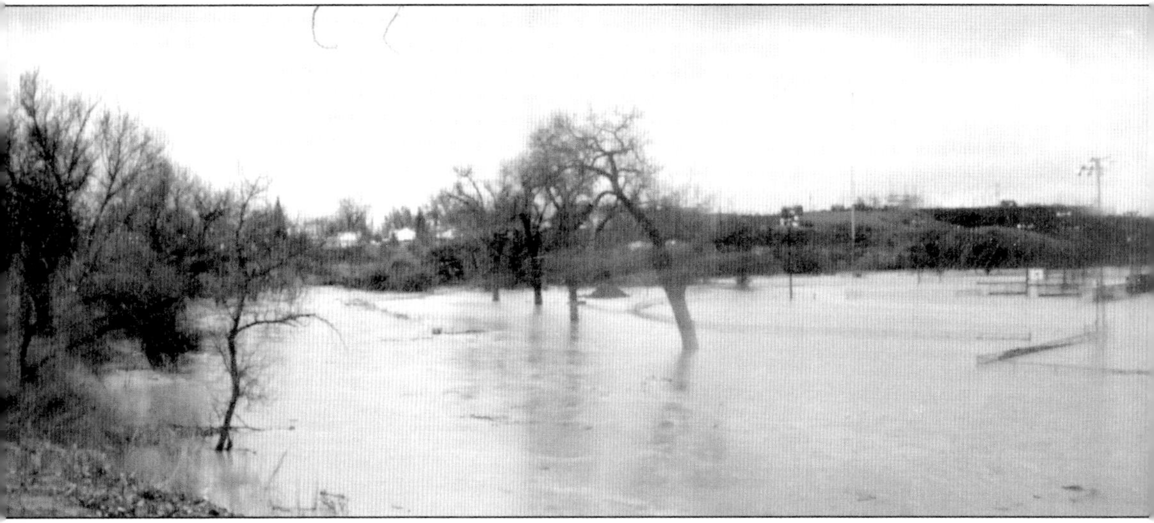

Over the years, the area around the Belle Fourche River has drastically changed. The once free-moving river is now controlled through the construction of the diversion dam and Orman Dam. Along the riverfront, within city limits, dikes have been built to help keep the city safe from flooding. Even with all these protections and changes to the river, its waters are still very

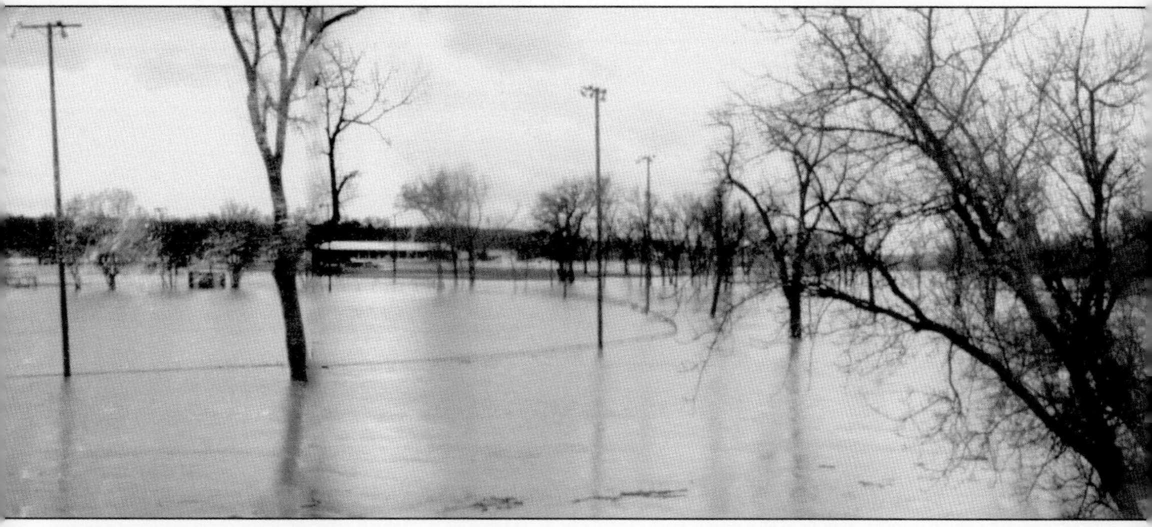

unpredictable, and the threat of flood is always present, as this 1995 photograph shows. Although this was the last major flooding of the river, the threat is present every spring when the winter snow starts melting. It is not a question of if the river will ever flood again but when it will, and the town must always be ready to face the worst.

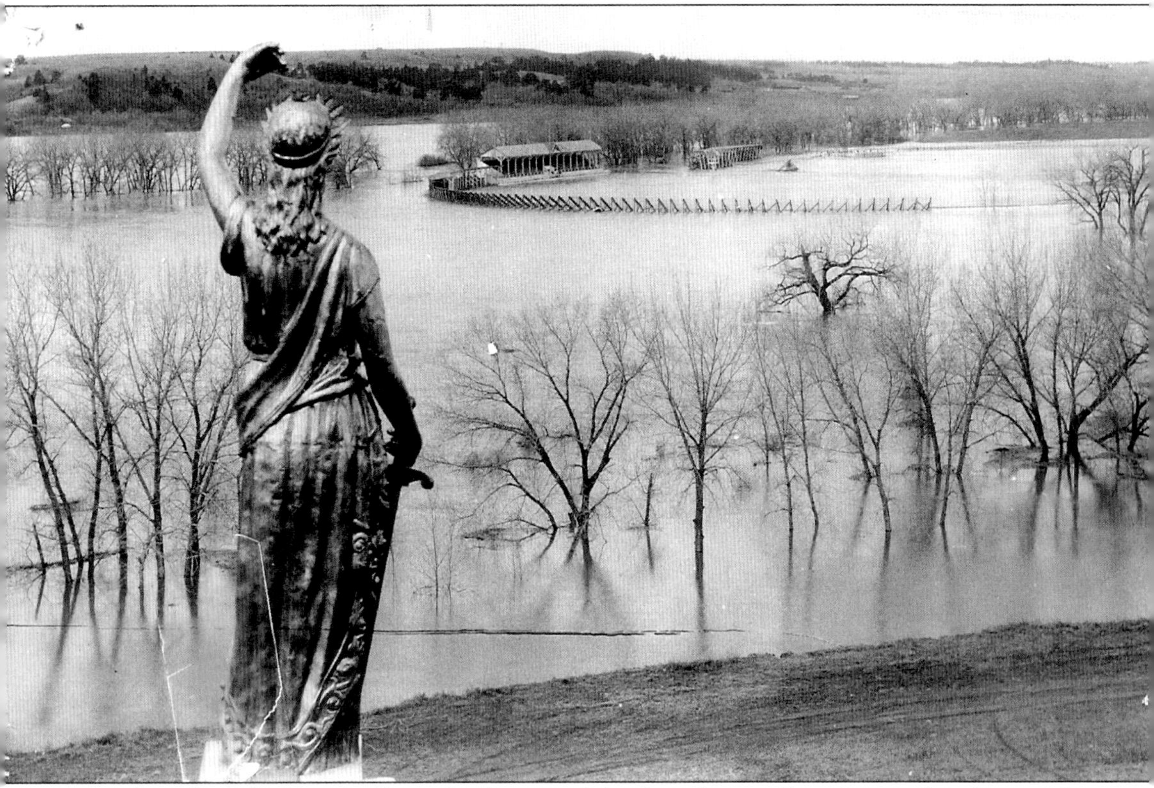

When the Belle Fourche River floods, one of the first places to be submerged is the roundup grounds, which the river forms a horseshoe around. This area is not protected from the river by any dikes, and in 1924, over $5,000 in damage was done to the rodeo grounds while the area was under three feet of water. This photograph was taken from the top of the Butte County Courthouse. Today the area houses a large sports complex that includes soccer fields, softball diamonds, and the rodeo arena.

Six

Community Services

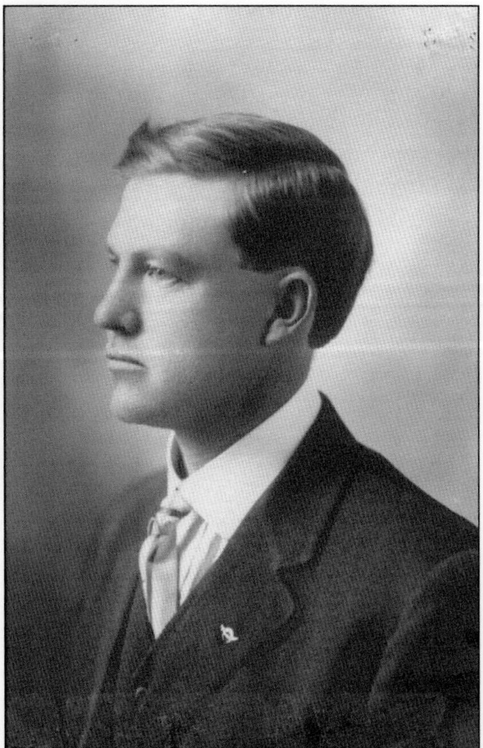

With the creation of towns in the Old West came structure and government. After the town became the seat of Butte County and was incorporated as a city in 1903, there became the need for a city government. Sam Mortimer was an early settler of the area, coming to the Black Hills around 1898. Mortimer served as the first mayor of Belle Fourche from 1903 to 1912. When elected, Mortimer was only 23 years old, the youngest mayor in South Dakota at the time and the youngest mayor in the town's history. Mortimer continued to be an outstanding member of the community until his death in 1959.

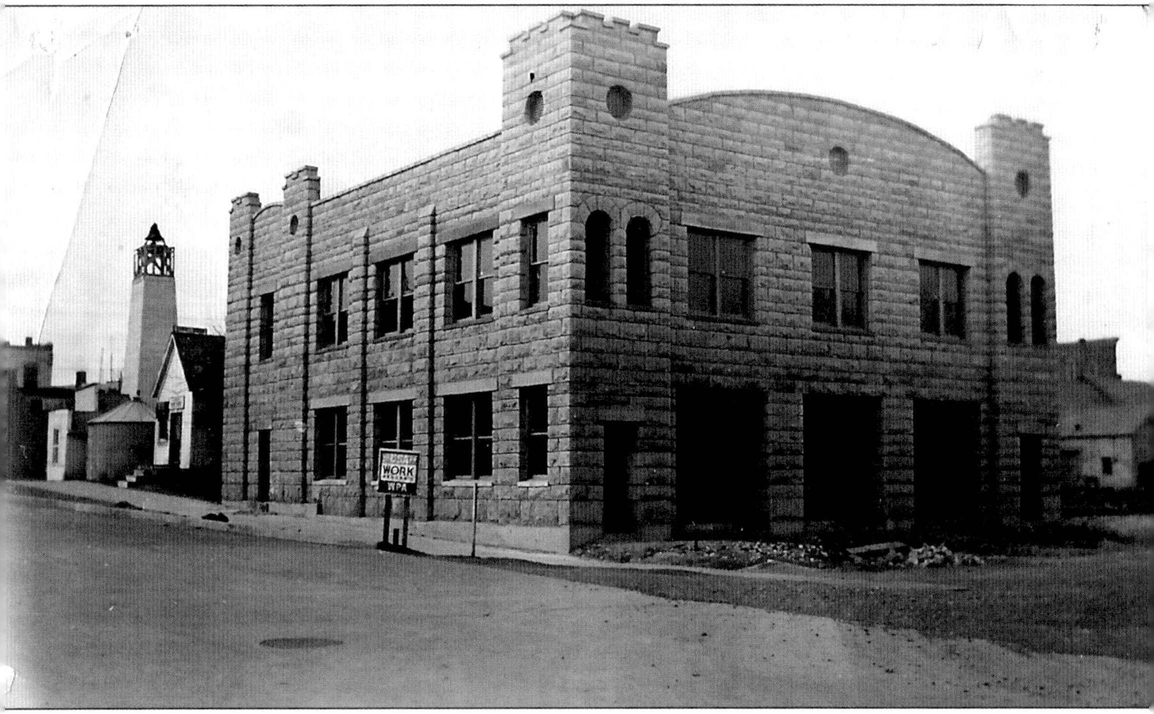

The Belle Fourche City Hall was built in the late 1930s as a Works Progress Administration (WPA) project. The WPA was an enormous New Deal agency, giving people jobs during the Great Depression. In 2007, the city approved the construction of a new city hall building, which will be only a block away. This new building is expected to be completed by the end of 2008, and the current building will be restored and used as a woodworking school. The preservation of this landmark is an important step toward preservation of the town's history. Previous landmarks in town had simply been torn down in the past to make way for newer, more modern buildings.

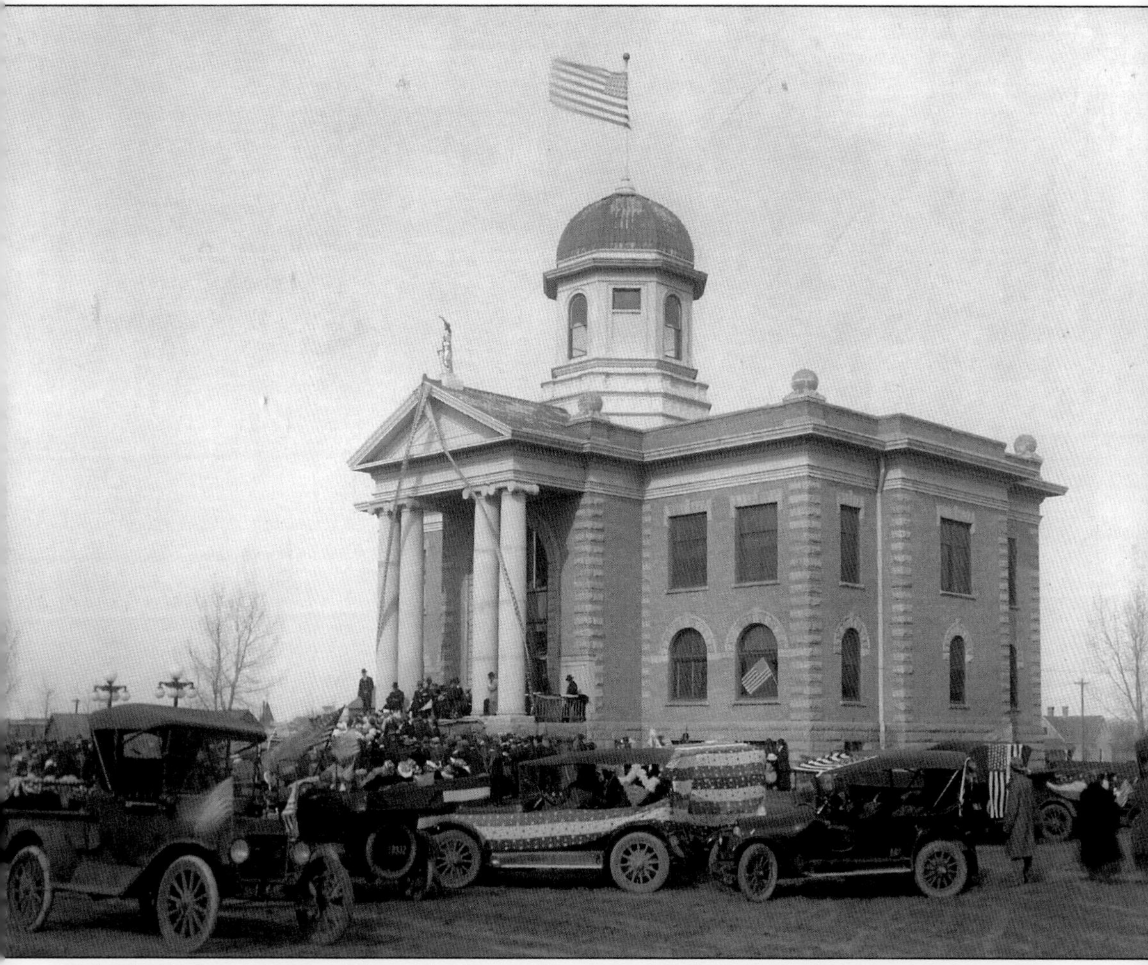

With the decline of Minnesela in the late 19th century, Belle Fourche became the dominant town in Butte County and ultimately became the county seat. When this happened, a new and impressive courthouse building was planned. This photograph shows the dedication of the new courthouse building in 1912. Although this building has been added to over the years, it is still used as the Butte County Courthouse.

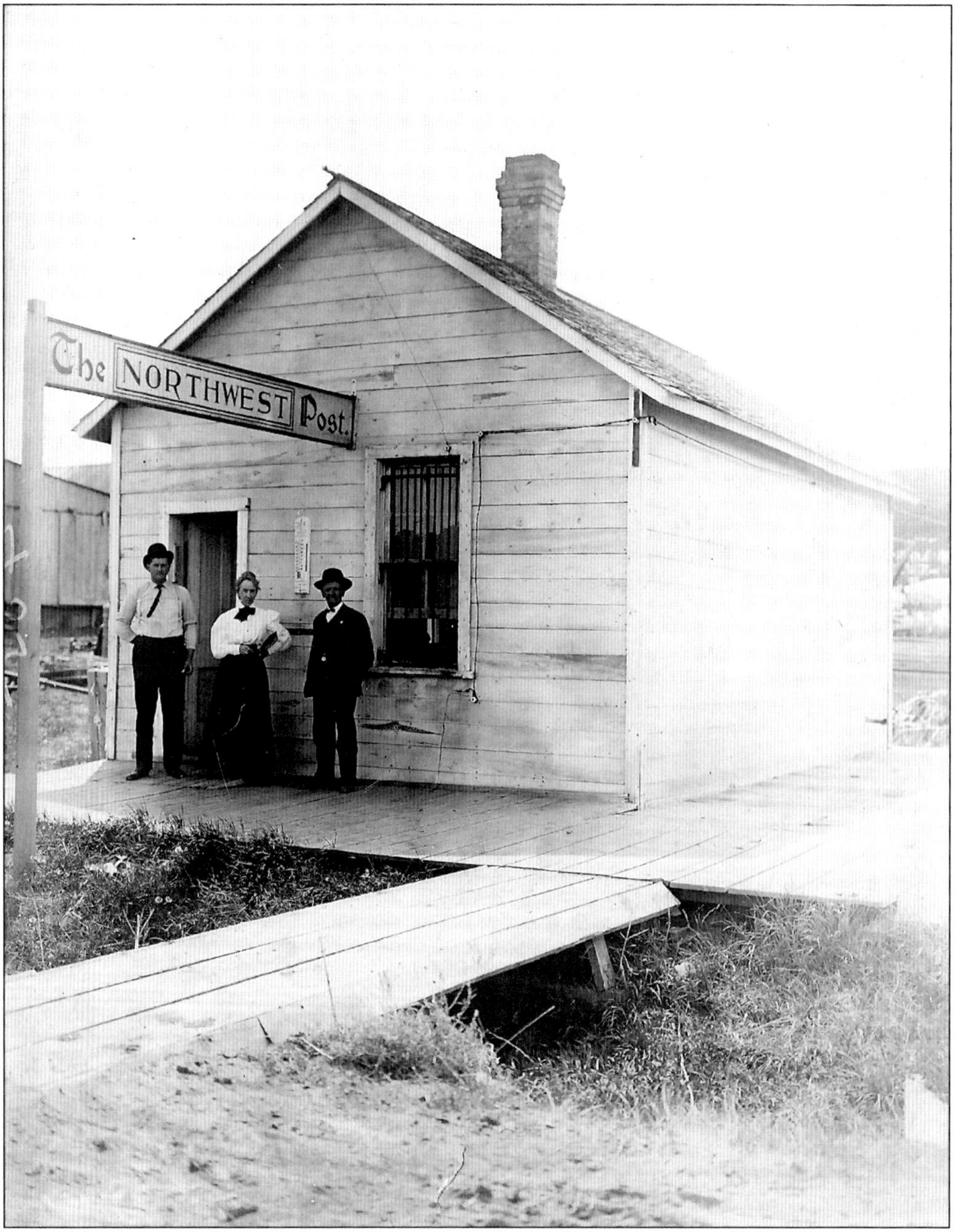

Whenever a new town springs up, a newspaper office generally is not far behind. The first newspaper in Belle Fourche was laid out in the lobby of the Belle Fourche Hotel shortly after the foundation of the town. The *Belle Fourche Bee* was the first newspaper in town, but it was not alone. The *Northwest Post* began publishing in 1902. Over the years, these newspapers changed hands many times; the *Northwest Post* actually was a daily newspaper for some time. Today there are two weekly newspapers in Belle Fourche, the *Belle Fourche Post* and the *Belle Fourche Bee*. This photograph depicts the *Northwest Post* office on Sixth Avenue. This building is no longer standing, and both newspapers today have an office on State Street.

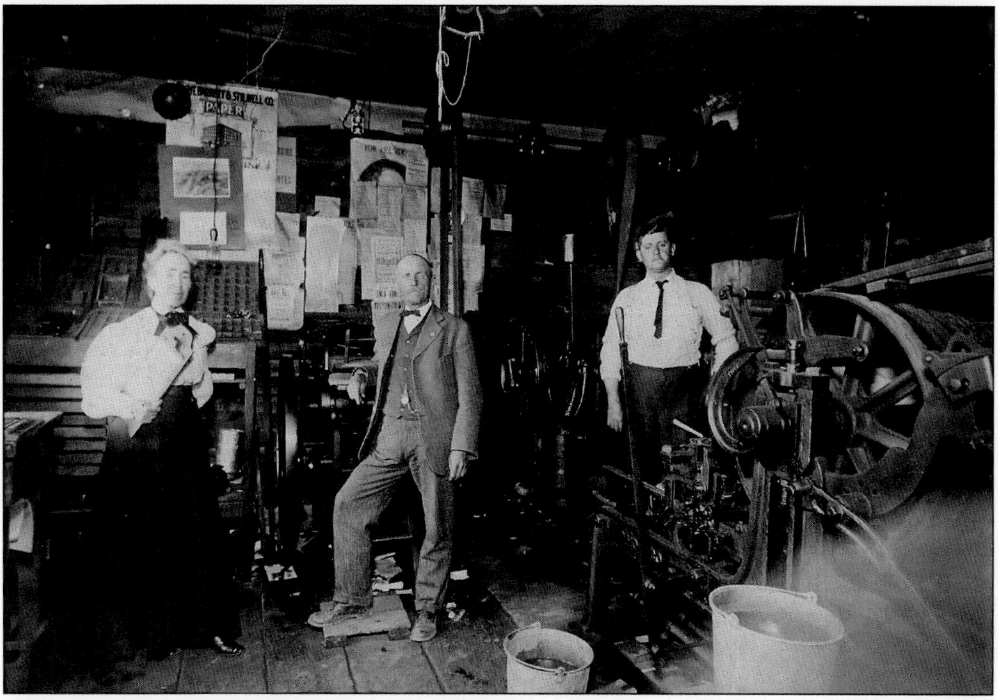

Here the staff of the *Northwest Post* pauses for a photograph around 1902. Notice the primitive and cramped conditions inside the office. The printing press at right is similar to a press once owned by the *Northwest Post* that is on display at the Tri-State Museum.

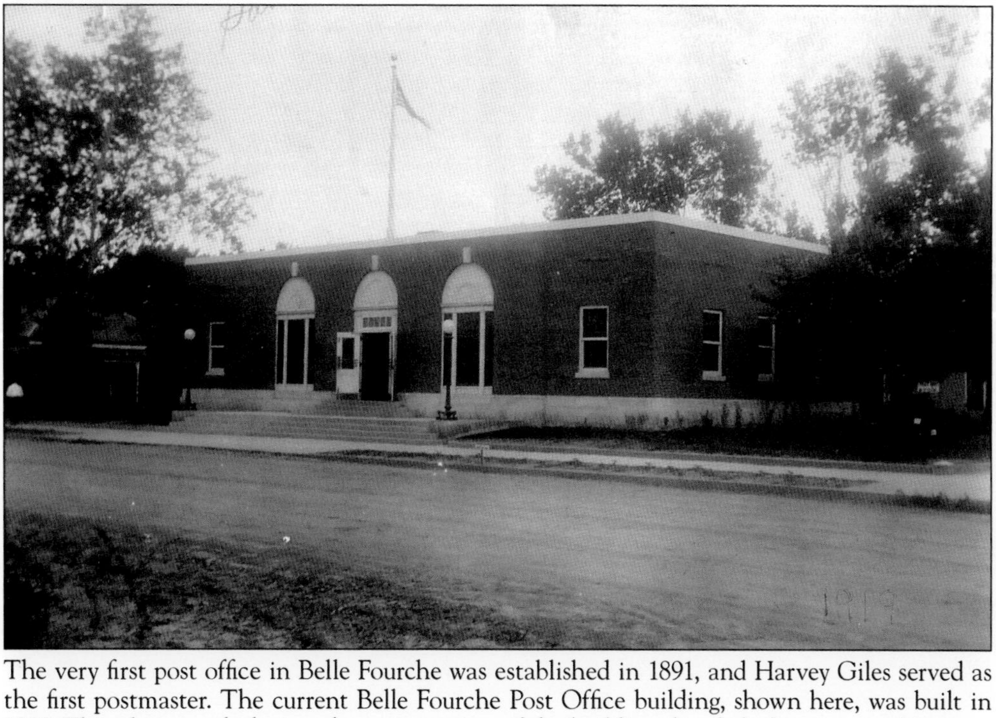

The very first post office in Belle Fourche was established in 1891, and Harvey Giles served as the first postmaster. The current Belle Fourche Post Office building, shown here, was built in 1919. This photograph depicts the construction of the building shortly before its completion.

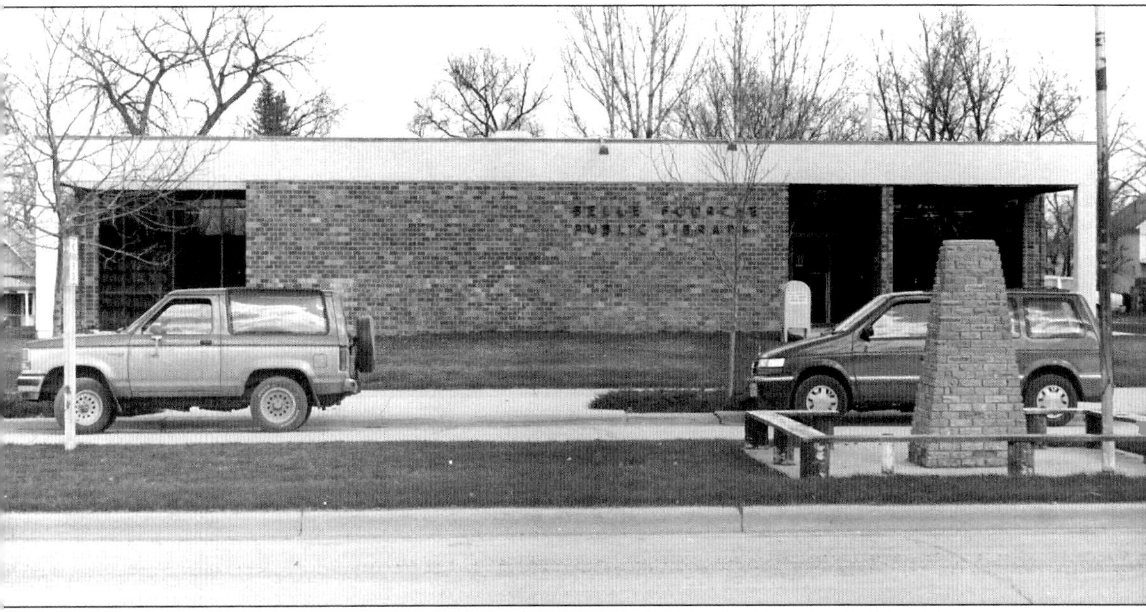

Belle Fourche is home to a wonderful public library. The Belle Fourche Public Library can trace its roots to a simple reading room in 1906, which operated with volunteers and donations. In 1939, the library formed a board of directors and began to submit budgets to the city, which the city council supported. In 1942, the library moved into the first schoolhouse in Belle Fourche. The building was remodeled and served as the library until 1978. Following a community vote on a bond, a new library was built in 1978. This is the current library facility, which is depicted in this photograph. The Belle Fourche Public Library has continued to expand and grow through the years and has a great collection of books and periodicals as well as microfilms documenting the history of Belle Fourche through its newspapers, films, and pictures.

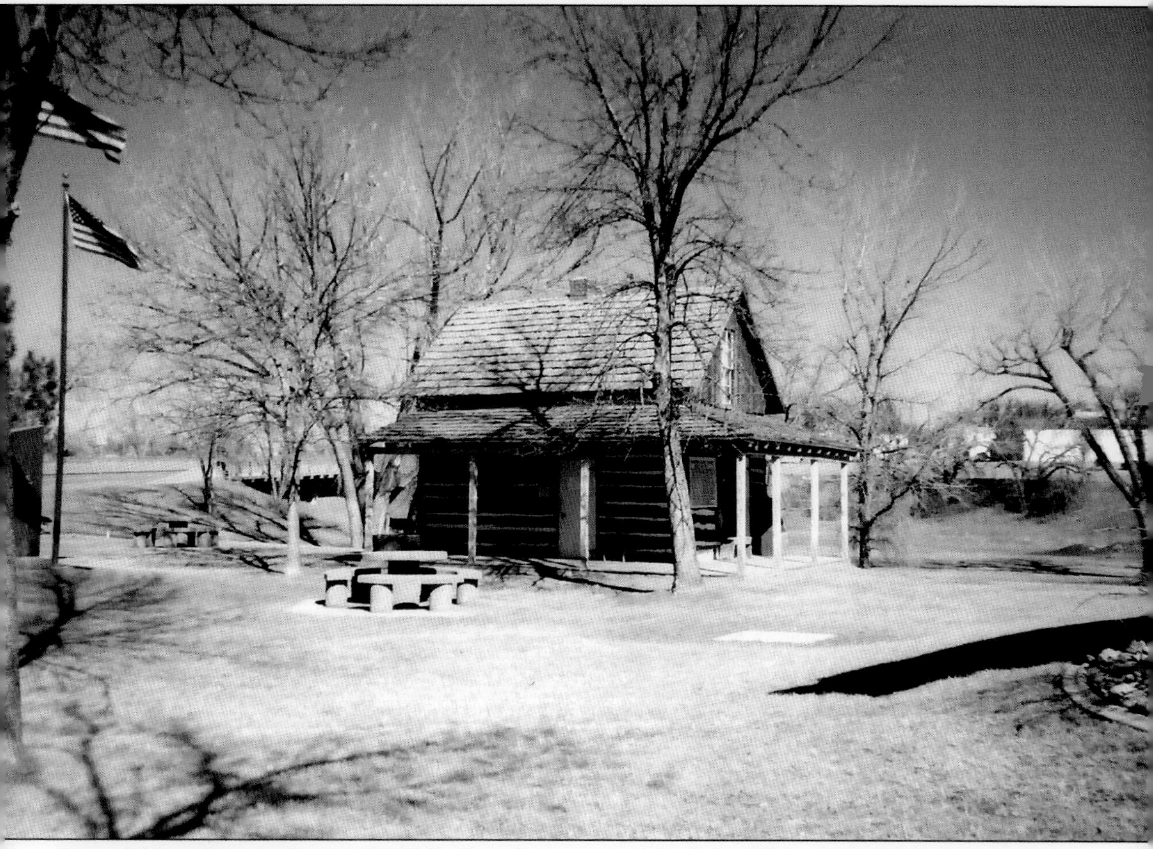

One of the earliest settlers in the Belle Fourche area was "Buckskin" Johnny Spaulding. He built a cabin nearby on the Redwater River in 1876, one of the earliest structures standing in the area. This cabin, which sat on private property, was donated to the Lions Club, which moved the cabin to a location across from the post office directly on Highway 212 and near the original site of the Tri-State Museum. The cabin was operated by volunteers and open to the public. In 2006, the cabin was again moved to the new Tri-State Museum and Visitor Center complex, where local groups such as the Questors and Lions Club have now renovated it. The cabin is open to the public during the summer, and there are many period artifacts from the area inside.

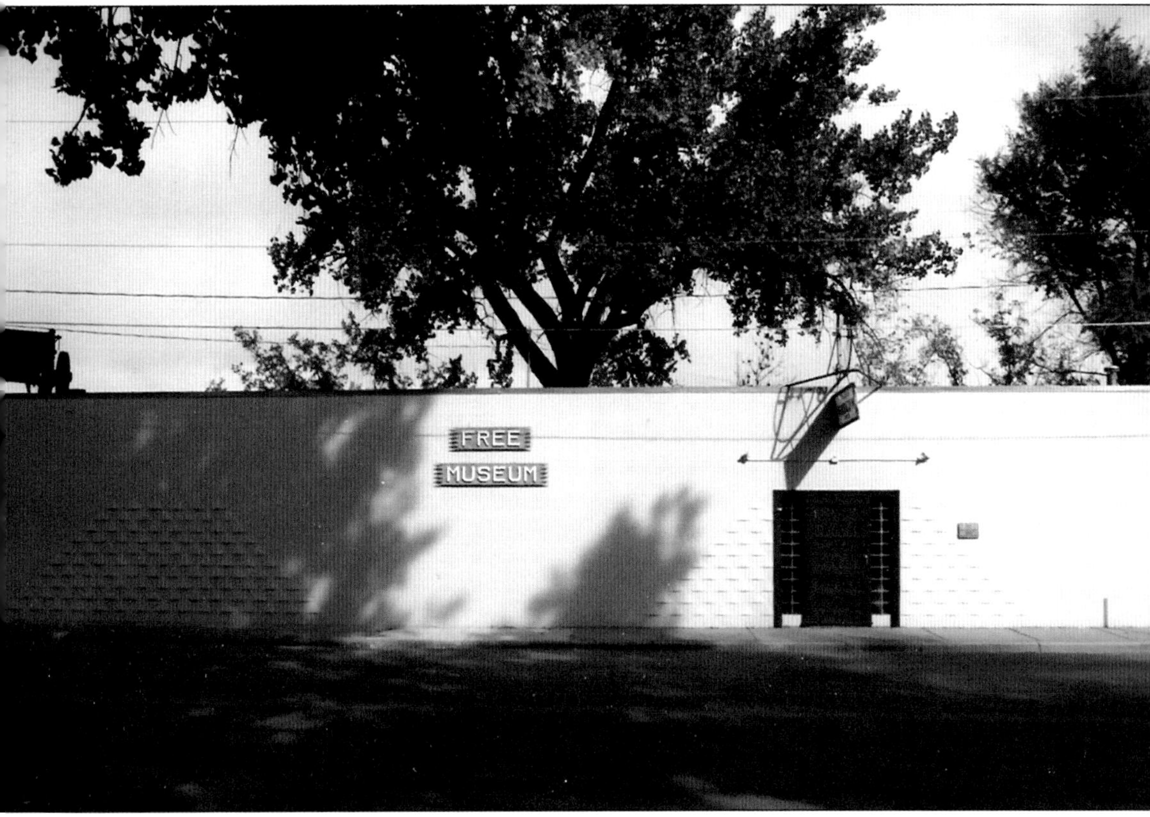

The Tri-State Museum was founded in 1955 when Bessie (Smith) Williams donated her husband's Western collection and $1,000 to start a museum in Belle Fourche. When the museum was first founded, the City of Belle Fourche bought a beautiful Victorian house in town to serve as the museum and the library. However, the building was sold after it quickly proved to be impractical for those uses. Instead this cinder block building was built to house the museum. The museum was mainly run by a dedicated staff of volunteers. Volunteers are presently an invaluable asset to the museum and the community. The first board of directors met in June 1955 and formed a nonprofit corporation. The museum was operated as a free museum, which it still is today.

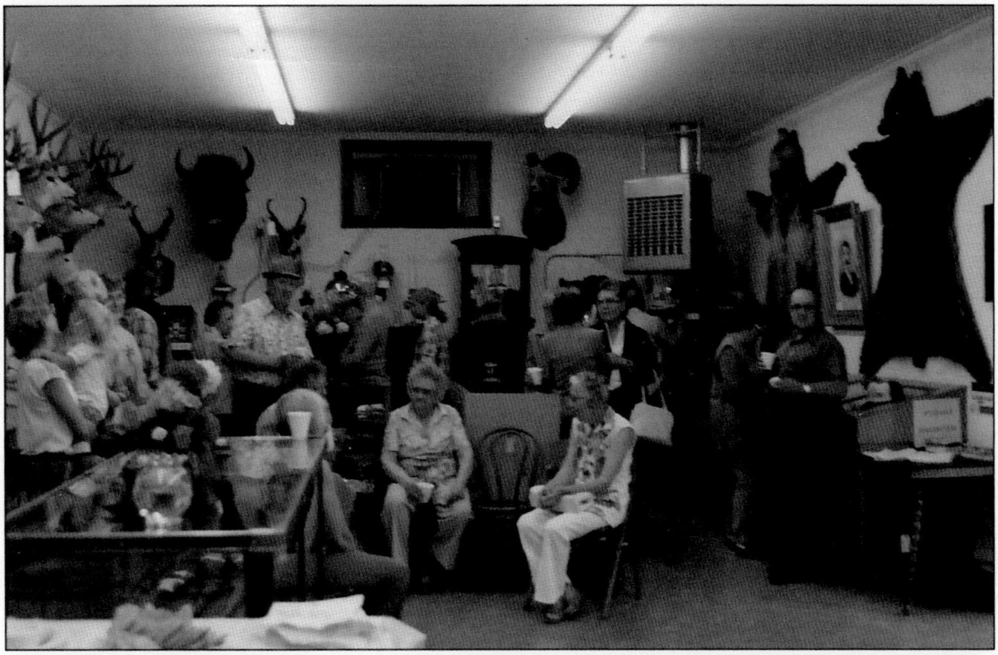

The original museum building, which was really nothing more than a cinder block rectangle, was added onto twice. This is the dedication of the final addition to the museum. Overcrowding is evident; however, it took over 30 years before the museum moved into its current facility.

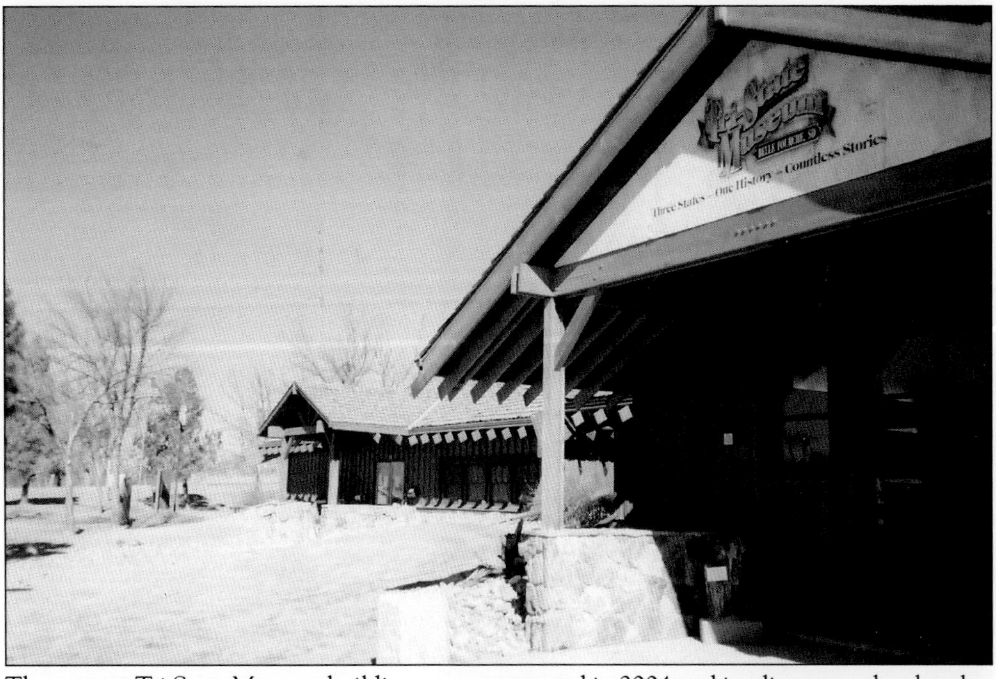

The current Tri-State Museum building was constructed in 2004 and is adjacent to the chamber of commerce and visitor center. The museum is operated as part of the City of Belle Fourche and runs programs throughout the year that serve over 10,000 people annually.

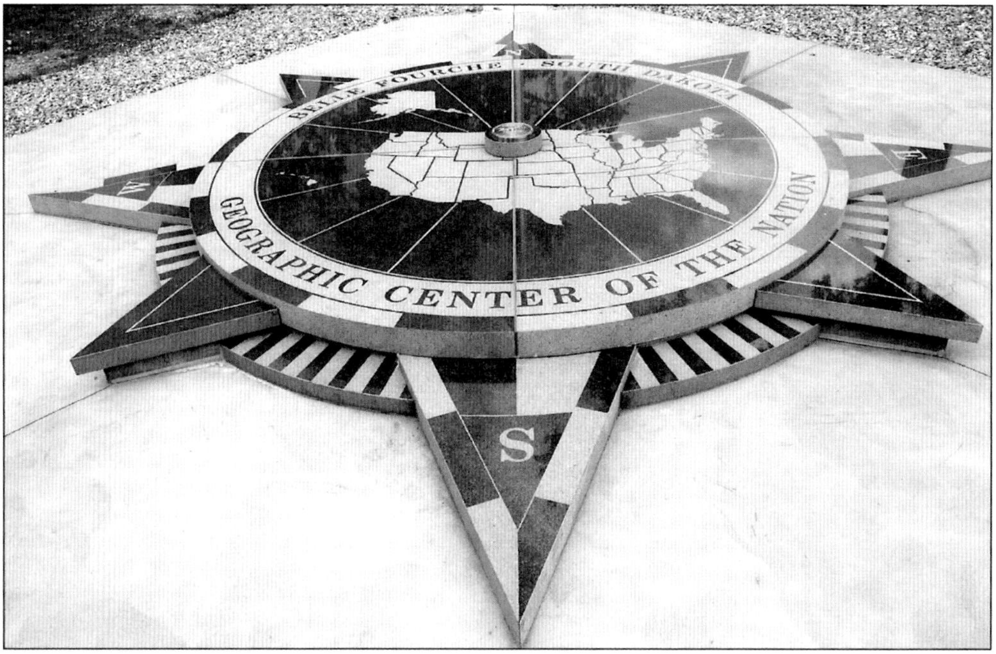

With the addition of Hawaii and Alaska to the Union, the geographic center of the nation shifted to a point just outside Belle Fourche. This sign was used to commemorate the spot until August 2007, when a new South Dakota granite monument was dedicated right outside the chamber of commerce and Tri-State Museum building.

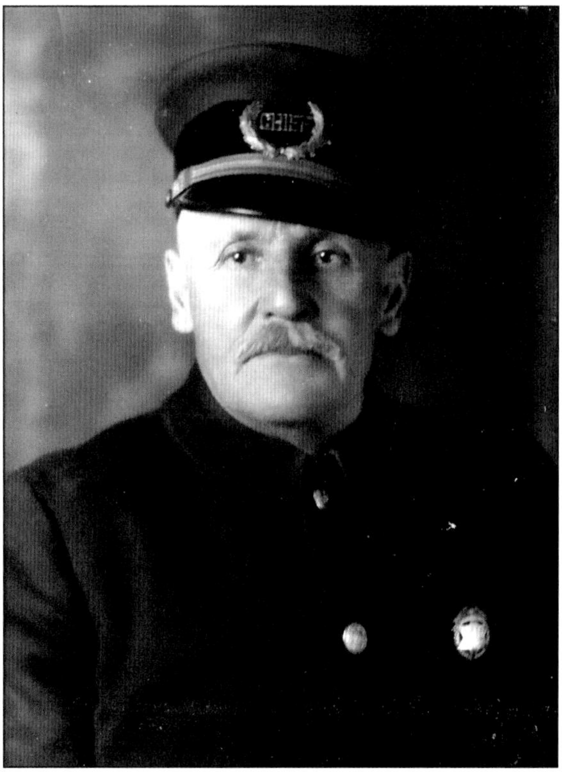

Hiram Hantz was an early lawman in Belle Fourche, first serving as deputy sheriff in 1913. In 1915, he was hired as the part-time police officer in town and served as police chief until his retirement in 1942. Hantz had the difficult task of policing the area during the politically unstable time of Prohibition, when he faced a lot of local opposition.

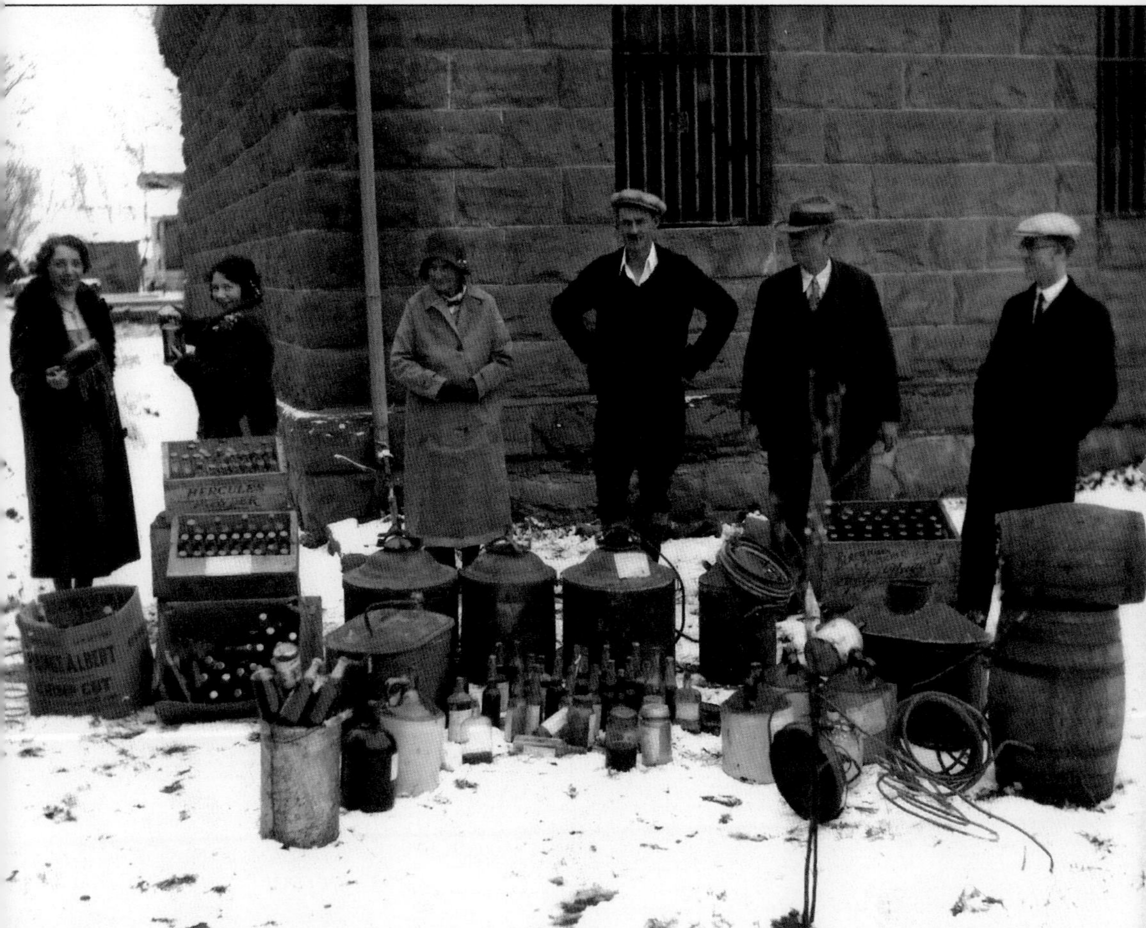

The Butte County Jail was an early addition to the city of Belle Fourche. It is made of sandstone quarried near Belle Fourche and sits near the Butte County Courthouse. The building is still standing today, but it no longer serves as a jail. It has since been converted into office space and is used by the Department of Game and Fish as its headquarters for the area. During Prohibition, the unpopular dry law was enforced in this area. This photograph shows bootlegging equipment and liquor sitting in front of the Butte County Jail, the spoils of a raid on a local bootlegger during Prohibition.

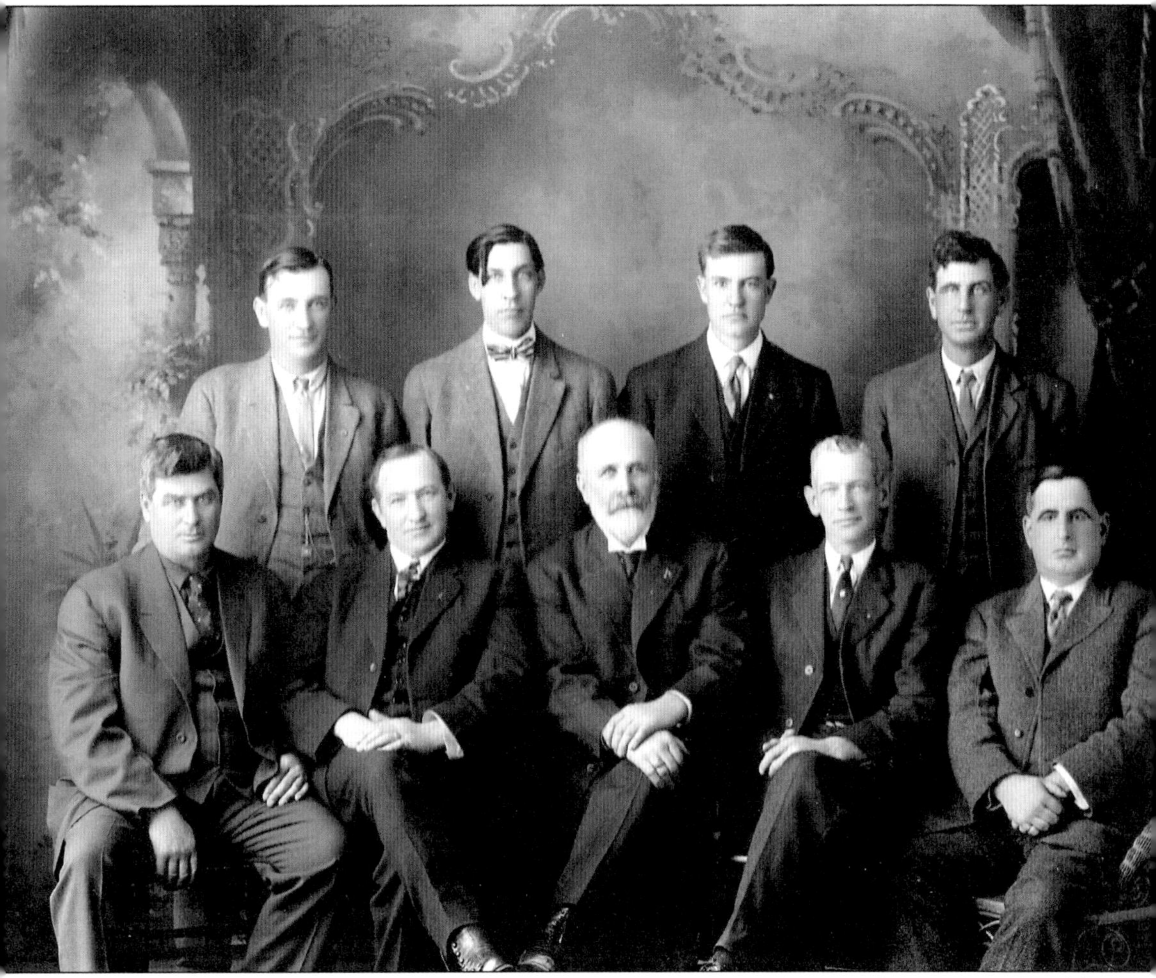

The men shown here were the first members of the Commercial Club in Belle Fourche. This club was an important part of promoting the town, which became increasingly important as more and more tourists began flocking to the Black Hills area. Today the Belle Fourche Chamber of Commerce and Center of the Nation Business Association serve this purpose. The chamber of commerce supervises the development of the new Center of the Nation Monument Park, which began in 2007 with the dedication of a new monument right outside the museum and chamber building. The monument was locally designed and made of South Dakota granite. Future plans for the park include an avenue of flags and new landscaping. From left to right are (first row) Wallace Butts, J. Noble, V. Bernard, T. H. Gay, and L. M. Simons; (second row) M. J. Smiley, H. O. Cooley, S. G. Mortimer, and Fred Harris.

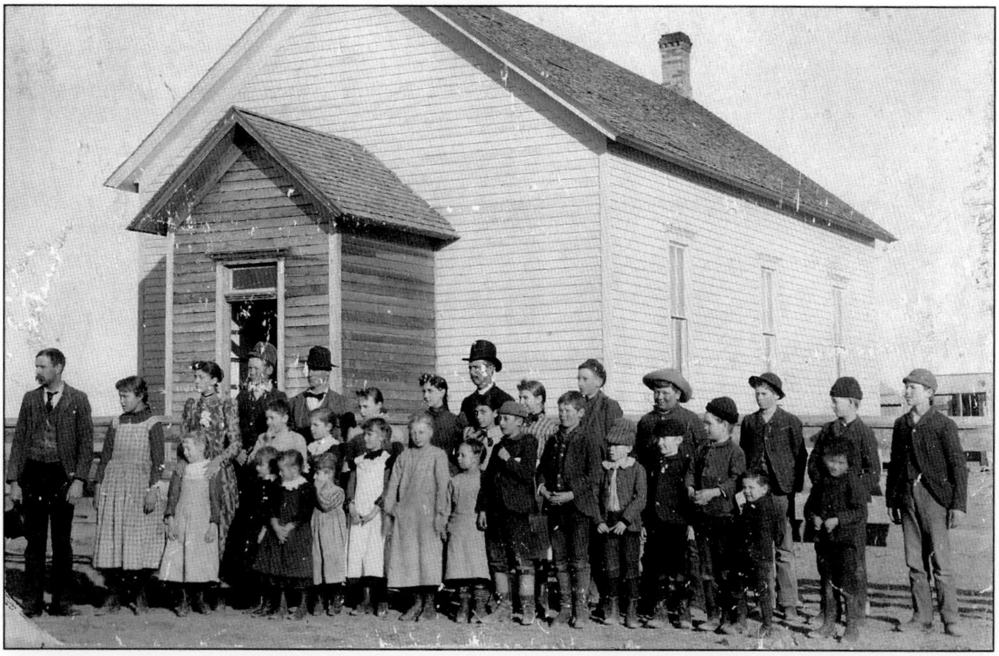

Before the foundation of Belle Fourche, Minnesela was a thriving town in Butte County. From around 1880 until the railroad approached the town around 1887, Minnesela was growing and prospering. Along with new businesses that came to town, schools were needed, and the first school in Butte County was built near Minnesela.

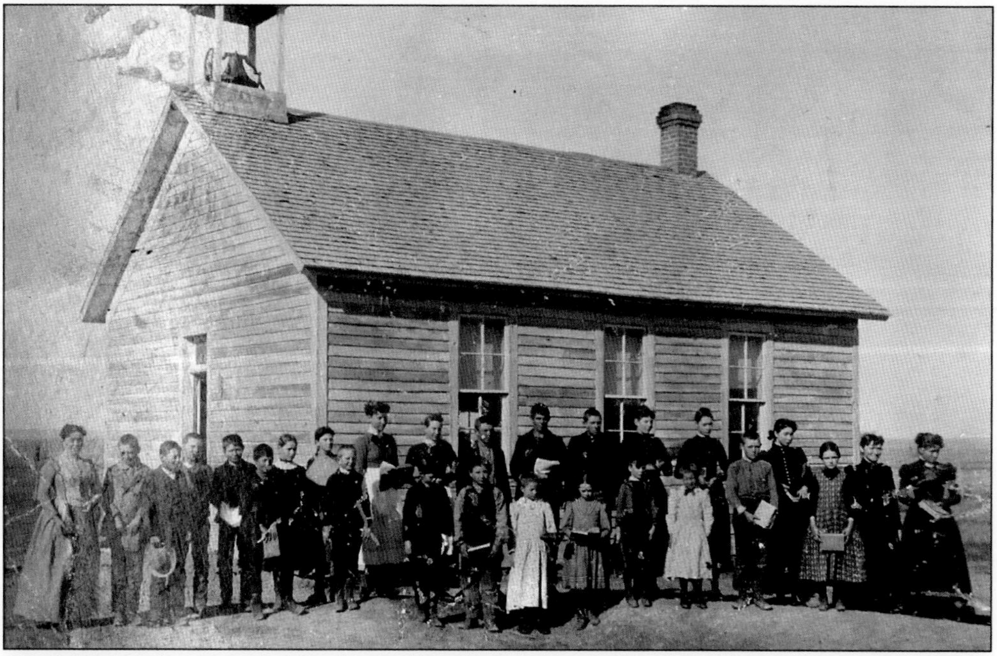

The hillside school, much like the Minnesela School, was an early rural schoolhouse in Butte County. Recently the Butte County Historical Society took possession of the school in order to preserve it. It currently sits on Jackson Street in Belle Fourche next to the Lincoln School and the police station. The historical society is now working to renovate the school.

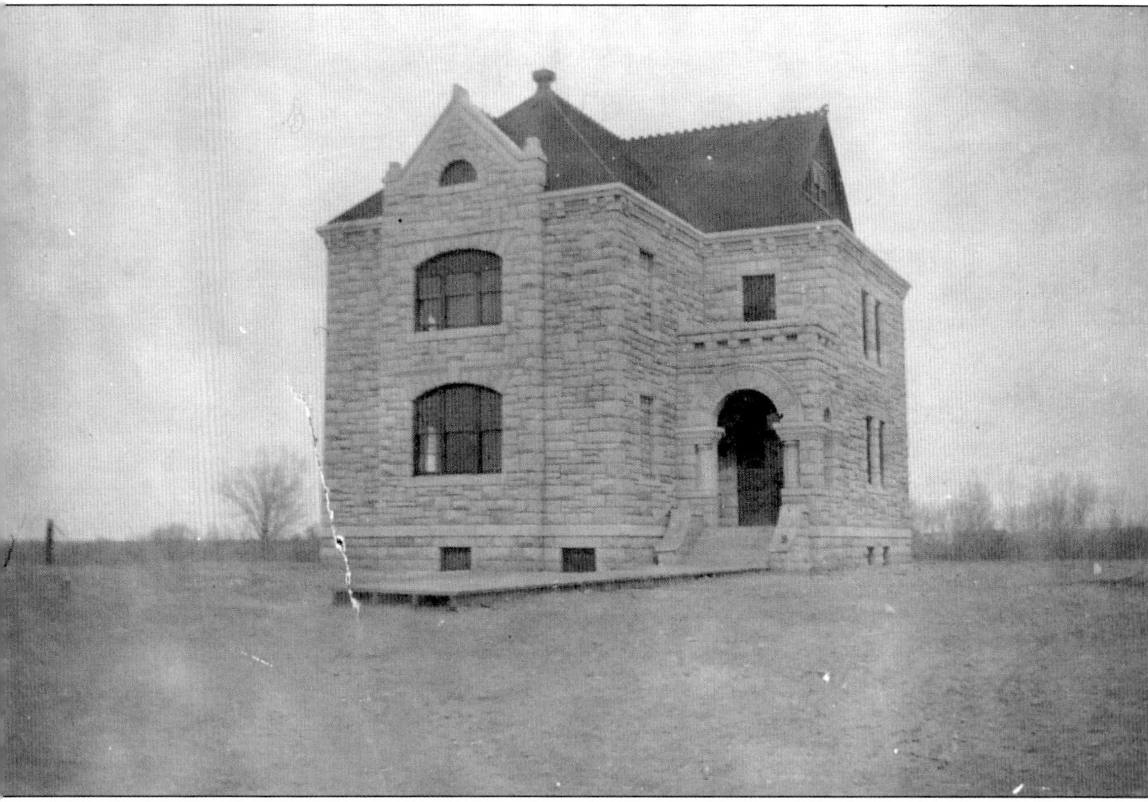

Education is an important aspect of life in Belle Fourche and western South Dakota. Ranching and new industries in the area brought growth to Belle Fourche, especially in the early part of the 20th century. With growth came the need for schools. This photograph shows the Washington School sitting alone in the early 1900s. The school was built as the first high school in Belle Fourche because the first schoolhouse was no longer large enough to handle the increasing enrollment in the city. The first students to graduate from this school received their diplomas in 1905. It was a senior class of three. The Washington School served as the city's high school until classes were moved to the Roosevelt School.

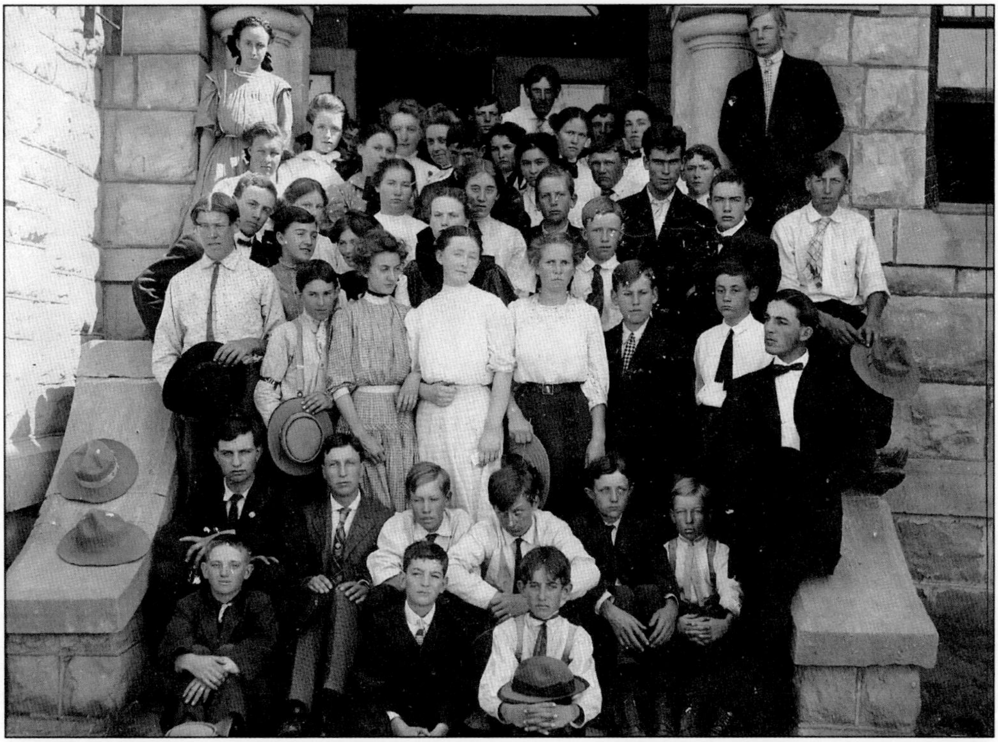

The top photograph, taken in 1908, shows the entire faculty and student population at the Washington School during that school year. There were only two teachers at the high school then. Below, the growth of the school district is evident. By 1931, the student body had grown considerably since 1908. Because of this growth, more space at the school was needed, and additions were made onto the school before the high school was eventually moved to the newer and bigger Roosevelt School.

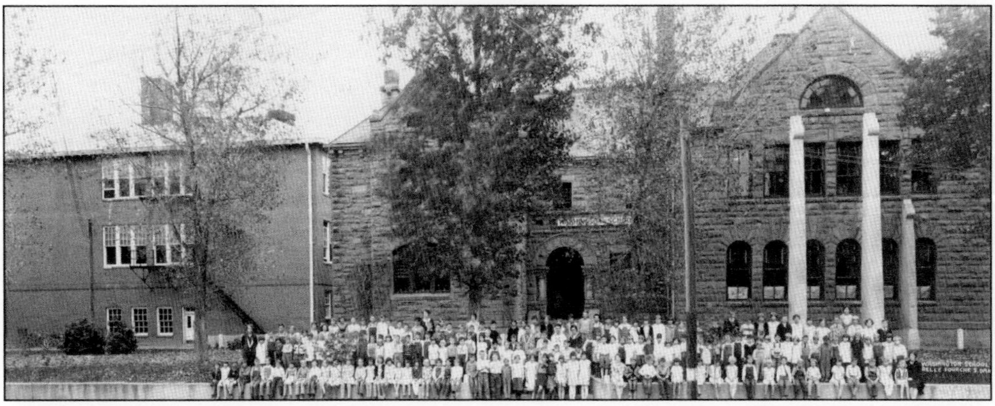

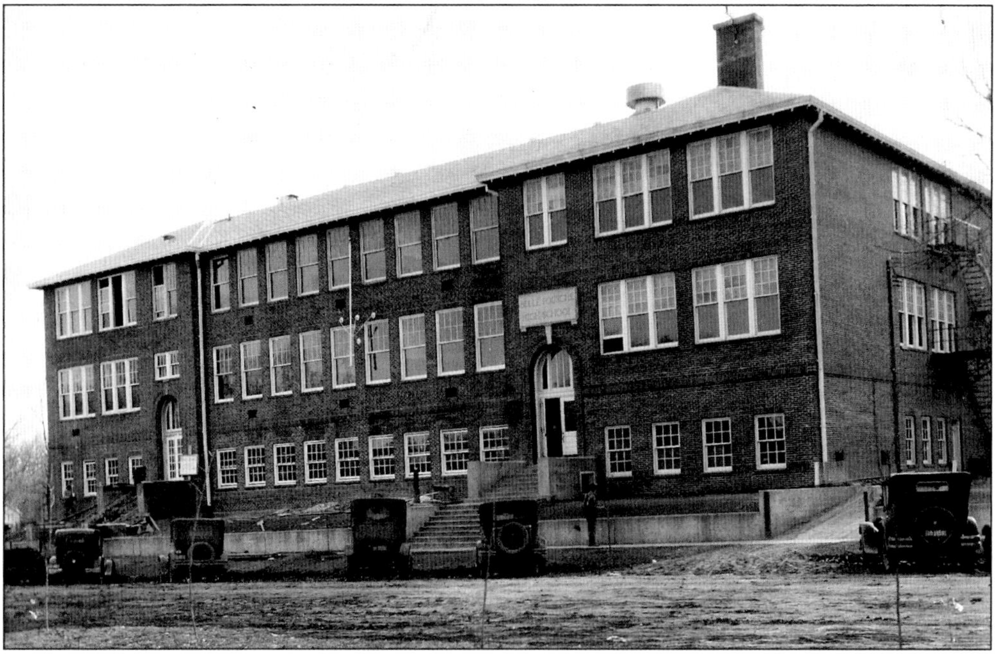

The Roosevelt School was built in 1920. It first housed the middle school and then the middle school and high school together, which was made possible through an addition that was built onto the school in 1929. This building housed the high school until 1954, when the new high school was built. It continued as the middle school until it was condemned as a school in 1989. Today this building is privately owned.

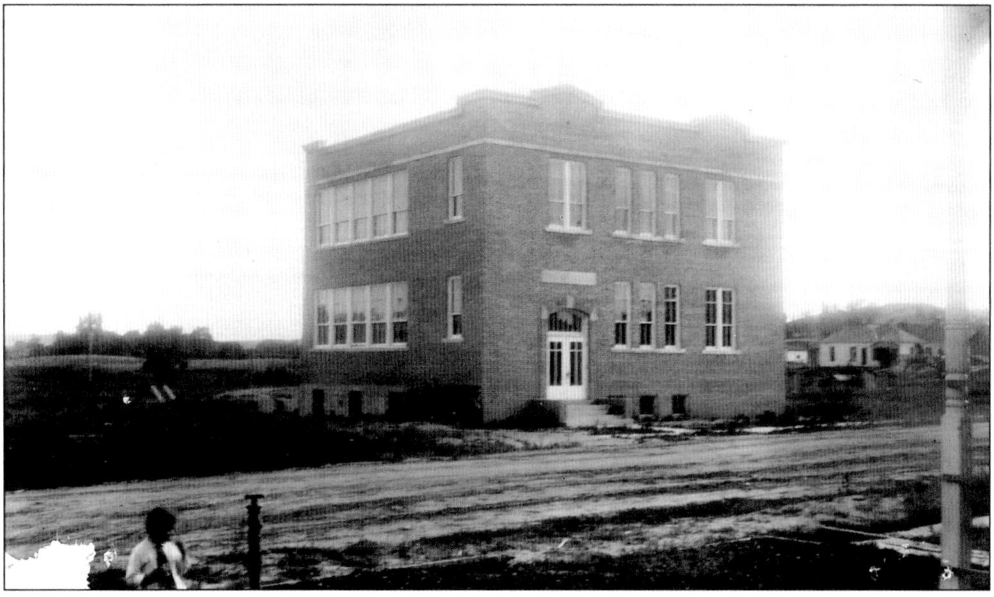

This shows the Lincoln School soon after its construction. It was built in 1919 because of increasing enrollment in Belle Fourche. At the time of its construction, as evident in this photograph, the Lincoln School was at the edge of the town. Today this building sits right in the middle of town near Herrmann Park and the Belle Fourche Police Station. In 2006, the Butte County Historical Society moved the Hillside School to a site adjacent to the Lincoln School.

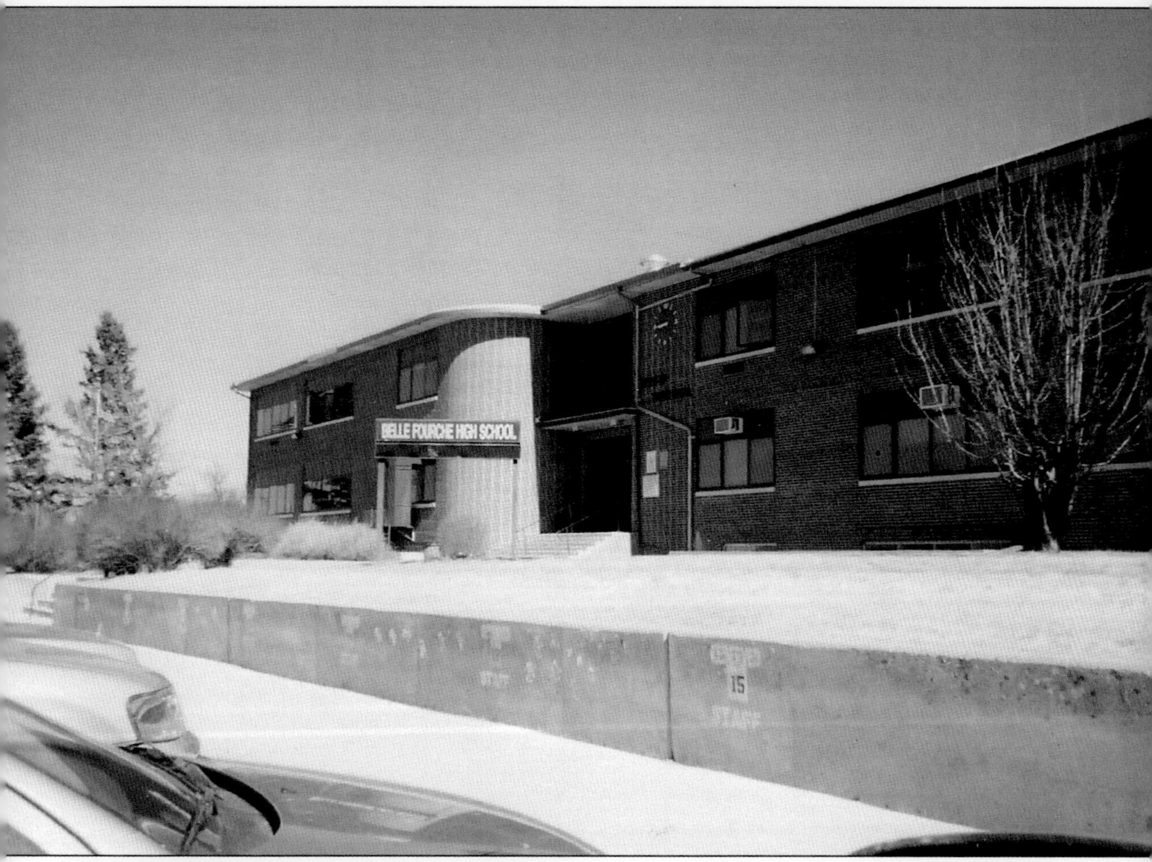

The current high school building sits conveniently next to the Belle Fourche Area Community Center. The school district now offers open enrollment, and the high school has benefited from this as enrollment has increased over the last several years. As of 2007, the high school, which houses grades 9 through 12, had a student enrollment of about 450 students and a teaching and support staff of around 50. The school also sits adjacent to an excellent football and track complex used for school-related activities and sports. The city has always invested in its education programs, and from the first graduating class in 1905, it has laid the groundwork for an amazing education system that will continue to grow and prosper in the future.

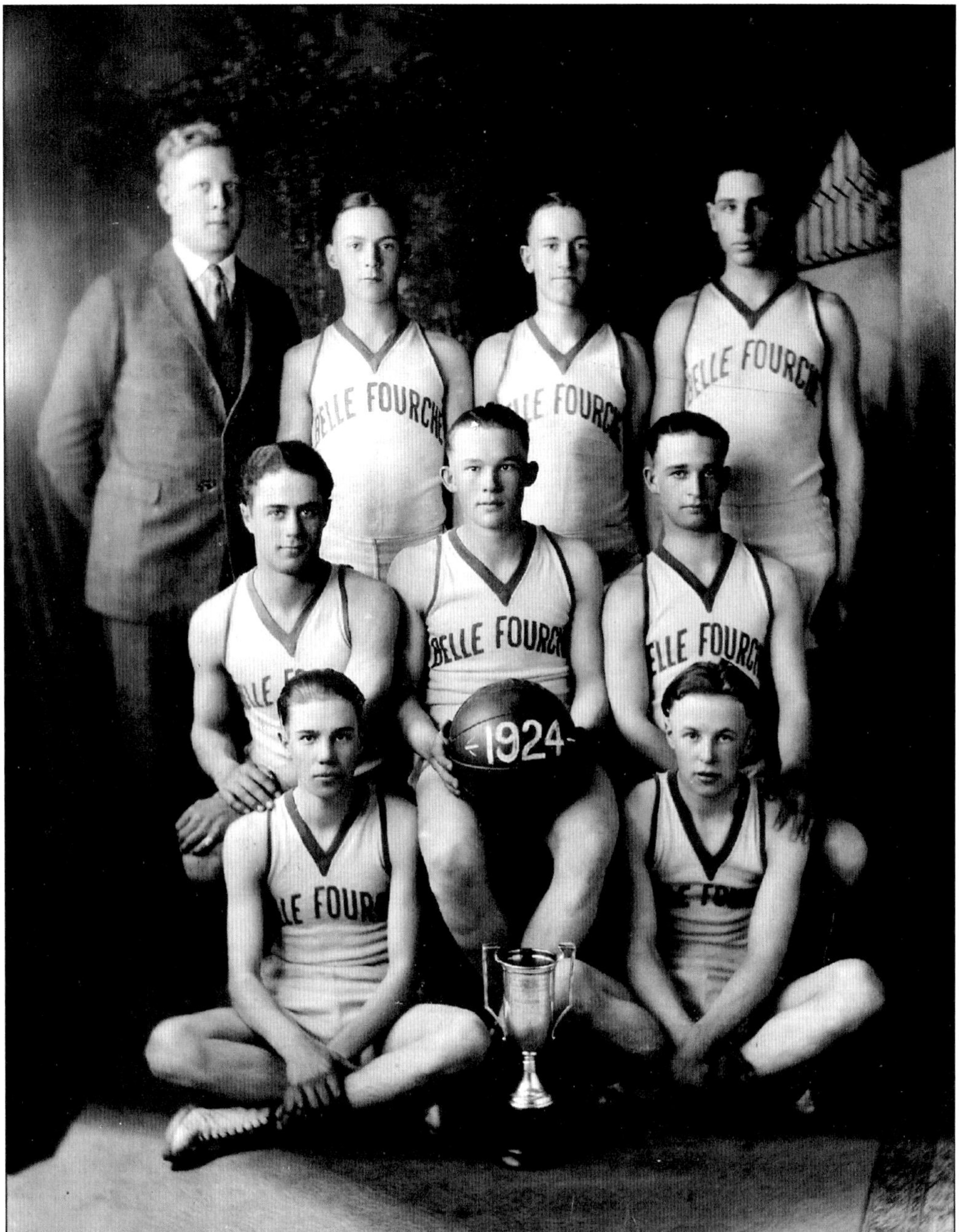

School sports have always been an important activity that Belle Fourche schools provide for their students. This photograph shows the Belle Fourche basketball team from 1924. This team made it to the state tournament, but it did not win. But in 1957, the boys' basketball team won the state tournament. It was the first time in the school's history that a state title was brought back to Belle Fourche, a feat which has since been repeated several times. In 2007, many members of the team and class of 1957 celebrated their 50th anniversary and spent time viewing a display at the Tri-State Museum that recognized the feat.

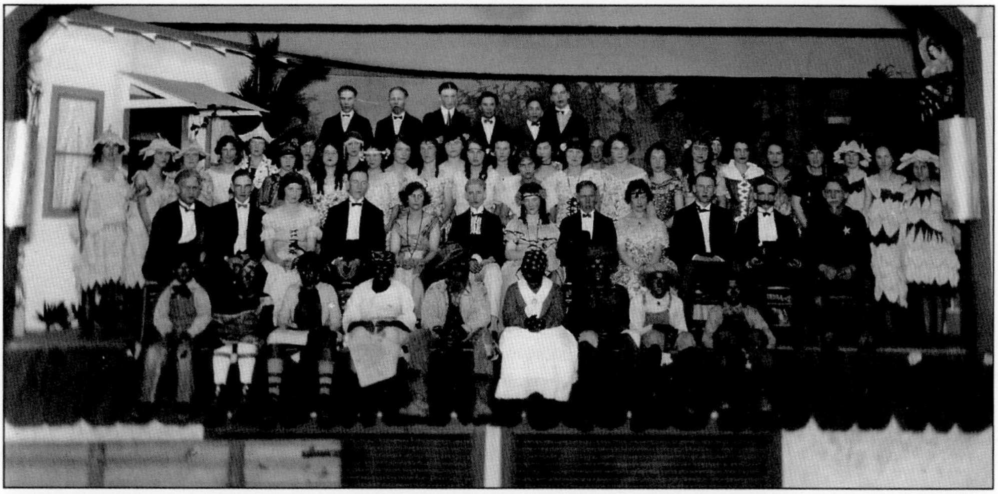

Extracurricular activities in town have always kept young people busy. Sports were an important activity but were not the only extracurricular activity popular in Belle Fourche. These photographs show the cast of a Belle Fourche school play around 1923 and an early high school band. Belle Fourche High School still has a very active theater department, and when the city built the Belle Fourche Area Community Center, it added a 500-seat theater to the design, which is used for school activities as well as concerts, speeches, and more. Bands are a unique part of Belle Fourche history. The school bands serve as an introduction for many youngsters into the world of music. Outside of school bands, Belle Fourche also has the Cowboy Band, which is comprised of members of all ages.

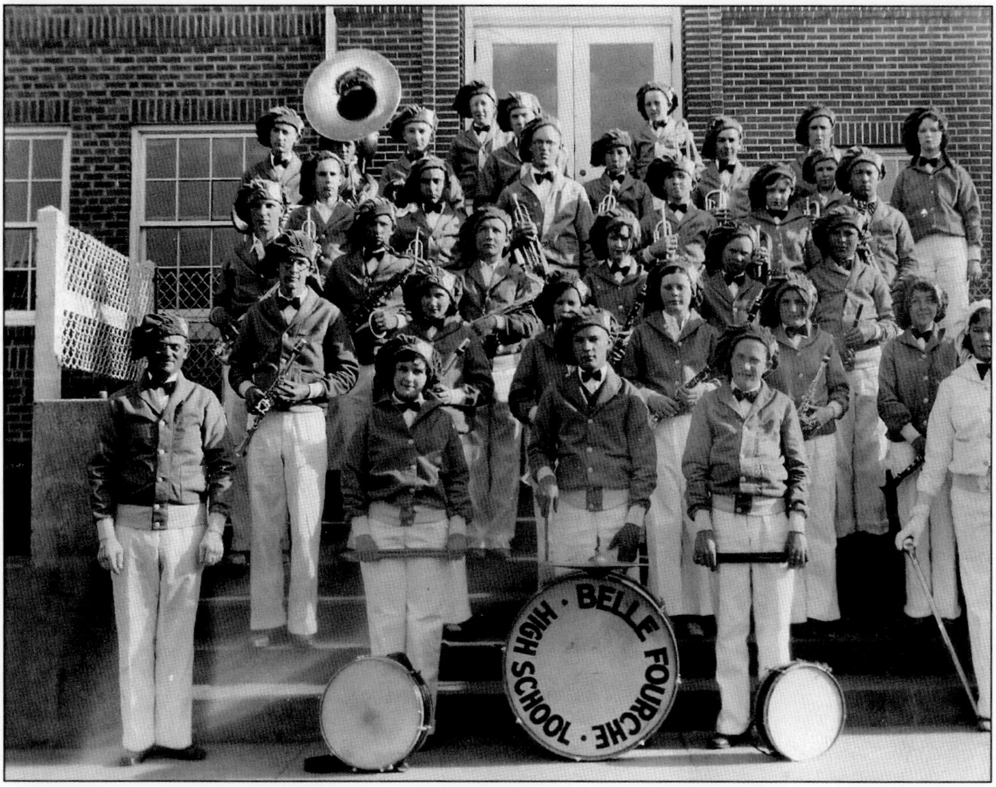

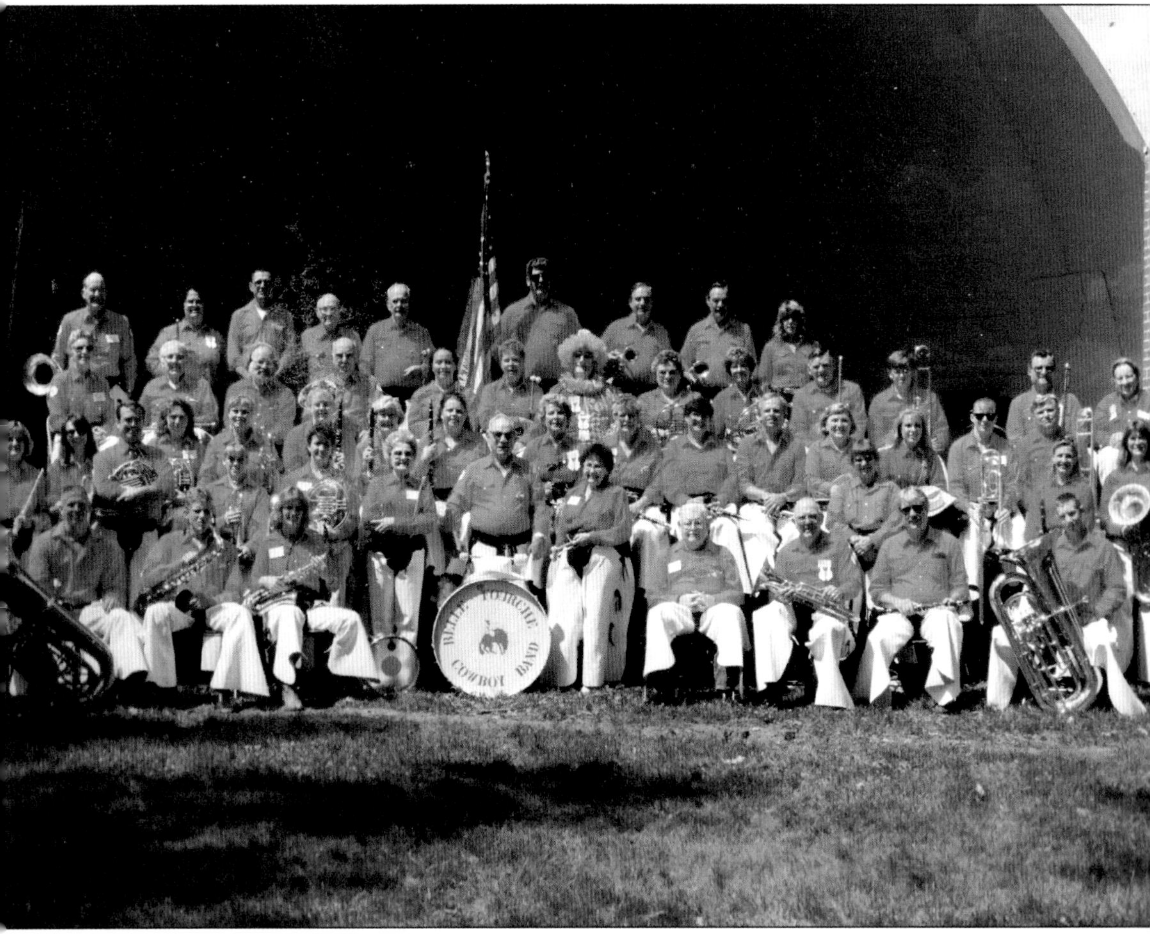

Organized in 1931, the Belle Fourche Cowboy Band has become a source of pride for this town. The band plays at the Black Hills Roundup, various parades, class reunions, and more. Members serve as unofficial ambassadors for the town. It is made up of people of all ages, and some come from other towns for the privilege to play in this great band.

BIBLIOGRAPHY

Black Hills Half Century Club of Belle Fourche, South Dakota. *Pioneer Footprints*. Sioux Falls, SD: Midwest-Beach Company, 1964.

Engebretson, Pat, Kay Heck, and Helen Herrett. *A History of Butte County, South Dakota*. Dallas, TX: Curtis Media Corporation, 1989.

Hennessey, Paul. *"Tin Horn Hank" Keenen and the World's Youngest Cowboy*. Pierre, SD: State Publishing, 1993.

———. *Tipperary The Diary of A Bucking Horse 1905–1932*. Pierre, SD: State Publishing, 1989.

Old Friends of Vale. *Cowboys and Sodbusters*. 1964.

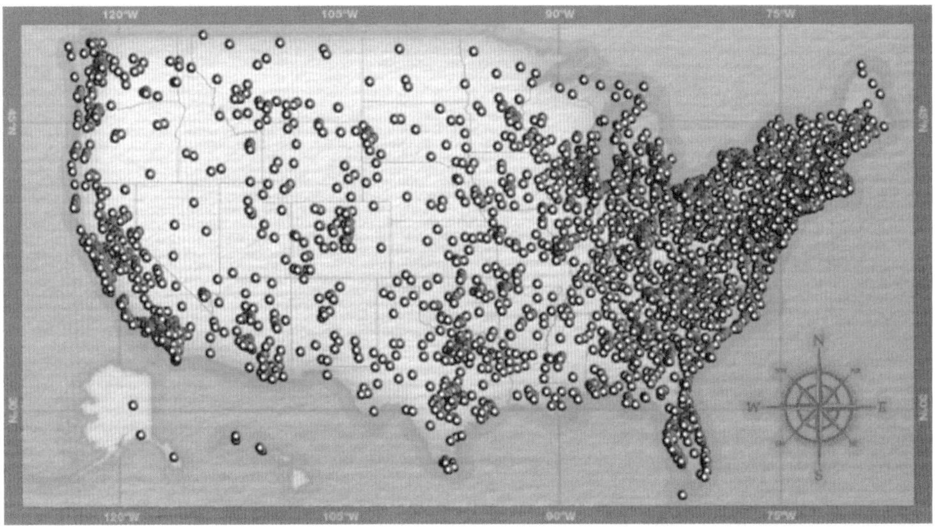